THE WAITER'S
HANDBOOK

THE WAITER'S HANDBOOK

GRAHAM BROWN
KARON HEPNER

HOSPITALITY
PRESS
MELBOURNE

Hospitality Press Pty Ltd
38 Riddell Parade
P.O.Box 426
Elsternwick Victoria 3185
Australia
Telephone (03) 528 5021 Fax (03) 528 2645

First published 1993. Reprinted 1993

National Library of Australia
Cataloguing-in-publication data:

Brown, Graham, 1947-
   The waiter's handbook.

   Includes index.
   ISBN 1 86250 430 X.

   1. Waiters – Handbooks, manuals, etc. 2. Waitresses – Handbooks,
   manuals, etc. 3. Table service – Handbooks, manuals, etc. I.
   Hepner, Karon. II. Title.

642.6

Cartoons by Dee Büman
Graphics by Alpha Research and Development (Australia) Pty Ltd,
Frankston, Victoria
Photography by R.W. Graphics, Burwood, Victoria
Designed by John van Loon
Typeset by Hospitality Press Pty Ltd
Printed in Australia by McPherson's Printing Group, Mulgrave, Victoria
Published by Hospitality Press Pty Ltd (ACN 006 473 454)

CONTENTS

Introduction

Acknowledgements

Foreword

Kraft Foodservice is proud to provide support to enable the publication of this excellent and timely industry reference manual.

Development of professionalism is of paramount importance in the hospitality sector to provide real long term career opportunities and to drive sustained industry growth.

Relevant education is the cornerstone for developing quality management and infrastructure. To that end Kraft Foodservice is fully committed to assist the industry to achieve its goals.

In recent times Australian hospitality has demonstrated it has the ability to equal the best in the world. Further investment, focus and professional education will ensure its rightful place amongst its leading global peers.

Our quality protects your reputation.

INTRODUCTION

The Waiter's Handbook has been designed as a basic training aid for waiters involved in the service of food and beverage.

Regardless of the styles of the establishments where waiters are employed, the skills of our industry do not differ in their basic application, but only in their interpretation. We believe that good professional service is as important in the café and the informal bistro as in the fine dining-room.

The term 'waiter' indicates a professional waiting person regardless of their sex or place of employment. The term 'professional' relates to a waiter who demonstrates both a positive hospitable attitude and the application of technical ability.

As a training manual *The Waiter's Handbook* was designed with both the beginner and the professional in mind. The book is designed to make clear the key objectives of professional food and beverage service and the essential techniques involved in their application.

The main text introduces the reader to all the equipment a waiter is likely to use and its application. There is also a chapter on beverage product knowledge. Food product knowledge, menu terminology and industry jargon are all covered in the extensive Glossary. The Glossary covers the terms and items most commonly found in today's menus which draw on so many different culinary traditions, as well explaining the long-established terms of classical French cuisine.

Techniques used throughout the book are described for a right-handed waiter. A left-handed waiter should reverse the techniques, except that all beverages are placed to the guest's right and both left- and right-handed waiters work anti-clockwise around the table.

Our book recommends that both food and beverage service should take place anti-clockwise round the table, starting with the guest on the right of the host, and finishing with the host. For various reasons some establishments choose to serve in the opposite (clockwise) direction. This, we believe, fails to allow for the custom of placing the principal guest immediately to the host's right. However, in this and in many other points of detail, there is room for differences of practice; the important thing is that there should be consistency within each operation.

Our aim has been to instil confidence in trainee waiters, and to provide the trained and more experienced with a reference work for use throughout their working careers.

Graham Brown and Karon Hepner

ACKNOWLEDGEMENTS

This book is the result of the hard work and generosity of a great many people and institutions. Among them we should especially like to thank Kraft Food Services (a Division of Kraft Foods Ltd) and in particular John Ubaldi (Director) and Rod Moffat (Business Manager) for the very generous contribution the company made towards the cost of the illustrations.

We should also like to thank Dandenong College of TAFE and AVS Catering Ltd for their strong support and encouragement while *The Waiter's Handbook* was being written and for the use of their equipment and facilities. The Windsor Hotel, the Melbourne Parkroyal, and the RACV Melbourne also helped by allowing us to make use of their premises and equipment.

Among the many helpful commentators on the typescript we must particularly thank Geoffrey Conaghan, Executive Director, Tourism Training Victoria, who made a great many invaluable suggestions and agreed to contribute the Foreword. Other exceptionally helpful and encouraging commentators were Dur-é Dara of Stephanie's Restaurant and Ian Ross, Editor of *Hospitality Foodservice*.

The Professional Waiters Guild, operating under the umbrella of the Catering Institute of Australia (Victorian Division) has also supported us and selected *The Waiter's Handbook* as its Official Handbook.

Domaine Chandon of the Yarra Valley (the Australian winery of Moët et Chandon of Epernay, France) and the wineries of the Goulburn Valley provided the wines used to illustrate this book and otherwise generously supported its publication.

Many of our professional colleagues, former students and friends gave their time to demonstrate techniques or to be used as models, suffering, without complaint, the long delays and the loss of their free time painstaking professional photography involves. They included Robert Saltalamacchia, George Foundas, Leonie Vanderheyden, Ray Van Gameren, Geoff Van Gameren, Claire Butcher, Pam Calderwood, Masumi Hiraga, Sally Kirkham, and Julie Buzasi.

The professional waiters who appear in the photograph on the front cover are Dianne Whelan, Mark Pascoe, Dimitrios Patrinios, Marjorie Harbour, Robert Saltalamacchia, Ashraf Doos, Michelle Fowler, Siew Ting, Mark McKenzie, Leonie Vanderheyden, and George Foundas.

Without the help of all these and many other generous helpers and advisers *The Waiter's Handbook* would be a very different book; we are extremely grateful to them all.

FOREWORD

Geoffrey Conaghan
Executive Director, Tourism Training Victoria
THE TOURISM AND HOSPITALITY INDUSTRY TRAINING BOARD OF
VICTORIA

Service in the 1990s will be a critical factor in determining the
success of any business in the hospitality industry. For the
individuals working in the industry their success and careers
will be determined by their ability to provide and understand
service, improve their service skills and develop the skills of
their teams.

As the major sector of Australia's tourism industry,
hospitality will be one of the key employment areas through
to the 21st century. The tourism industry's strategic human
resource report **Tourism 2000** has predicted that over 50
per cent of all new jobs in the tourism industry will be in the
hospitality sector.

This further enforces the emerging Australian trend to
career food and beverage service staff rather than the casual
and temporary staff of old. As opportunities increase so too do
demands for experienced, skilled professionals able to provide
the service which will attract customers, improve productivity
and increase sales.

Waiters are found at all levels on the industry career
path and in industrial award classifications. Cafés, suburban
pub bistros, club dining-rooms, function centres, hotel banquet rooms and fine-dining restaurants all link to create
employment opportunities and career paths in a number of
different waiter roles. This range of jobs provides career
opportunities within the occupation of waiter and has
employment and career links to a range of other positions in
the hospitality sector of the tourism industry.

While all establishments are different, they all have the
common need for quality service which is appropriate to the
style of business. *The Waiter's Handbook* is successfully
framed in a number of relevant contexts — customer service,
technical skills, processes and procedures, product knowledge,
team work, sales and service, skill levels and career paths.
Each is woven into a framework which makes this book the
most comprehensive resource for food and beverage service
staff available in Australia or overseas.

The Waiter's Handbook is a timely publication for the Australian hospitality industry. It arrives at a time when service has joined product and price as a key consumer consideration. It also leads the way to assist business and individuals identify the appropriate mix of skills and knowledge required to develop and maintain good service in a wide range of operations. Most importantly, *The Waiter's Handbook* presents the opportunities for skill upgrading and career development for Australia's growing ranks of career food and beverage professionals.

1

HOSPITALITY AND THE WAITER

1.1 Waiters are employed in a huge variety of establishments in the hospitality industry, but, no matter what type of restaurant or other venue they work in, the waiter's basic role does not differ.

The number of food and beverage service staff, and their positions in an establishment's hierarchy, depend on the size of the operation and the services it offers, but the function of the waiting staff, large or small, remains the same. So does the need for the waiters to be professional in what they do.

In any establishment, large or small, formal or informal, the industry demands that the waiting staff should have a professional attitude to their jobs.

When you have read this chapter you will have a basic understanding of:
- Different types of food and beverage operations
- The role of the waiter
- The classification of food and beverage service employees
- The organization of food and beverage service staff
- The need for high standards of personal presentation and hygiene.

Why should waiters who work in coffee shops or who serve counter meals in pubs feel any less professional in their role than waiters who offer silver service?

Guests have a right to professional service no matter how much they are spending.

1.2 DIFFERENT TYPES OF FOOD AND BEVERAGE OUTLETS

The hospitality industry offers employment to people of differing personalities, backgrounds and skills through a wide diversity of the types of outlets serving food and beverages.

Hospitality may be defined as meeting the needs of guests in a variety of establishments including all the following at which service staff or waiters are employed:

○ *Coffee shops* which offer coffee, snacks, and often light meals through to supper items. Coffee shops require fast service to ensure a fast turnover of customers.

○ *Food halls/food courts* have taken over from traditional cafeterias. They offer a wide variety of foods which guests are able to select for themselves. Service staff are responsible for clearing the eating areas.

○ *Bistros/pubs (counter meals)*. This style of service applies in casual or pub environments. The food, usually main meals, is either collected by the guests from a counter or served by service staff, but an essential element of this type of meal service is speed.

○ *Casual dining restaurants (bistros)*. Here appearance and atmosphere provide an environment for casual dining but table service is offered. Informal restaurants do not always have licences to serve liquor, but they may have BYO facilities. Service staff must be capable of friendly informality in their dealings with guests while remaining professionally efficient.

○ *National or 'ethnic' restaurants*. In these popular establishments the style of the service may be as much a part of the cultural experience offered to guests as the food itself.

○ *Functions (receptions/banquets/conventions)*. In these cases the number of guests and the style of function varies enormously so they demand extreme flexibility from both management and service staff.

○ *Fine dining restaurants* usually have a suitably comfortable or impressive ambience for the fine cuisine on offer. Service staff are expected not only to be discreetly professional in what they do but also to be highly skilled, and knowledgeable.

1.3 THE ROLE OF THE WAITER

The term waiter includes food and beverage service personnel of either sex.

It is the role of the professional waiter to ensure that guests enjoy a satisfactory total dining experience; the job involves much more than simply serving food or beverages.

To fulfil this role adequately a waiter needs a range of qualities and attributes, including a pleasant personality, honesty, efficiency and punctuality. Also a waiter must always be fastidious about self-presentation and personal hygiene.

A professional waiter will also have a good knowledge of the products being served, what they consist of and how they are presented. Good waiters will also understand the organization of the establishment in which they are working, and how other members of the team contribute to the dining experience of the guests.

1.4 *The Australian waiter*

While the role of the waiter is essentially the same everywhere — to ensure that guests have a satisfactory dining experience — this requires differences in approach in different circumstances. In Australia, where people are in general less formal in their dealings with each other than in older societies like those in Europe or Japan, the strict formality of the traditional European waiter is often not appropriate. This does not mean that Australian waiters should be any less attentive to the needs of their guests, simply that they can and should project the self-confident unservile individuality that is a most attractive aspect of the Australian character.

Australian waiters should not try to imitate other service cultures as good Australian service concentrates on the specific needs of the guests — service without servility.

1.5 *Duties of the waiter*

The work of the waiter includes
- preparation and maintenance of the work area
- maintaining good customer and staff relations
- making recommendations and assisting guests in making selections
- order taking and recording
- service and clearing of food and beverages.

1.6 *FOOD AND BEVERAGE INDUSTRY AWARD CLASSIFICATIONS*

In Australia food and beverage service employees are classified into grades. Each grade has a definition, identifying major tasks one would perform at that grade. The level of pay you receive generally depends on the nature of the work you are actually doing, rather than the grade level at which you may be qualified to work.

At some of the higher grades you are now expected to undergo specific training programmes accredited by the Australian Hospitality Review Panel (AHRP). This is a national body operating under the auspices of Tourism Training Australia, which grants industry recognition to training programmes which meet minimum training requirements and achieve industry standards.

The 1992 Federal Hotels Award classification structure is detailed in the following table. The structure enables people to build a career in either beverage or waiting or a combination of both, depending on where they are working and what their career aspirations are. Similar arrangements are in place for the other Awards in the hospitality industry. For details you should contact your local Department of Labour.

CLASSIFI-CATION	DEFINITION	TYPICAL JOB TITLES
Food and Beverage Attendant Grade One	An employee who is engaged in any of the following: ○ picking up glasses ○ emptying ashtrays ○ general assistance to Food and Beverage Assistants of a higher grade **not** including service to customers ○ removing food plates ○ setting and/or wiping down tables ○ cleaning and tidying associated areas.	○ Bar useful ○ Busboy ○ Function porter
Food and Beverage Attendant Grade Two	An employee who has not achieved the appropriate level of training and who is engaged in any of the following: ○ supplying, dispensing or mixing of liquor, including the sale of liquor from the bottle department ○ assisting in the cellar or bottle department ○ undertaking general waiting duties of both food and/or beverage, including the cleaning of tables ○ receipt of monies ○ attending a snack bar ○ engaged in delivery duties.	○ Bar attendant ○ Assistant cellar person ○ Waiter ○ Function waiter ○ Cashier ○ Snack bar attendant ○ Bottleshop attendant
Food and Beverage Attendant Grade Three	An employee who has the appropriate level of training and is engaged in any of the following: ○ supplying, dispensing or mixing of liquor, including the sale of liquor from the bottle department ○ assisting in the cellar or bottle department where duties could include working up to four hours per day in the cellar without supervision ○ undertaking general waiting duties of both food and beverage, including cleaning of tables ○ receipt of monies ○ taking reservations, greeting and seating guests ○ assisting in the training and supervision of Food and Beverage Attendants of a lower grade ○ engaged in delivery duties.	○ Waiter or bar attendant in charge ○ Senior waiter ○ Senior bar attendant ○ Senior bottleshop attendant Persons at Grade 3 would be undertaking similar types of functions to Food & Beverage Attendants Grade 2. Because they have met the training requirements for Grade 3, however, they are more skilled and are able to perform a broader range of functions.

CLASSIFI-CATION	DEFINITION	TYPICAL JOB TITLES
Food and Beverage Attendant

Grade Four | An employee who has the appropriate level of training and is engaged in any of the following:
- full control of a cellar or liquor store
- mixing a range of sophisticated drinks
- supervising food and beverage attendants of a lower grade. | - Cellarperson
- Cocktail bar attendant
- Bar supervisor
- Coffee shop or restaurant supervisor
- Bottleshop supervisor |
| Food and Beverage Attendant

Grade Five | An employee who has completed an apprenticeship in waiting or who has passed the appropriate trade test and as such carries out specialized skilled duties in a fine dining-room or restaurant:
- serving food using silver-service techniques
- arranging, preparing, and serving food and beverages from trolleys
- guéridon cooking and carving. | - Silver-service waiter
- Chef de rang |
| Food and Beverage Supervisor | An employee who has the appropriate level of training, including a supervisory course, and who has the responsibility for supervision, training and co-ordination of food and beverage staff, or stock control for a bar or series of bars:
- undertaking budgeting
- staff costing and operational reporting
- preparing staff rosters
- initial menu planning
- maintaining service standards. | - Head bar attendant
- Bar(s) supervisor
- Head waiter
- Maitre d'hôtel
- Restaurant supervisor |

Source: Tourism Training Australia.

1.7 THE ORGANIZATION OF FOOD AND BEVERAGE SERVICE STAFF

While most jobs advertised will refer to the formal classifications of the Award listed in 1.6, those classifications do not detail the actual duties of each job. These will vary from establishment to establishment, according to its size, the nature of its business and the traditions of the organization. Positions commonly found include:

- Food and Beverage Manager
  In larger operations a Food and Beverage Manager is usually responsible for the success of the food and beverage operations from a business point of view. He or she will be responsible for such matters as compiling the menus (in consultation with the kitchen) to make sure

that the required profit margins are achieved, purchasing food and beverage items and deciding portion sizes, and staff recruitment and training.

○ Restaurant Manager

In operations where there are several bars and restaurants, such as a large hotel, each restaurant may have its own manager responsible to the Food and Beverage Manager. He or she will be responsible for the work of the staff within that restaurant and for seeing that the policies of the Food and Beverage Manager are carried out. Either the Restaurant Manager or the Head Waiter will be responsible for staff duty rosters.

○ Head Waiter

The Head Waiter is responsible for all the service staff in the restaurant and for seeing that all the preparation, service and clearing work is efficiently carried out. In smaller establishments he or she may also be responsible for taking reservations and for greeting and seating guests. In larger establishments there may be a special Reception Head Waiter with these duties.

○ Station (Head) Waiter

The Station Head Waiter or Captain is responsible for the service of a **station** or group of tables. He or she takes the orders and carries out the service at the tables of the station, assisted in larger establishments by less experienced and knowledgeable staff. Each station may have its own workstation or sideboard. (This sideboard is also called the waiter's 'station'.)

○ Waiter

If the stations are looked after by a service team, less experienced waiters are responsible to the Station Head Waiter. They perform duties such as plate service of dishes and the service of sauces, sometimes assisted in the simplest tasks by a trainee.

A trainee waiter is sometimes called a **commis** (pronounced *commie*) waiter. He should not be confused with a commis cook, that is a cook in training, working under the chef.

○ Wine Waiter

The wine waiter is a specialist, responsible for the service of all alcoholic drinks to the tables. He or she must, of course, have a thorough knowledge of the wines on the establishment's wine list, and be able to recommend wines suitable to accompany the various menu items. And, of course, know how to serve them correctly.

A **sommelier** (pronounced *som-may-lee-ay*) is another word for a specialist wine waiter.

Award Grade	Popular Terminology
	FOOD & BEVERAGE MANAGER
	RESTAURANT MANAGER
6	CAPTAIN, STATION WAITER, HEAD WAITER
5	WINE WAITER, SOMMELIER
4	WAITER
3	
2	COMMIS, APPRENTICE, WAITER IN TRAINING
1	

The industrial award grades (left) and popular terminology (right). The relationship of the popular terminology and the Award classifications may vary in detail from one establishment to another.

1.8 PRESENTATION AND HYGIENE

One all-important aspect of the professionalism of waiting staff is the attention they give to personal hygiene and presentation. A waiter when at work, in or out of uniform, must invariably be absolutely clean and tidy in all respects. This is the first and most obvious sign that waiters are professional in their approach to their work.

The first (visual) impression of waiting staff received by guests comes from the waiters' appearance. First impressions are extremely important for the commercial success of an establishment.

Good grooming and meticulous attention to personal hygiene not only express a positive attitude to guests but also build self-confidence in the individual waiter.

High standards of personal hygiene are also essential for all workers involved in the service of food and beverages for health reasons.

High standards of hygiene in the waiting staff are also essential if guests are to enjoy their dining experience. Their enjoyment will be considerably lessened if their food or drinks are served by a waiter with bad breath or dirty finger nails.

Waiters must select their footwear with care and pay attention to good posture when standing and moving. It is almost impossible for a waiter with sore feet or an aching back to maintain a pleasant and helpful attitude to the guests.

Waiters' hairstyles should be suitable to the establishment in which they are working. In general they should be in tune with current fashions, but hair must be tidy and should be swept away from the face. This projects an air of self-confidence and is also more hygienic.

Unobtrusive jewellery, make-up and perfume may all be used, but with discretion. They must not be over-done.

Whether the waiter's uniform is provided by the establishment or not, it is the waiter's responsibility to make sure that the uniform is kept clean and well-presented at all times.

When uniforms are being selected it is important that their size and design make adequate allowance for the extensive body movement a waiter's work demands. Natural fibres are preferable to man-made ones because they allow the body to breathe and they are safer in case of burns.

2

THE MENU

2.1 The words 'the menu' have at least three meanings for the waiter. The menu means:

- the range of food items served in an establishment, including their organization into a number of courses
- the arrangement by which the items are offered (the type of menu, as in 'set menu', 'à la carte menu', etc.), and
- the physical object on which the list of these items (and courses) is written for guests to choose from.

This chapter is concerned with the menu in the first two of these senses. The handling of the menu as a physical object and its presentation to guests is dealt with in a later chapter (see 6.2-6.4).

When you have completed this chapter you will have a basic understanding of:

- The framework of the modern menu
- The sequence of the courses
- Food items which are not part of the framework of courses
- The different types or classes of menu.

Why bother to provide a menu if the descriptions of the menu items are not true to the items served?

2.2 THE STRUCTURE OF THE MENU

There is necessarily a menu of some kind or other for any meal, however simple. For example, cornflakes followed by toast and marmalade is a popular breakfast menu. However the menu this chapter is concerned with is the menu for a main meal of the day, luncheon or dinner.

The classical French menu or 'classic menu' had more than twelve courses*. It offered the diner a wide variety of items served in a well-understood traditional sequence. Modern menus have fewer courses but they may cause confusion as to the appropriate sequence of service.

Menus are laid out so that the different courses appear in the order in which they would normally be served. They are usually presented in a framework of five courses, as follows:

* See 'classic menu' in the Glossary.

- appetizers
- soups
- entrées
- main courses
- desserts.

Appetizers are such items as hors-d'oeuvres, pâtés, or oysters natural, which are designed to stimulate rather than to satisfy the appetite.

Soups may be thick (*potages*) or thin (*consommés*). The less common French word *soupe* (with an *e*), often used as *soupe du jour* (soup of the day), can mean either a thick or thin soup. Soups are usually hot, but can be served chilled, as a vichyssoise, for example, is.

In the classical French menu the *entrée* was a course served between the fish and the main meat courses. In the modern menu the term is used to cover such items as small helpings of pasta dishes, seafood crêpes, elaborate salads, miniature sausages, or fish (if not chosen as the main course). The entrée is a course which certainly does more than stimulate the appetite but which is not so substantial as to make the main course unwelcome.

Many Australian establishments list all the first three of these courses under the general heading of 'starters', or sometimes 'entrées'.

The term 'entrée' can cause even more confusion because it is sometimes, especially in the USA, used to mean the main course itself although the word literally means 'entrance', or 'way in', i.e. a starter.

There is, fortunately, no possible confusion about what the main course is. It is the most substantial course of the meal. Guests usually choose their main courses first and then select other courses to suit it. Similarly, when chefs design menus, they usually start with the principal or main course and then plan the other courses to complement it.

Dessert is another term which can cause confusion. In the modern menu it is used to mean the sweet course at the end of a meal, although the term is occasionally (particularly in Britain) reserved for fruit and nuts, etc. served after the sweet dish or pudding has been cleared.

2.3 Sequence of courses

In most formal circumstances the courses are served in the order assumed in the standard modern menu, but this structure may not readily apply to the menus actually offered in many less formal or non-traditional establishments. When this is so it is the responsibility of the waiter to determine in what order the guests wish their courses to be served.

2.4 ITEMS OUTSIDE THE MENU STRUCTURE

Not all the food items served with a meal are included in the formal structure of the menu.

2.5 Pre-dinner food items

Items served before the first course may include:
- canapés
- crudités
- bite-sized hot or cold hors-d'oeuvre items.

2.6 Sauces and accompaniments

Now that our eating habits draw on so many different cultural traditions, the range of different sauces and accompaniments available is huge. It is appropriate for some of these items to be placed on the table for the guests to help themselves; others should be offered to the diners by the waiter (see 8.6).

It is the waiters' responsibility to make sure that their stations' mise-en-place includes the necessary sauce and accompaniment items, such as different kinds of mustard, coarse-ground black pepper, chutneys, ketchups, etc. appropriate to the menu of the establishment.

2.7 Cheese

Cheese may be ordered prior to dessert (as is the usual custom in France, for example), in place of dessert, or after dessert, depending on the guest's preference. While one guest may prefer cheese to be served while still enjoying table wine, another may prefer cheese to be served later, with coffee and port.

The correct procedure for serving cheese and the appropriate accompaniments depend on the types of cheese being served. Fashions change in what accompaniments are considered 'appropriate', and different establishments have different practices. There is no one correct procedure applying to all establishments.

2.8 Accompaniments to coffee

Like pre-dinner food items, accompaniments to coffee are not included in the menu framework, but are an addition to it.

The range of items that may be offered with coffee is limited only by one's imagination. The service of after-dinner mints is standard practice, but many establishments now treat their coffee accompaniments as their personal signature. These items may be petits fours, personalized chocolates, biscuits or glacé fruits, for example.

2.9 *TYPES OF MENU*

The different types or classes of menu are distinguished by the variations in the selections offered and by their pricing structure.

2.10 *A la carte menu*

An à la carte menu is a menu which offers choices in each course and in which each item is individually priced and charged for. Menu items when selected by the guests are cooked to order. The literal meaning of the French words *à la carte* is 'from the card'.

The term à la carte when applied to a restaurant is often misinterpreted. The term does not relate to a particular type of establishment nor to its pricing or to the services it offers; the term refers solely to the type of menu, and to the fact that the food is cooked to order.

2.11 *Table d'hôte*

A table d'hôte menu is a menu which offers some (usually limited) choice and is charged at a fixed price per person for the whole menu. *Table d'hôte* is, literally, French for 'the proprietor's (mine host's) table'.

A modestly-priced 'business lunch', in which three or four items only are offered in each course and the guest pays a fixed price for the whole meal, would be a typical use of the table d'hôte menu.

More exclusive restaurants also often make use of the table d'hôte menu as its limited number of menu items allows the chef to select fresh ingredients of the best quality and to treat each dish with maximum attention. Because a more limited range of choice has to be catered for than in a typical à la carte menu there is less wastage.

Table d'hôte menus are also popular for festive occasions, for example Christmas Day or Mother's Day.

2.12 *Set menu*

A set menu is one which offers set items (one for each course) pre-arranged by the host. Set menus are utilized predominantly for functions, for example, weddings and banquets.

2.13 *Carte du jour*

Carte du jour literally means 'card of the day'. It offers choices available for a particular day only. It allows the chef to offer a list of 'specials' or variations in addition to a pre-printed à la carte menu, or it can be used as a table d'hôte menu prepared for use on the one day only.

2.14 *Cycle menu*

A cycle menu is a group of menus which are rotated on a set cycle. Cycle menus are usually used in the institutional sector of the industry, for example in hospitals, prisons, on airlines and in employee food-service operations (works canteens, etc.).

The cycle menu is used to avoid boredom for both customers and staff, and also to ensure that the diet of the people eating in the institution is sufficiently varied to be healthy. In a hospital, for example, the cycle would be set to fit the average length of stay of the patients.

Menus should not be designed to a seven-day cycle as this results in the same items always being served on the same day of the week, producing a boring predictability.

A la carte menus

Table d'hôte menus

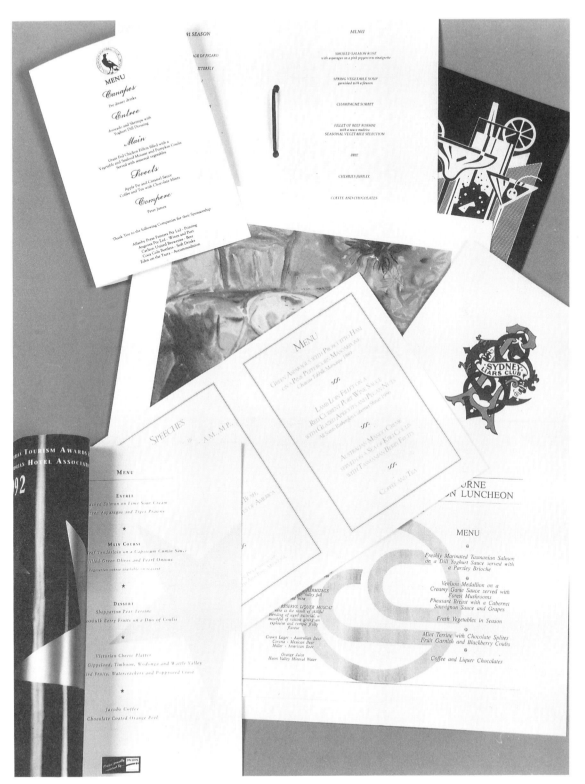

Set menus

3

FOOD SERVICE EQUIPMENT

Why should a guest be embarrassed by having to use inappropriate equipment for a particular dish?

3.1 There is a huge variety of cutlery and tableware in use in hospitality establishments today. Not only does the basic cutlery come in a variety of styles, but the range of specialist equipment is almost endless. This chapter does not attempt the almost impossible task of describing every piece of equipment a waiter may encounter; what it does is to introduce all the equipment used by waiters commonly found in modern establishments. Remember though that there is a great variety of possible styles so that the illustrations are only representative of examples of particular pieces of equipment; other styles may be equally common and valid.

When you have read this chapter you should be familiar with:

○ The appearance and use of the various types of cutlery used for the eating and service of food
○ The various types of crockery and tableware used for the eating and service of food
○ The various pieces of equipment required for the preparation of food in the dining-room.

Glassware and beverage-service equipment are dealt with later, in chapter 13 (see 13.2, 13.3, 13.4, and 13.7).

3.2 CUTLERY

Basic cutlery (silverware) items

Large fork (table fork)
Used as
○ Main fork or joint fork
○ Serving fork (see 8.2)

Large knife (table knife)
Used as
○ Main knife or joint knife

Small fork (dessert fork)

Used as
- Entrée fork
- Pasta fork
- Salad fork
- Dessert (or pudding) fork
- Fruit fork

Small knife

Used as
- Side knife (for buttering bread or spreading pâté)
- Entrée knife
- Cheese knife
- Fruit knife

Steak knife

(Note the serrated edge)

Fish knife

Used for
- Fish
- Serving delicate or large items (see 8.3 and 8.7)

Fish fork (webbed fork)

Used for
- Fish

Large spoon (tablespoon)

Used for serving (see 8.2)

Medium spoon (dessert or pudding spoon)

Used for
- Desserts (see 4.13 and 6.13)
- Pasta

Soup spoon

Small spoon (teaspoon)

Used for
- Tea and coffee
- Cocktails (e.g. prawn or fruit cocktails)
- Ice creams
- Dessert coupes
- Sugar spoon

3.3 Other cutlery items sometimes placed on the table

Parfait spoon
Used for
- Desserts
- Ice cream

Grapefruit spoon

Oyster fork

Snail (escargot) **fork**

Snail (escargot) **tongs**

Lobster (crayfish) **picks**

Lobster (crayfish) **cracker**

Butter knife
Used for serving butter or pâté.

Cheese knife
Used for serving cheese

Tea-strainer

Sugar tongs

3.4 *Cutlery items used for serving*

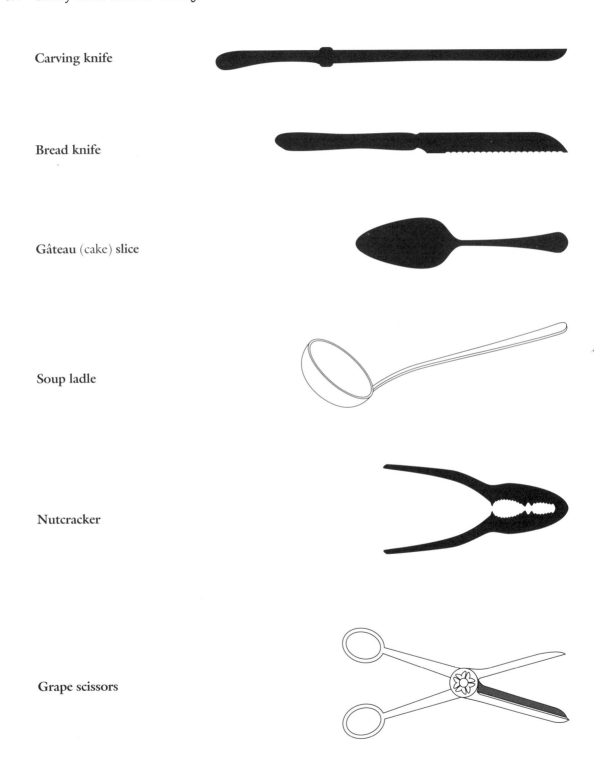

Carving knife

Bread knife

Gâteau (cake) **slice**

Soup ladle

Nutcracker

Grape scissors

3.5 *TABLEWARE*

Common items of tableware (also called crockery or china) include:

Cover plate
Used as a presentation or showplate in the setting. Can be a simple large plate also used as a service plate or an under-plate for service.

Large plate (dinner plate)
Used for the main course. Oval plates are sometimes used instead of round ones.

Middle-sized (entrée) **plate**
Used for entrées, and also for salads, cheese and fruit. Can be oval instead of round.

Small (side) **plate**
Used for bread and bread rolls, also for cheese, fruit, and cake.

Soup bowl
Used for cream soups, also as an oatmeal (porridge) bowl, for breakfast cereals, and as a pasta bowl.

Consommé bowl and **saucer**
Used for clear soups. Note that the consommé bowl is always served on a matching saucer.

Large soup tureen (with lid)
Often used for service from a guéridon rather than on the
table (see 10.4).

Coupe
A stemmed vessel, made of glass, silver, or stainless steel.
Used for cocktails (seafood or fruit), desserts, ice cream.

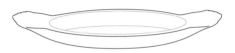

Ravière
Oval or rectangular dish, used primarily for pasta or for
presenting hors d'oeuvres.

Ramekin
Comes in various sizes. Used for baked eggs, custards and
soufflés.

Tea or **coffee cup** and **saucer**
Sizes vary considerably. Some establishments use a smaller
size for coffee than for tea.

Demitasse and **saucer/small coffee cup** and **saucer**. Often
used for black or Turkish coffee. (*Demi-tasse* is French for
'half-cup'.)

Coffee pots
Various styles including:

Long spout

Cona pot (Cona is a trade name)

Plunger

Tea pot

Hot water pot

Sugar bowl

Milk or **cream jug**

Salad bowl (individual)

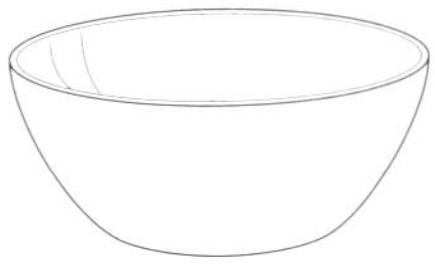

Salad bowl (for table service)

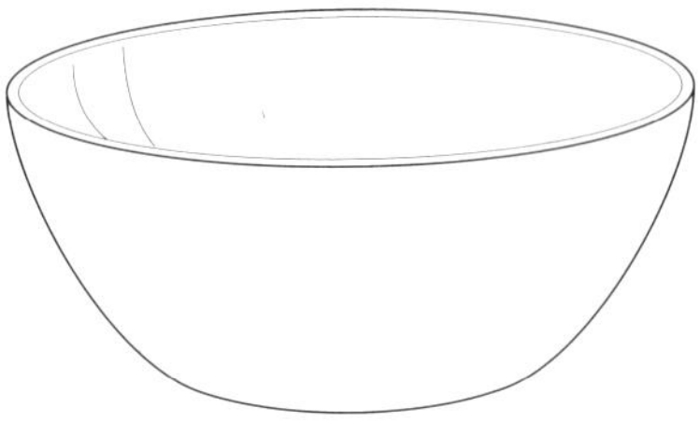

Kidney plate
Crescent-shaped, used for salads or sometimes vegetables.

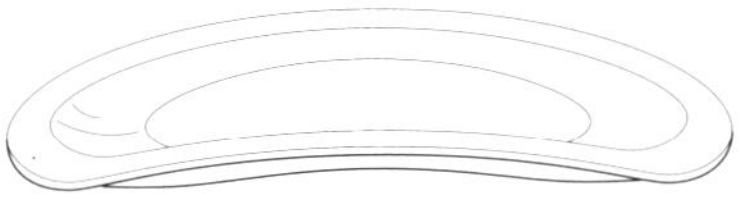

Oyster or **mussel plate**

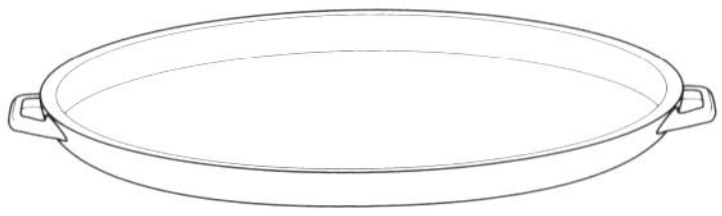

Snail (escargot) **plate**

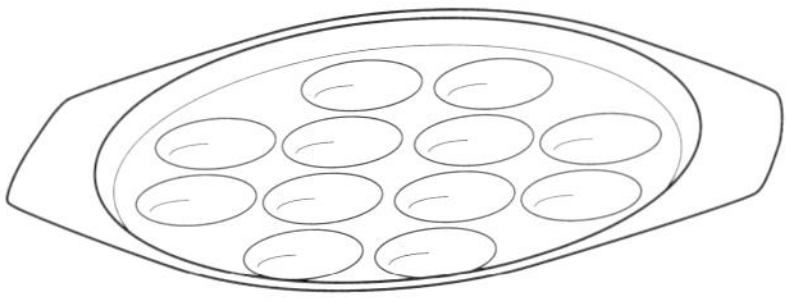

Sauce-boat (saucière)

Serving flats, platters
Varying sizes

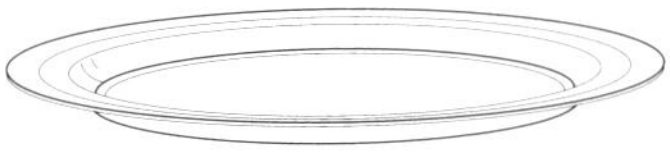

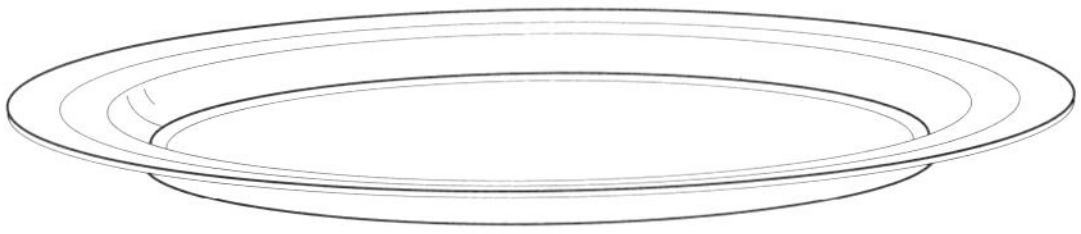

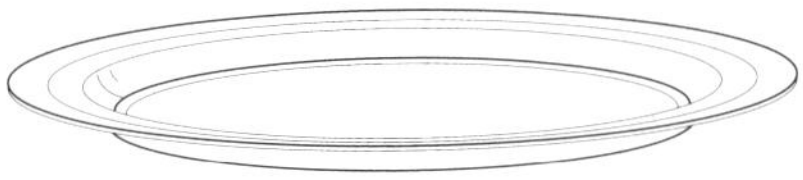

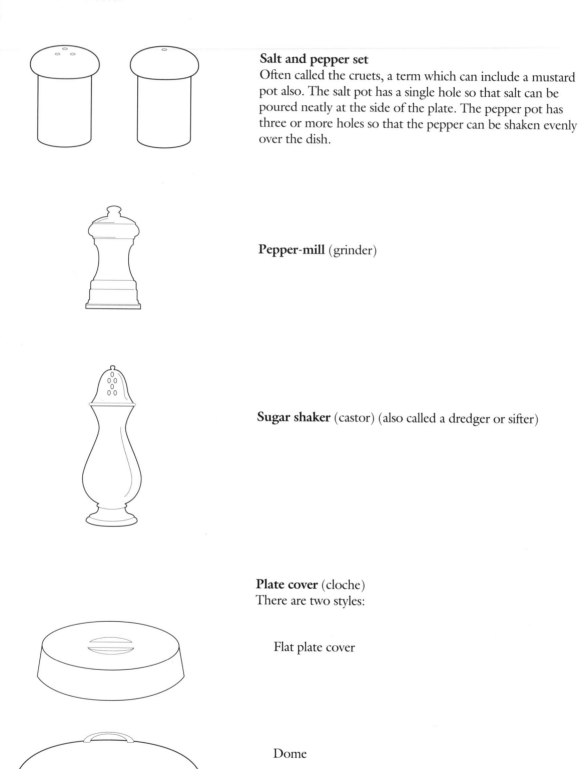

Salt and pepper set
Often called the cruets, a term which can include a mustard pot also. The salt pot has a single hole so that salt can be poured neatly at the side of the plate. The pepper pot has three or more holes so that the pepper can be shaken evenly over the dish.

Pepper-mill (grinder)

Sugar shaker (castor) (also called a dredger or sifter)

Plate cover (cloche)
There are two styles:

Flat plate cover

Dome

Butter dish

Butter pad

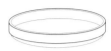

Bud vase

3.6 *LARGE EQUIPMENT*

Warming racks (guéridon service)

Guéridon trolley

Flambé trolley

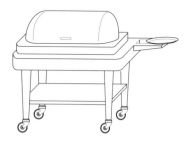

Carving trolley (dome) (see 12.16)

Chafing dish/Flambé pan (see 12.13)

Réchaud (cooking lamp or warmer) (see 12.12)

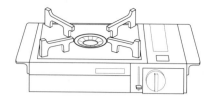

1. Gas cylinder burner

2. Spirit lamp

FOOD SERVICE PREPARATION

4.1 A guest's first impression can make or break the total dining experience. Careful and thorough preparation of the dining area before guests arrive is therefore essential. While standards are set by management, it is the responsibility of all employees to maintain those standards by demonstrating individual professionalism in their work.

On completion of this chapter you should have a basic understanding of the following:
- Taking reservations
- The use of floor plans
- The need for an appropriate atmosphere
- Clothing tables
- Preparation of service stations
- The laying of covers
- A variety of napkin folds.

4.2 TAKING RESERVATIONS

Before you take a booking make sure you know the answers to the types of questions you are likely to be asked, for example:
- What kind of cuisine do you offer? (French, Italian, Cantonese, etc.)
- What style of menu do you offer? (À la carte or table d'hôte?)
- Do you accept cheques? Or credit cards? Which cards?
- Are you licensed or BYO? Or both? If BYO, is there a corkage charge? If so, what is it?
- When are you open? For both lunch and dinner?
- Are children welcome?
- Can you cater for disabled people in wheelchairs?
- Are you air conditioned?

Who suffers when guests call you over and complain that their glass is chipped, or that there is lipstick on the edge of the glass, or that there is no salt in the shaker?

Guests are inconvenienced and their dining experience may be spoiled, but it's the waiter who suffers!

- Is there a non-smoking area?
- Do you have car-parking facilities?
- Do you cater for functions?
- How do I find your establishment?

Before beginning to take the booking make sure you have the reservation book in view. The first things to be clarified are *when* the table is required and *how many* people there are in the party. Only when you have established that a suitable table is available when one is wanted, continue taking the reservation, asking for the following additional details:

- The host's name. (Have it spelt out if you are not sure.)
- The time of arrival.
- A contact telephone number.
- Any special requirements.

Confirm all the details by repeating the name, the date, the time of arrival, the number in the party and the contact phone number. Make sure all the details have been clearly written into the reservations book.

Complete the conversation with a show of hospitality — 'Thank you Mr Bryans. We look forward to seeing you on Thursday evening'.

4.3 FLOOR PLANS

The floor plans for a restaurant or a function are dictated by the number of covers and the style of the service to be offered. When these have been established a floor plan is prepared by the dining-room supervisor as a guide for the set-up of the dining area and to assist in the seating of guests.

Key points to consider when preparing a floor plan are:

- To position the tables so as to allow for sufficient movement by guests and service staff.
- To consider the placement of covers to avoid guests complaining of inappropriate placement, for example near doorways, kitchens, toilets, behind pillars or in draughty areas.
- To accommodate guests' specific needs, for example a business meeting, handicapped guests, honeymoon couples, family groups, etc.

4.4 SETTING THE MOOD

The total dining experience is much affected by the atmosphere created by management for the guests. The mood of the dining environment should reflect the time of day, the location, and an atmosphere that is consistent with the desired character of the establishment.

Key points to be considered by management or staff in setting the dining atmosphere are:

○ *Lighting:* daylight or bright lighting is preferred for daytime meal services.

Subdued light is more appropriate for evening dining.

Candlelight can enhance the mood for evening dining but should not be used for daytime events.

○ *Views:* tables should be set to take best advantage of the views from the dining-room (subject to the limitations of space).

○ *Music:* background music can be appropriate to set the mood. (In dining-rooms where music is played special consideration must be given to the placement of tables.)

○ *Decor:* the decor should be consistent to create a harmonious atmosphere.

Colour selection plays an important part in the dining experience. Some colours are warm, others cold; some are romantic, others business-like, and so on.

While individual waiters may have no control over the colour and general decor of the dining-room, they are often responsible for the details. Live plants and fresh flowers, for example, make a major contribution to the overall presentation and to the mood a room encourages. They must be carefully placed, well-presented and well-maintained.

4.5 *HOW TO CLOTH A TABLE*

There are many different sizes and styles of table and tablecloths used in the industry, and there are different ways of folding tablecloths adopted by different laundries. There can therefore be no one correct technique of clothing tables. The tablecloth fold used in the following procedure for clothing a table is called a concertina fold. It is one of the more commonly-used folds. The procedure as described assumes that the table has four legs at the corners of the table.

4.6 *Clothing procedure*

○ Check the table for steadiness: and position it for ease of access for service. Should the table be unstable it must be stabilized.

○ Stand centrally between two legs of the table.

○ Position the folded cloth on the table with the two woven edges towards you and the two folds of the concertina facing away from you.

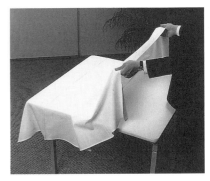

Clothing a table before service

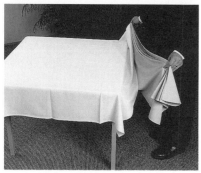

Changing a cloth during service

- Position the vertical centre crease in the centre of the table, holding the concertina fold.
- Lean across the table and release the bottom layer of the cloth to hang over the far edge of the table.
- Re-position the horizontal crease of the cloth in the centre of the table.
- Release the hold on the centre fold and draw the top fold towards you.
- Having centred the cloth both vertically and horizontally, the cloth should now be positioned with an equal drop all round, with the folds of the cloth covering the legs.

4.7 *Changing a cloth during service.*

Cloths often have to be changed during food service, when guests are present at other tables and new covers are to be laid, or when there has been a serious spillage. In these circumstances cloths must be changed with a minimum of fuss, and, most importantly, without at any time exposing the bare tops of the tables to view. The procedure is as follows:

- Remove any articles remaining on the table to the sideboard.
- Stand centrally between two legs of the table.
- Holding the concertina fold, position the vertical centre crease of the clean cloth in the centre of the table.
- Lean across the table and allow the bottom layer of the clean cloth to hang over the far edge of the soiled cloth.
- Take the soiled cloth in both hands, holding it between the little and ring (fourth) fingers.
- Concertina the soiled cloth towards you while opening the clean cloth above it.
- Fold the soiled cloth and remove it discreetly.

4.8 STATION MISE-EN-PLACE

Mise-en-place (French for 'put in place') can be defined as the equipment and food that is prepared ready for service before service begins. Station mise-en-place is the preparation of a waiter's workstation in a food-service area, housing all the equipment required for service.

A waiter's station, whether it is simply a clothed table or a special sideboard equipped with shelves, drawers and, sometimes, a hot box (plate/food warmer), should carry the following:

- All the necessary cutlery, for example, side knives, soup spoons, main (table) knives and forks, sweet spoons and forks, tea and coffee spoons.

- service gear (tablespoons and forks)
- crumbing down equipment
- service plates
- tea/coffee service equipment (milk jugs, sugar bowls, cups and saucers, teaspoons, etc.)
- glassware (tumblers, wine glasses — white and red)
- underliners (an underplate lined with a doily or napkin)
- bread service equipment (and butter — see 4.9)
- napkins
- service trays
- toothpicks
- menus
- wine lists
- spare docket books and pens (a docket and pen will be carried by the waiter)
- waiter's friend (usually carried by the waiter — see 13.4)
- condiments (sauces, pepper-mill, etc.)
- clean table linen
- additional items to meet the specialist requirements of the establishment.

If the sideboard is equipped with a plate/food warmer, it must be turned on approximately 15 minutes before service begins.

Items from the service station used during service should be replaced or replenished during or at the end of the waiter's shift, or at the beginning of the next shift, as decided by the supervisor.

4.9 PREPARING BUTTER

Butter is prepared before the guests arrive. Chill individual portions of butter, whether they are curled, sliced, or moulded, by placing them separately in iced water. This prevents the pieces of butter from sticking together. After they have been chilled place the portions of butter on butter plates and keep them in the refrigerator until they are required for service. Take the butter plate to the table when you are serving the bread (see 5.7).

4.10 HOW TO LAY A COVER

A 'cover' may be defined as:

- A place setting at a table for one guest, laid to suit the type of menu offered.
- The number of guests to attend a function — 'There will be 75 covers at the Rotary dinner', or to indicate the seating capacity of a dining area — 'The Lawson Room seats 50 covers'.

There are two principal types of cover — à la carte/basic cover, and set menu cover. The difference will be explained below. But whatever the type of cover to be laid, the following rules apply:

○ All cutlery and glassware should be cleaned and polished before they are placed on the table.

○ The main knife and fork should be positioned 1cm from the edge of the table and 25-29cm apart (depending on the size of the establishment's dinner plates).

○ Sideplates are always positioned to the guests' left.

○ Side knives are placed on the sideplate, to its right-hand side and parallel with the main knife and fork so that a bread roll can be placed on the plate.

○ The blades of all knives on the cover should face left.

○ The first or only wine glass is positioned 2.5cm from the tip of the main knife. Additional glassware is positioned at a 45° angle to the left of the first glass. (See 4.14 .)

○ A folded napkin is placed in the centre of the cover. (See 4.16.)

4.11 TYPES OF COVER

A la carte/basic cover

An à la carte menu features a variety of dishes individually priced. The guests then select the dishes they would like, usually up to and including the main course.

The basic à la carte cover — the lay-up performed before the guests arrive — is for a main course only. After the guests have ordered, this basic cover is then corrected to suit the customers' actual orders (see 6.12).

An à la carte cover includes:

○ main knife and fork
○ sideplate
○ side knife
○ table centre items (including bud vase or candlestick, cruets, ashtray, tent card and table number)
○ wine glass
○ napkin.

A la carte cover/basic cover

4.12 Set menu cover

A set menu features pre-arranged items at a fixed price for the whole meal. Because it is known in advance what will be served to the guests, the cutlery and glasses for the whole meal are laid in advance. The cover illustrated is for a set menu offering a plated appetizer, soup, a fish entrée, and a main course.

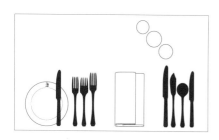

Set menu cover, with no dessert gear

The cutlery required for this menu is:
- entrée knife and fork
- soup spoon
- fish knife and fork
- main knife and fork
- sideplate
- side knife
- glassware
- napkin.

Note that the various items of cutlery are set so that the cutlery used for the first course is outermost, and the remaining cutlery is set in the order in which it will be used, working inwards from the outside.

4.13 DESSERT CUTLERY

Dessert gear (the dessert spoon and fork) is not usually laid before the meal begins, but corrected (placed) after the main course has been cleared. It may also be set across the top of the cover before the meal. This alternative will require the waiter to move the fork and spoon down just before the course is served (see 6.13).

As an alternative to laying the dessert spoon and fork prior to the meal, we suggest that dessert gear should be taken to the table on a service plate and laid only when needed for the sweet course. This will allow additional room on the table and ensure that the cutlery will be absolutely clean when the time comes for it to be used.

Note that not all desserts require a spoon and fork; some may require a fruit knife and fork, or a small spoon.

Set menu cover, with dessert gear

Set menu cover, with small spoon

4.14 GLASSWARE

The wine glasses, like the cutlery, are also set in the order in which they will be used. They are set in at an angle of 45° from the first glass to be used, which (as already noted) is placed about 2.5cm from the tip of the main knife.

Should the table not have sufficient room for the glassware to be set in a row, it may be set in a triangle.

Wine glasses: standard setting

Wine glasses: triangle setting

4.15 *BISTRO COVER*

A bistro cover is a simplified setting to suit a less formal style of dining. The simplicity of this cover makes it suitable for buffets, counter meals, or barbecues.

The cutlery used and the exact placement of the equipment will vary according to menu and the style of the establishment.

4.16 *NAPKIN FOLDS*

A folded table-napkin is placed on the table for the guests' use and to contribute to the appearance of the cover and the whole dining environment. The way in which the napkin is presented depends on the type of establishment and the type of service.

It is an advantage if napkin folds are kept simple as less handling is involved. Less handling makes for more hygienic napkins (as well as being less time-consuming). However, some establishments require more elaborate folds for aesthetic reasons.

Detailed below are examples of some commonly used professional napkin folds. Either starched linen or paper napkins can be used for folding.

A professionally folded napkin will stand by itself without the aid of cutlery or glassware.

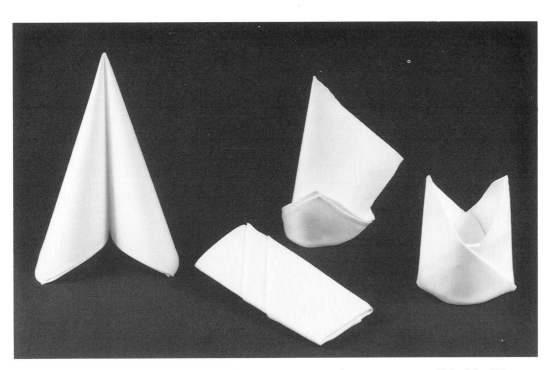

| Sail | Bistro | Cone | Bishop's hat/Mitre |

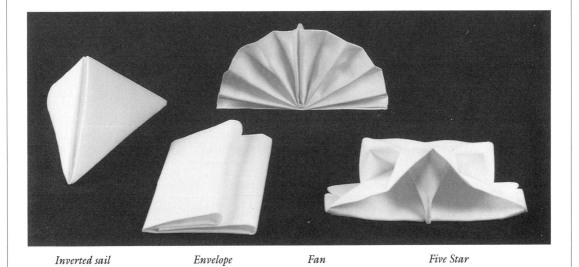

| Inverted sail | Envelope | Fan | Five Star |

Napkin folds

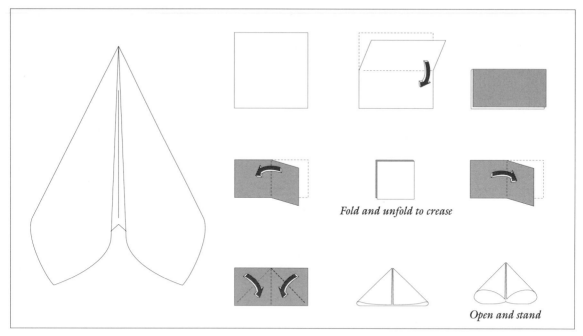

Sail

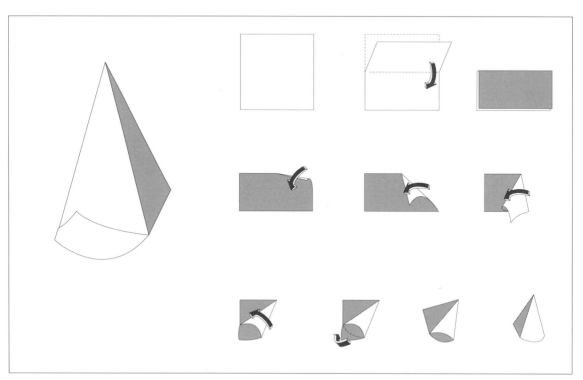

Cone

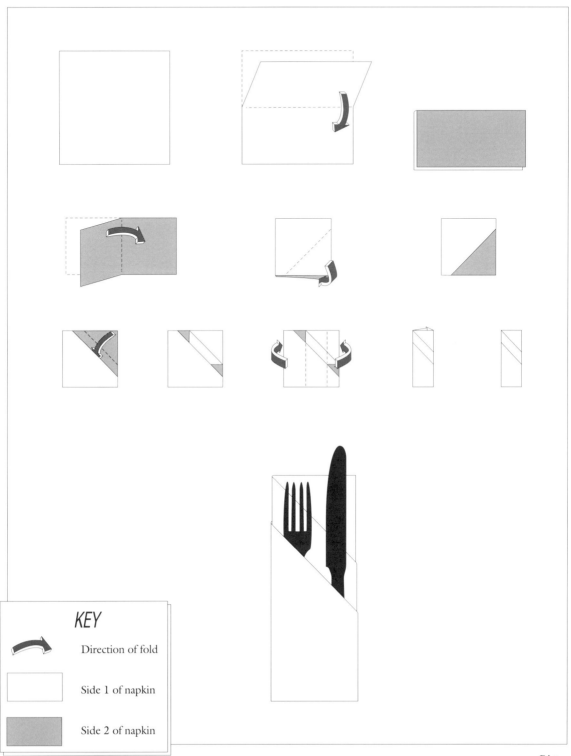

KEY

Direction of fold

Side 1 of napkin

Side 2 of napkin

Bistro

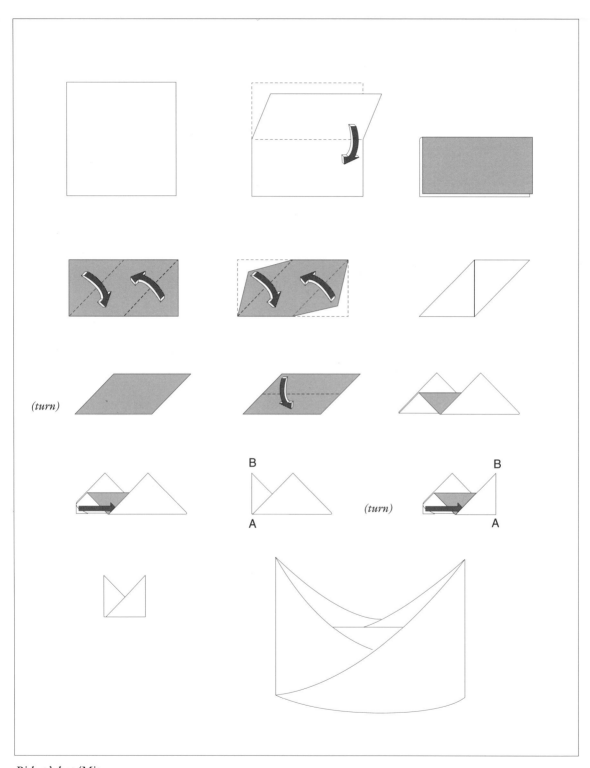

(turn)

(turn)

Bishop's hat/Mitre

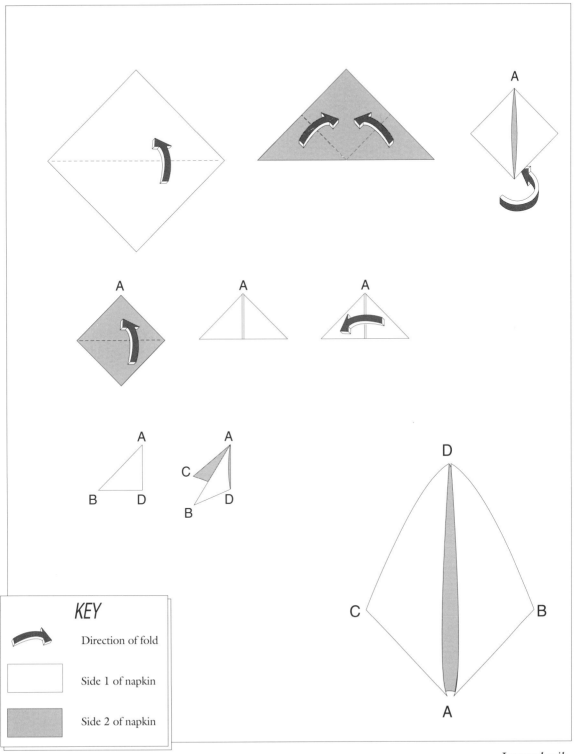

Inverted sails

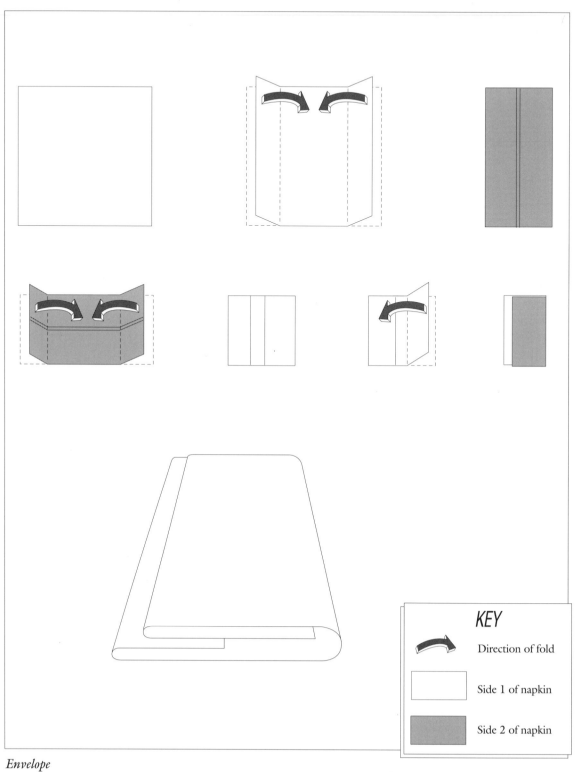

KEY

Direction of fold

Side 1 of napkin

Side 2 of napkin

Envelope

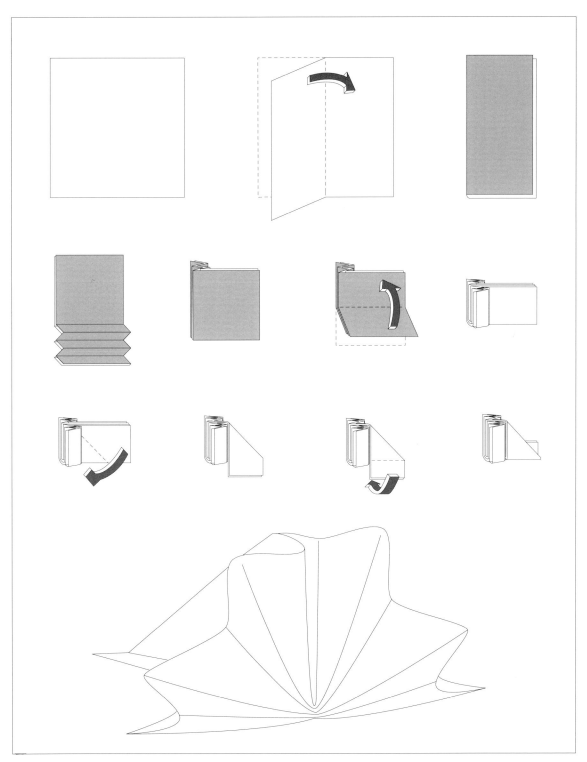

Fan

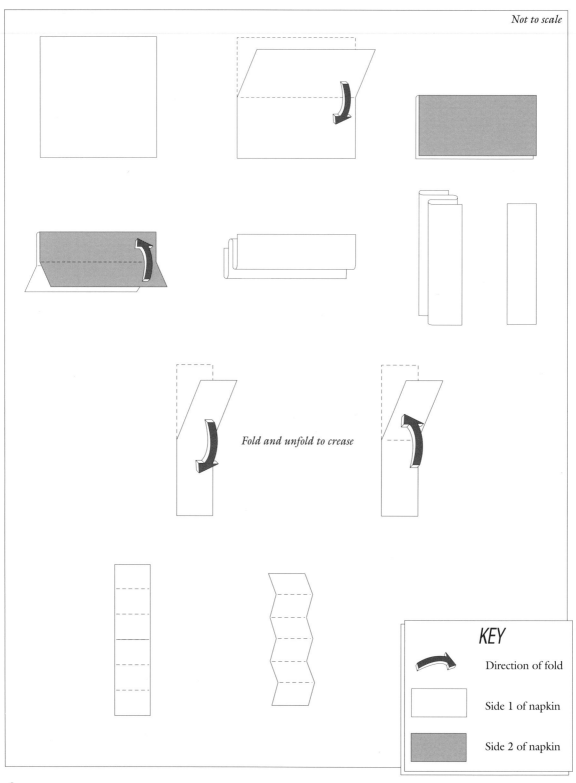

Not to scale

Fold and unfold to crease

KEY

Direction of fold

Side 1 of napkin

Side 2 of napkin

Star

(stretched view)

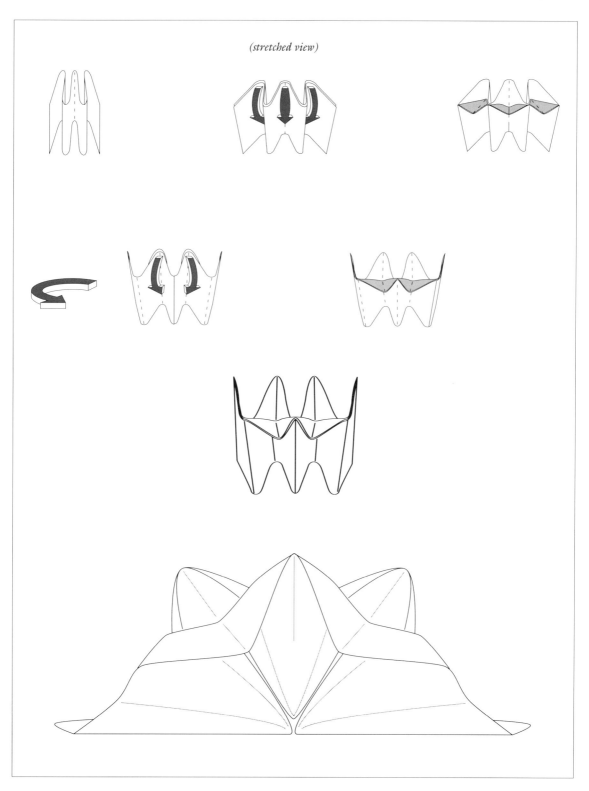

5

FOOD SERVICE PROCEDURES: THE PRELIMINARIES

The objective of food service is to meet the needs of guests and to ensure that their dining experiences are both pleasurable and memorable. Why then should a guest be inconvenienced by the service? A guest who has to duck and dive throughout a meal to make way for the service will only remember that the service was not pleasurable.

5.1 Food service procedures vary considerably throughout the industry. Whether an establishment offers traditional services, modern service, or its own particular variation, is of little importance; what matters is that the establishment is consistent in the services it offers.

Because of the great variety of food service procedures in use today, many people entering the industry for the first time become confused about what are the 'correct' practices. The answer is, of course, that no one set of techniques is correct in all circumstances. What we have tried to do in this and the following chapters is to present common-sense solutions to the various problems and challenges of service which will be applicable in most circumstances, but the reader must always be aware that in some establishments other techniques and practices may be required.

On completion of this chapter you should have a good understanding of the following:

○ The order of service
○ Greeting and seating guests
○ Opening napkins
○ Service of water
○ Service of bread
○ Taking orders for pre-dinner drinks
○ Serving pre-dinner drinks

5.2 THE ORDER OF SERVICE

The 'order of service' is a sequential check-list of services from the arrival to the departure of the guest. It will differ in detail depending on the style of the establishment and the services it offers.

The sequence of service will take into account the particular tasks to be performed to achieve a smooth flow of service to suit the special needs of each guest.

Many points must be considered when an order of service is defined, for example whether iced water will automatically be offered, whether hot or cold towels will be provided, and how the food and beverage services are to be co-ordinated. (There may be a specialist wine waiter.)

If several groups of guests arrive simultaneously at tables which are the responsibility of a single waiter then it is necessary to read the differing needs of the various groups and adjust the order of service to ensure that the tasks can be performed without overloading the station.

5.3 CHECK-LIST OF SERVICE

A written check-list of service ensures the consistency of the services offered and acts as a guideline to part-time and new waiting staff. What follows is an *example* of such an order of service from the time the guests are taken to their table.

- Greet and seat the guests.
- Open the napkins.
- Offer iced water.
- Take pre-dinner drink orders.
- Serve the bread and butter.
- Offer the menu and suggest specials and inform the guests of variations to the menu.
- Take the food order up to and including the main course.
- Offer the wine list.
- Transfer the food order to the kitchen and cashier dockets and place the order with the kitchen.
- Take the wine order.
- Serve the wine.
- Correct the covers, up to and including the main course.
- Serve the first course.
- Clear the first course.
- Top up wines, and open fresh bottles as ordered.
- Serve additional starter courses (for example a second entrée).
- Clear the course preceding the main course.
- Call away the main course.
- Serve the salad.

- Serve the main course.
- Enquire (after the guests have had the opportunity to taste the food) whether the meals are satisfactory.
- Clear the main course.
- Clear the sideplates, salad plates and butter dishes.
- Check and, if necessary, change ashtrays. (If ashtrays are being used they should be changed regularly throughout the meal, especially just before food is served — see 11.6 and 11.7.)
- Brush/crumb down.
- Offer hot (or cold) towels.
- Offer the wine list for the selection of dessert wines (or, if the guests prefer it, continue to serve the wine selected earlier).
- Offer the menu for dessert, suggesting specials and inform the guests of variations to the menu.
- Take dessert or cheese order.
- Transfer the dessert order to the kitchen and cashier dockets and place the order with the kitchen.
- Correct the covers.
- Serve the dessert wines or other beverages selected.
- Serve the dessert or cheese course.
- Take the order for coffee/tea. (The coffee/tea may be served with the dessert/cheese course if requested by the guest or as a separate service.)
- Transfer the coffee/tea order to the cashier docket.
- Take the after-dinner drinks order.
- Correct the cover.
- Serve the after-dinner drinks.
- Serve the coffee/tea.
- Serve the petits fours.
- Prepare the guest's account.
- Offer additional coffee/tea.
- Present the guest account when it is requested.
- Accept payment and tender change.
- Offer additional coffee/tea.
- Farewell your guests.

5.4 GREETING AND SEATING GUESTS

First impressions are extremely important. Guests arriving at a restaurant gain their first impression of the establishment substantially from the willingness of the staff to acknowledge their presence and the greeting they receive. If the greeting is both warm and efficient guests will immediately feel that they can expect the rest of their experience to be pleasurable, and they will feel confident that they will be in the hands of reliable professionals.

Offer the guest a chair

The waiting service begins with the greeting and seating of the guests.

In larger establishments guests may be received by a head waiter or supervisor and taken to the table (after checking reservations, etc.) where they are introduced to their table waiter, who takes over responsibility for their service. In smaller restaurants a single waiter will be responsible for the whole operation. In either case the procedure is as follows:

- Acknowledge new guests as soon as they arrive.
- Approach the guests with an appropriate welcome, for example, 'Good evening'.
- If the guests have come to eat, enquire whether they have a reservation. Check the reservation. If no table has been booked, check that one is available.
- When checking the reservation, note the host's name — the table will usually have been reserved in the name of the host. It is important to establish who the host is. (The host may, of course, be female or male.)
- Show the guests to their table.
- Offer the guests a chair to encourage them to be seated.

Opening a napkin

5.5 OPENING NAPKINS

Opening the napkin for your guests ensures that the napkin is out of the way when drinks and food are to be served. Some guests will open their own napkins as soon as they sit down, others will wait for you to open theirs for them. The technique is:

○ Pick up the napkin with the right hand from the guest's right.

○ Shake the napkin from its fold into a triangle.

○ Place it across the guest's lap with the longest side of the triangle closest to the guest.

○ Move anti-clockwise around the table opening the napkins, opening the host's last.

5.6 WATER SERVICE

Iced water may be offered to the guests after the greeting/seating procedures. The purpose of serving iced water is to refresh the guests' palates, and allow them time to select a pre-dinner drink.

Iced water is a valuable addition to the meal experience, and is appreciated by guests. It should always be available, although in some establishments it may not be the practice to serve it unless it is asked for. (Some countries, including the USA and Japan, require fresh water to be made available, and visitors from those countries will expect iced water to be available without their having to ask for it.) The procedure for serving water is:

○ The water glass is positioned to the right of the wine glass above the table knife.

○ Water is poured from the guest's right.

Serving iced water

- Move anti-clockwise round the table pouring the water, serving the host last.
- Continue to offer water throughout the meal, as required. In some establishments jugs of iced water may be left on the table for the guests to help themselves.

5.7 BREAD SERVICE

Bread, in some form or other, is usually served as soon as the guests are seated. It may be placed in a basket on the table, or served individually (silver service). The advantage of the individual service of bread is that it leaves more room on the table. The silver service technique is:

- Carry the bread basket and butter plate in the left hand, using the two-plate method (see 7.5).
- Place the butter plate in the centre of the table.
- Transfer the bread basket to the flat of the left hand.
- Serve from the guest's left.
- Hold the left hand (with the bread basket) down over the edge of the sideplate.
- Transfer the bread from the basket to the sideplate, using service gear (see 8.4).
- Move anti-clockwise around the table, serving the host last.

5.8 PRE-DINNER DRINKS

Pre-dinner drink (apéritif) orders should be taken as soon as possible after guests have been seated. The waiter should encourage the guests to try something a little adventurous or different by suggesting speciality cocktails or beverages, allowing guests time to consider their preferences.

- Offer the drinks/cocktail list, or suggest a variety of the beverages available.
- Assist the guests in making their selections by explaining what is in the various cocktails and what they are like.
- Record the orders in sequence round the table, anti-clockwise.
- Note any special requirements (no ice, etc.).
- Record the sales following the house control system.
- Place the order with the bar.

Carry the drinks to the table on the tray

5.9 Serving pre-dinner drinks

- Arrange the drinks in sequence of (anti-clockwise) service on a drinks tray.
- Carry the drinks to the table on the drinks tray.
- Hold the tray on the left hand away from the table (see 15.11).

Serving pre-dinner drinks

○ Serve the drinks in sequence around the table anti-clockwise, serving the host last.

○ Place each drink to the right of the guest's wine glass.

Your guests should now be comfortably settled and ready to turn their attention to the menu.

6

TAKING ORDERS AND CORRECTING THE COVERS

6.1 Once the guests are comfortably settled, and have been provided their pre-dinner drinks and bread, they are ready to turn their attention to the menu and to selecting what they want to eat. The menu is offered, the order is taken, and the cover is corrected.

When you have completed this chapter you should have a thorough understanding of the following:

○ Presenting the menu
○ Food sales and sales techniques
○ Taking food orders
○ Use of a service plate
○ Correcting the covers.

6.2 PRESENTING THE MENU

A waiter should not simply take orders and serve what is ordered. The waiter's job is more pro-active — waiters should make things happen. They are salespeople as well as service people.

Presenting the menu is a time for suggestive selling. The waiter has the opportunity actively to sell items on the menu, and 'specials' and side dishes which may not be on it. At no other time does the waiter have so much of the guests' attention, and it is an opportunity not to be missed.

Before presenting the menu you must understand all the items on it and be able to describe how they are cooked and served. (You may find the Glossary helpful for this.) You must also know the details of the daily specials.

Guest: What would you recommend today?

Waiter: Everything is good!

Well, that was a big help, wasn't it?

Presenting the menu

Menus should be offered in such a way as to encourage the guests to select their meals reasonably quickly, without appearing to put any pressure on them to do so.

6.3 *Different forms of menus*

Menus come in different forms. In traditional restaurants the menu is usually presented in a cover, but in less formal establishments it can be written on a blackboard, or a card, or a souvenir place-mat, or almost anything else.

Particular venues may well have devised their own methods to suit the form in which their menus appear and the style of the operation. Of course, these special 'house rules' must be followed by the waiting staff.

6.4 *The technique of presenting a menu*

If the menu is in a cover, it should be opened before it is presented to encourage the guests to read it and make their selections.

- ○ Carry the menu on the flat of the left arm.
- ○ Open the menu from the top with the right hand.
- ○ Present the menu to the guest's right.
- ○ When all the guests have received a copy of the menu, suggest items which do not appear in the menu or any variations to the menu items.

6.5 DESCRIBING AND RECOMMENDING DISHES

You are now likely to be asked questions about the specials, and about the items on the menu. You must be able to describe the dishes, and how they are cooked and served, concisely, accurately, and attractively.

You may also be asked to make recommendations. Be prepared to assist the guests in making their selections. To say, 'Everything is good!' is not helpful. Establish what sort of dish the guest may want — fish or meat, hot or cold — and then direct the guest to those dishes which seem most appropriate.

6.6 *The waiter as salesperson*

This is the time when the waiter's skill as a salesperson comes into play. 'Hard sell' techniques are seldom effective. Sales are made by suggesting items which the guests might well have ordered had they known of them. What you are providing is better service — making the guests' experience more complete and enjoyable, rather than a series of sales pitches. You might helpfully say, for example, that the fish of the day is fresh from the market, or that buffalo steaks are a new menu item and have proved very popular.

It is a basic sales technique not to invite negative answers. Instead of saying, 'Would you like a starter?' which invites the answer 'No', rather ask, 'What would you like to start with?'.

Some establishments (in particular American-based chain restaurants) give detailed instruction to their waiting staff in sales techniques; in others the whole emphasis is on helpful service without any mention of the word sales — 'sales' might almost be thought of as a dirty word — but the effect of good service should be the same in either case: contented guests and profitable food sales for the establishment.

To be an extremely effective salesperson the waiter need only be sincerely helpful, friendly, attentive and enthusiastic, and have a thorough knowledge of the menu and be able to describe and recommend suitable items.

6.7 *CHILDREN*

Unruly bored young children are the waiter's (and their parents') nightmare. Give them something to eat or do as quickly as possible: paper, pens, crayons if you can manage it, at the very least some bread and butter to eat. They must be kept waiting for their food as little as possible. Serve their main course when the adults are served their entrées.

6.8 *TAKING AND PLACING FOOD ORDERS*

Food orders are taken as soon as the guests have made their selections. You must be alert to the signs that the guests are ready to order so that they are not kept waiting. They may, for example, close their menus and place them on the table.

6.9 *Order-taking techniques*

To ensure prompt service and fulfilment of the guests' orders, the waiter must record all the necessary information, so that there is no doubt which guest ordered what.

Orders can be taken in various forms, depending on how many guests there are at the table, and the procedures of the establishment. Some establishments have pre-printed forms which simply have to be ticked. Often the waiter will have to use a blank docket.

The way the order is taken must serve three functions. It must be clear to the kitchen what dishes are to be prepared (and whether there are any special requirements). The waiter must be able to see which dish is to be served to which customer. And when the bill is prepared it must be clear what has been ordered and consumed. The essential is *clarity*.

The great enemy of clarity is the use of personally-devised abbreviations. If abbreviations are used they must be consistent and in a style agreed by *both* the waiting and kitchen staff. Avoid letter abbreviations; use at least part of the name of the dishes ordered — according to the agreed style.

6.10 *Procedure for order-taking*

- Ensure the guests are ready to order.
- Take the order of the guest on the right of the host first, and work anti-clockwise round the table, finishing with the host's order.
- Take the order, up to and including the main course.
- Note any special requirements (for example a special dietary requirement, such as no milk to be used in the preparation of the dish, or a service requirement, such as meals required very quickly because the guests are going on to a show).

- Repeat the order to the guests to make sure that the order is correct.
- Transfer the order to the kitchen docket (using either a manual or a computer system), including the special instructions.
- Record the sale, for billing purposes, following the house control system.
- Place the order with the kitchen.

The service plate

6.11 *USE OF THE SERVICE PLATE*

A service plate is a dinner plate, covered with a folded napkin to reduce noise. It is used to carry all small items used in food service to and from the table — cutlery, cruets, etc.

Service plates should be readily available at all service points. At no time should waiters carry cutlery in their hands.

- Carry the service plate on the flat of the left hand.
- Use the right hand to lift the items from the service plate and place them on the table.

SAMPLE OF A SIMPLE MANUAL ORDER-TAKING DOCKET SYSTEM

Waiter order pad

A small plain jotter pad may be ruled up by the waiter to accommodate the orders of all guests at each table.

Indicate table number

Indicate position of guests at the table by numbering them down the page, starting with the person on the right of the host, moving anti-clock-wise around the table. The host is the last person to order. (See diagram of table.)

Note re host. (Waiters sometimes indicate a characteristic of the host on their ordering pad to assist in remembering the order of service.)

2		
1	Soup	Steak MED Salad only
2	Paté	Veal
3	Soup	Fish
4 Bow tie	Prawns	Steak MR No sauce

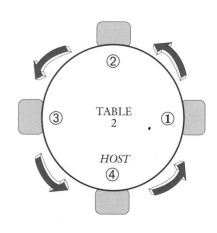

Establishment control docket

Duplicate docket with carbon. The orders are transferred by the waiter from the order pad to the control docket. One copy goes to the kitchen; one goes to the cashier.

Control serial number

THE UNICORN			0241
Date 6/12	**Server** Jan	**Number of Guests** 4	**Table Number** 2
2	Soup		
1	Paté		
1	Prawns		
2	Steak	1 MR – No sauce 1 MED – Salad only	
1	Veal		
1	Fish		

Rule off the close of each course

Using the waiter's order pad to ensure correct:
- ordering
- placement of gear
- placement of food

Orders are taken starting with the person on the host's right moving anti-clockwise round the table and finishing with the host.

The order for each guest is written across the pad up to, and including, the main course.

The waiter reads across the pad when correcting the cover to ensure that the total correction up to, and including, the main course has been completed for each guest before moving to the next guest.

2/		
1	Soup	Steak MED salad only
2	Paté	Veal
3	Soup	Fish
4 Bow tie	Prawns	Steak MR No sauce

The total quantity of each menu item is transferred to the official control docket.

Assuming plate service, the plated food would be placed in the waiter's left hand starting with the prawns, followed by the soup and then the pâté in a three-plate method. The remaining soup would be carried in the right hand. The plated food is now positioned to allow the waiter to place the correct plate (soup) in front of the person on the right of the host, moving anti-clockwise and serving the second and third (pâté and soup) plates. The prawns for the host are placed last.

If the main item on the plate is turned so that it is closest to the waiter when it is picked up, then the plated meal will automatically be in the correct position and will be placed with the main item correctly placed closest to the guest.

Correcting the covers

6.12 *CORRECTING THE COVERS*

To correct a cover is to adjust the cutlery originally laid to meet a guest's specific order.

Covers are corrected after the orders have been taken and placed with the kitchen. They are corrected up to and including the main course.

Guests use the outer cutlery for their first courses and move inwards for each succeeding course.

Cutlery for the dessert and the cheese is corrected after those orders have been taken later in the meal.

○ Prepare the cutlery for each guest, up to and including the main course, on a service plate.

○ Starting with the guest on the right of the host, move anti-clockwise, correcting the covers.

○ Correct the knife section of the first guest and the fork section of the next guest by standing between them.

○ To adjust the cutlery, lift the item not required and replace it with the correct item. Place the items required in sequence of use, that is with the first-course items on the outside and the items for the later courses inside and nearer the plate in the order in which they will be used.

○ Pick up the cutlery holding it between the thumb and the index finger at the neck or join between the handle and the top of the gear. This will ensure that no finger prints can be seen on the cutlery after it has been placed.

○ All cutlery used when adjusting the covers is placed parallel to the main gear. This applies to dessert spoons and forks when the covers are adjusted for the dessert and cheese orders as well as to the cutlery used for the earlier courses.

6.13 *Dessert gear*

As we have already noted (see 4.13), dessert gear is usually placed or corrected after the main course has been cleared, just before the dessert course is served. This means that the dessert gear must be brought to the table and placed. The procedure is:

- Arrange the required dessert gear for the whole table on a service plate and take it to the table.
- Correct the cover by standing between each pair of guests and placing a spoon to the right of the guest on your left and a fork to the left of the guest on your right. Move anti-clockwise round the table repeating the procedure.
- If the dessert cutlery required is only a small spoon and not a full-size dessert spoon and fork, the small spoon is placed to the right of the cover.

If the dessert gear was placed on the table across the top of the cover as part of the cover for a set menu it must be moved down before the dessert course is served. Stand between two guests and move the spoon of the guest to your left and the fork of the guest to your right, repeating the procedure round the table as you would have done had you brought the dessert gear to the table on a service tray.

7

STYLES OF SERVICE: PLATE SERVICE

Why should guests have to experience delays in the service of food to their table caused by a waiter's inadequate skills?

7.1 The manager of a food-service establishment has the choice of a number of different styles of service. Management should select a style of service to complement the type of food being served, taking into account the effectiveness of the service to accommodate both the guests' and the establishment's needs.

An operator who understands the various service styles can utilize a particular service, or combine two or more different styles of service, to achieve greater productivity (and profitability) and enhance guest satisfaction.

The two most commonly used food-service styles are plate service and silver service.

The various styles of service and the techniques required by them are all explained in detail in this or later chapters. They are:

○ Plate service (this chapter)
○ Silver service (chapter 8)
○ Guéridon service (10.5-10.6)
○ Family service (10.7-10.8)
○ Smorgasbord service (10.9)
○ Buffet service (10.10)
○ Cafeteria service (10.11).

These styles of service can be used in new and interesting ways to encourage custom. Cafeteria service, for example, is used in modern food halls, while guéridon service is used imaginatively for salads and desserts in some bistros and delis. Silver service is commonly used instead of the usual plate service at large tables at banquets.

In plate service the food is plated in the kitchen or at a service point and served to the guest on the plate. In silver service the food is presented on serving dishes and is transferred from a serving dish to the plate in front of the guest with the use of a spoon and fork — the 'service gear'.

There are of course variations on these two basic techniques. For example, the main food item, perhaps the meat, can be placed on the plate in the kitchen and served using the plate service technique, and then the vegetables can be served at the table using the silver service technique. This constitutes a combination of the two service techniques, not a new technique.

This chapter deals with plate service techniques and procedures. Silver service technique is explained in the next chapter.

When you have completed this chapter you should have a thorough understanding of:

○ Plate service procedures
○ The use of service cloths for carrying hot plates
○ Two-plate carrying technique
○ Three-plate carrying technique
○ The use of underliners.

7.2 *PLATE SERVICE SKILLS AND TECHNIQUES*

Plate service is a basic and commonly-used form of service. It demands that the waiter should be skilled in carrying plates without disturbing the food arranged on them. The methods used to carry the plates depend on the number of plates to be carried.

In professional plate service no more than four plates are carried at a time. It is possible to carry more than four plates but, as this relies on balance, it is not usually considered professional service.

The two professional methods most utilized in the industry are the two- and three- plate carrying techniques. These involve carrying either two or three plates in the left hand, leaving the right hand free. The right hand can be used to carry another plate, thus allowing three or four plates to be carried at once.

When plates are cleared the same plate-carrying techniques should be used (see chapter 9).

All professional waiters must be proficient in plate carrying and clearing techniques.

In modern plate service plates are placed from the guest's right

7.3 *PLATE SERVICE PROCEDURE*

Traditional plate service required food to be served to the left of the guest, and that the empty plates should be cleared from the right. In modern plate service, however, plates are both placed and cleared from the guest's right as this causes the least disturbance to the guest.

Modern plate service practice has come about because dining space is now more intensively utilized than in the past, and there is less room for movement between guests. The plate-service waiter can unobtrusively place a plate of food in front of a guest from the right, while holding other plates in the left hand safely behind the guest's head. (Left-handed waiters reverse the technique and serve and clear from the left.)

The modern plate service practice of both placing the plates and clearing them from the guest's right has been adopted by leading colleges and establishments throughout the world. However, there are restaurants which still offer traditional plate service from the left. Waiters must, of course, conform to the 'house rule' on this point.

Modern plate service does not interfere with beverage service as food and beverage service do not take place at the same time.

Unless otherwise instructed serve the guest immediately to the right of the host first and then move anti-clockwise round the table serving each guest in turn, regardless of sex. The host should be served last. Note, though, that in some establishments you may be required to serve ladies before gentlemen, or this may be requested by the guests.

7.4 *THE SERVICE CLOTH*

Service cloths should be used to protect the hands and wrists from burning when you are carrying hot plates.

○ Place the cloth along your left hand and forearm, with the open section of the cloth inwards; the cloth should not protrude beyond the tips of the fingers.

○ Fan the end of the cloth open to protect the hand: this allows both the two-plate and three-plate carrying methods to be used (see 7.5 and 7.6).

○ A second folded service cloth should be held in the right hand to protect it, when holding plates or transferring them from the left hand to the table.

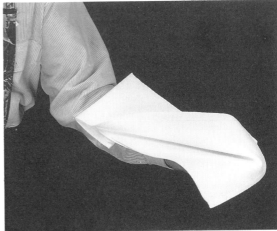

Using a service cloth to carry hot plates

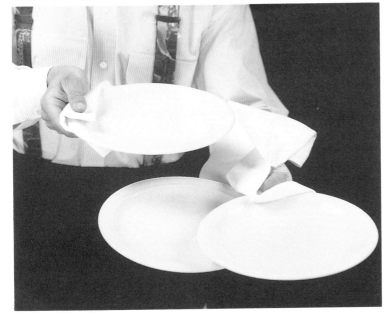

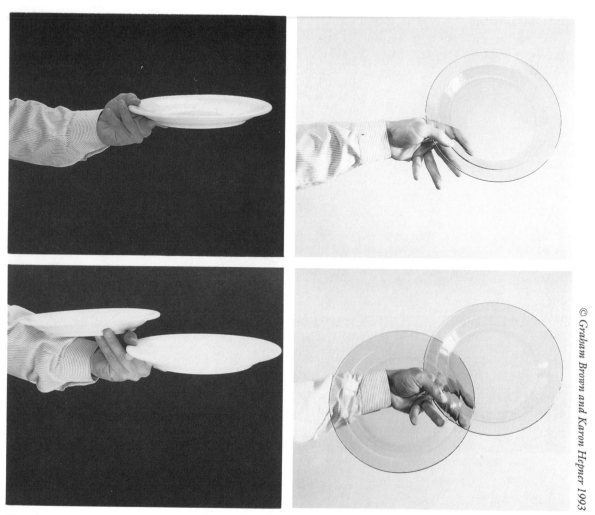

Two-plate carrying technique

7.5 *TWO-PLATE CARRYING TECHNIQUE*

- Plates are picked up so that when they are placed the main item will be on the side of the plate facing the guest. Remember that the first plate to be picked up in the left hand will be the last to be placed on the table.
- Hold the first plate between your thumb, index finger and the middle finger of your left hand. If the plate is hot use a service cloth. (See 7.4.)
- Then place the second plate on a platform above the first plate, supporting it by your ring (or fourth) finger, your little finger and the base of your thumb and lower forearm.
- You may carry a third plate in your right hand, also in a service cloth.

- Carry the plates to the table away from your body, with the shoulders held back, so that the plates are not resting against the front of your body.
- Only bring the plates in front of your body when limited access to the table requires it.
- To place the plates in front of the guests, position yourself at the back right-hand corner of a guest's chair, holding your left hand (and its plates) out of the way behind the guest's head.
- Leaning forward, place the plate in your right hand in front of the guest from the guest's right.
- The plate should be placed so that the main item (the meat, fish, etc.) is immediately in front of the guest, and the vegetables further away at the 'top' of the plate.
- Move behind the next guest to your right and transfer the second plate to your right hand and place it in front of the guest from the guest's right.
- Continue anti-clockwise round the table repeating the procedure.

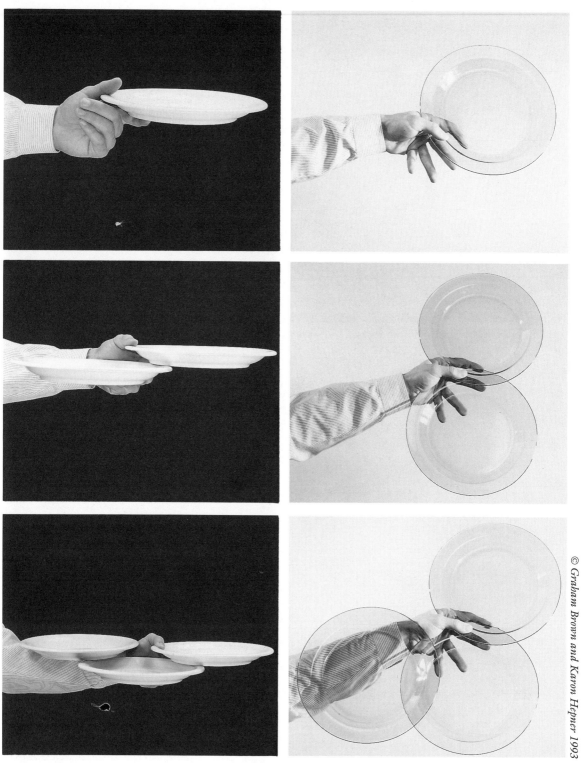

Three-plate carrying technique

7.6 *THREE-PLATE CARRYING TECHNIQUE*

If four plates must be taken to the table at the same time, three plates should be carried in the left hand using the three-plate carrying method.

○ Hold the first plate between your thumb, index and middle fingers of the left hand (as in the two-plate technique). If the plates are hot use a service cloth (see 7.4).

○ Place the second plate into the crease of the palm of your left hand under the edge of the first plate, supporting it by your ring and little fingers.

○ Place the third plate so that it sits on the flat of your forearm and the rim of the second plate.

○ Carry the fourth plate in your right hand.

○ Carry the plates to the table, holding them away from your body, with your shoulders held back, so that the plates are not resting against the front of your body.

○ The plates should only be carried in front of your body when limited access to the table requires it.

○ To place the plates in front of the guests, position yourself at the back right-hand corner of the guest's chair, holding your left hand and its plates out of the way behind the guest's head.

○ Leaning forward, place the plate in your right hand in front of the guest from the guest's right, using your right hand.

○ Move behind the next guest to your right and transfer the third plate to your right hand and place it in front of the guest from the guest's right.

○ Continue anti-clockwise round the table repeating the procedure.

Three-plate carrying technique

7.7 *UNDERLINERS*

An underliner or underplate is a plate placed under the service equipment (the vessel containing the food) when it is served to guests. Underliners are not primarily intended to enhance the appearance of the food being served; their purpose is to make it easier to carry and clear service equipment that is difficult to handle, and to provide something for guests to place their used cutlery on when the service equipment itself is not suitable for that purpose.

It is usual for a doily or napkin to be placed on the underliner to prevent the service equipment from sliding.

Underliners should only be used for a specific purpose. They are often used when serving items in soup bowls and coupes. They should also be used when serving natural oysters on ice to prevent condensation.

Underliners used for soup bowls and coupes

8
SILVER SERVICE

Obviously this 'waiter' hasn't mastered the basic silver-service skills — he's using kitchen tongs instead of a spoon and fork!

8.1 Silver service is the technique of transferring food from a service dish to the guest's plate from the left with the use of service gear. 'Service gear' usually means a serving spoon and fork, but occasionally it consists of knives, especially fish knives. Silver service requires the waiter to be able to use the service gear to serve the food with one hand.

Professional silver service depends on mastering the technique of using service gear held in one hand to transfer items to the guest's plate from a service dish held in the other hand.

When you have completed this chapter you will understand:
○ The technique of using a serving spoon and fork
○ The technique of using knives for service
○ Silver service of bread rolls
○ Silver service procedures for the main meal
○ Silver service of sauces
○ Silver service of delicate or large items.

Silver service takes place from the left of the guest

8.2 *USE OF A SPOON AND FORK*

- Place a fork over a spoon in your right hand, both facing up. They should rest across your middle, ring, and little fingers with the base of the gear resting in line with the bottom of the little finger, leaving the index finger and thumb free to move the gear. The handles should not protrude beyond your little finger.

- Slide your index finger between the fork and the spoon, and hold the fork between the tip of your index finger and the tip of your thumb so that you can lift the fork with your index finger and thumb.

- Holding the fork between the tips of your index finger and your thumb, raise the fork from the bowl of the spoon, keeping the ends of the handles of the fork and the spoon together with your little finger.

- At no time allow the index finger and thumb to slide more than half-way up the handles of the gear.

- You can now lift food items with the spoon and hold them firmly in place with the fork while you transfer them to the guest's plate.

- Pick the food up from the side, drawing the gear towards you as you lift it.

- If the item to be moved is small or very thin, you can remove your index finger. This enables the fork to be pressed more tightly against the spoon, holding the item firmly. To release the item insert the tip of your index finger to separate the gear.

- For large round items, such as bread rolls, you may turn the fork, enclosing the item.

- The tops of some items, broccoli hollandaise for example, must not be touched when they are served. In those cases turn your hand so that you can pick up the item from its sides.

Some waiters thread the fork through their fingers when using the service gear for silver service. To the novice this may seem an easier and safer technique, but it has its limitations and is not recommended for professional service. It is much too slow, for example when several different items requiring different service gear have to be served quickly one after the other. Also it is difficult to apply when two knives are being used as the service gear (see 8.3, 8.7).

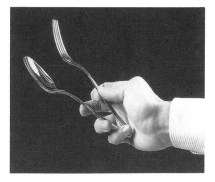

Holding the service gear

For large round items turn the fork

8.3 USE OF KNIVES FOR SERVICE

Two knives, preferably fish knives, are sometimes used for the service of soft or large items requiring more support than can be given by a service spoon and fork.

- Hold the two knives in the same fashion as a spoon and fork.
- Fan out the knives to give greater support to the item you will be moving.
- Place the knives under the food item, supporting it while you transfer it to the guest's plate.

8.4 SILVER SERVICE OF BREAD ROLLS

- Hold the bread basket on the flat of your left hand.
- Silver service takes place from the left of the guest.
- Place your left hand low above the edge of the guest's sideplate (no more than 5cm above the plate).
- Hold the bread roll in the service gear and transfer it to the sideplate.
- Move anti-clockwise round the table offering a bread roll to each guest.

8.5 SILVER SERVICE PROCEDURE — THE MAIN MEAL

- Place clean hot plates in front of the guests from the right from a stack carried in the left hand.
- Hold the serving dish on a service cloth on the flat of your left hand, with your hand under the centre of the service dish.
- Calculate the size of the portion allowed for each guest, and decide how it should be presented, considering the other items to be served. (For example, two green vegetables may be separated by a white item, giving a satisfactory visual balance.)
- As before noted, silver service takes place from the left of the guest. (From the right the service plate would present a barrier between the guest's plate and the waiter's right hand used for transferring the food items.)
- Hold the serving dish over the guest's plate, no more than 5cm above it.
- Place the main item of the course to the front of the guest's plate.
- Place the vegetables around and behind the main item away from the guest in the pattern already decided for plate presentation.
- Note that no items are placed on the rim of the plate.
- Garnishes are placed to enhance the presentation.

Place clean hot plates in front of each guest

○ If you are serving small items such as Brussels sprouts, transfer a small number at a time. You can then position them carefully on the plate.

○ Pick up food items on the side of the serving spoon closest to you (its left side) and release them from the same side of the spoon. When a food item is being picked up from the serving dish, the service gear is moving towards you; when the item is released on the guest's plate the service gear is moving away from you.

○ Plate presentation should be consistent: the different food items in a dish should always be presented in the same pattern to all guests who have selected that dish.

○ Move anti-clockwise round the table serving each guest in turn, with the host last.

When a food item is picked up from the serving dish the service gear is moving towards you

When the item is released on the guest's plate the service gear is moving away from you

8.6 *SILVER SERVICE OF SAUCES*

In silver service, accompanying sauces should not be carried on the same serving dish as the food. They are offered and served separately, using a sauce-boat (*saucière*) and a serving spoon or special ladle. Sauces are never poured direct from the sauce-boat. A spoon (or ladle) is always used to serve them.

- Carry the sauce-boat on an underplate on the flat of your left hand, with the lip of the sauce-boat facing to the right.
- Serve the sauce from the left of the guest.
- Lower the underplate over the guest's plate, so that it is not more than 5cm above it.
- Hold the serving spoon (or ladle) in your right hand with the handle of the spoon above the lip of the sauce-boat.
- Draw the spoon across the sauce-boat towards you to collect the sauce.
- Carry the spoon away from you to sauce the appropriate item. Note that the sauce should only cover one third of the item.
- Other accompaniment items, such as mustard or apple sauce, are placed to the left of the main item.
- Move anti-clockwise round the table offering the sauce or accompaniment to each guest in turn, with the host last.

Draw the spoon across the sauce-boat towards you to collect the sauce.

8.7 *SILVER SERVICE OF DELICATE OR LARGE ITEMS*

Two knives, preferably fish knives, are used to serve delicate or large items which are difficult to handle with a service spoon and fork.

- Two (fish) knives take the place of the service spoon and fork.
- Hold the knives in your right hand in the same way as a service spoon and fork, and fan them out (see 8.3).
- Transfer the food item to the guest's plate with the fanned knives.
- Remove the knives when the food touches the plate.
- In addition to the knives, carry a set of ordinary service gear (a serving spoon and fork) on the serving dish to serve the vegetables and garnishes.

Hold the knives in your right hand and fan them out

9

CLEARING THE TABLE

'Is this the same waiter who has been so helpful and knowledgeable?'

9.1 The same clearing techniques are used for both plate service and silver service. They rely on a similar plate-carrying techniques; the two-plate and three-plate techniques already described (7.5 and 7.6).

On completing this chapter you should understand and have mastered:

- ○ Clearing procedures
- ○ Two-plate clearing technique
- ○ Three-plate clearing technique
- ○ Clearing sideplates
- ○ Clearing soup bowls and oddly-shaped dishes.

9.2 *CLEARING PROCEDURES*

When a course is cleared it is usual for the whole table to be cleared at the same time when all the guests have finished. Guests usually indicate that they have finished by placing their cutlery together on the plate. As they don't always do this you must be alert to other signs from the table that everyone has finished, and if necessary you must ask guests about whom you are doubtful whether they have finished or not.

Once you have established that all the guests have finished the course, clear the plates using one of the following techniques.

9.3 *TWO-PLATE CLEARING TECHNIQUES*

- ○ Start with the person to the right of the host.
- ○ Standing at the back right-hand corner of the guest's chair, lean forward and pick up the used plate and cutlery with your right hand.

Clearing the table. These guests have indicated that they have finished by placing their knives and forks together on their plates.

○ Transfer the plate to your left hand, holding it between the thumb and index finger. Place your thumb over the end of the fork handle. Use the knife to move the scrap items to the front of the plate.

○ Place the knife under the handle of the fork at right angles to it.

○ Moving anti-clockwise round the table, place yourself behind the next guest. Holding your left hand (and the first guest's empty plate) behind the guest, lean forward and pick up the second used plate and its cutlery.

○ Transfer the second plate to your left hand. Position it on a platform above the first plate, supporting it with your ring finger, your little finger and the base of your thumb and lower forearm.

○ Place the fork alongside the other fork on the first plate, and, using the knife, push the scraps down off the second plate onto the front of the first plate to join the scraps already there.

○ Place the knife alongside the knife on the first plate.

○ Moving anti-clockwise round the table, collect the remaining plates and cutlery. Stack the plates on the second plate and arrange the cutlery on the first plate, following the same procedure as for the second plate.

○ The number of plates which can be collected in this way will depend on the waiter's skill and experience. When you have collected as many plates as you can confidently carry, take the plates and cutlery to the station (sideboard) and place them on a tray for removal, or take them directly to the dish-washing area, according to the practice of the establishment.

Two-plate clearing technique

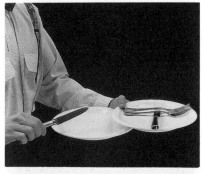

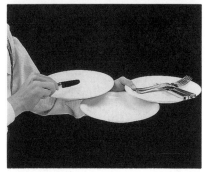

Three-plate clearing technique

9.4 *THREE-PLATE CLEARING TECHNIQUE*

The three-plate clearing method is similar to the two-plate method, with the added advantage that the scrap food items and the used cutlery are carried on separate plates.

○ Start with the person to the right of the host.

○ Standing at the back right-hand corner of the guest's chair, lean forward and pick up the used plate and cutlery with your right hand.

○ Transfer the plate to your left hand, holding it between the thumb and index finger. Place your thumb over the end of the fork handle. Use the knife to move the scrap items to the front of the plate.

○ Place the knife under the handle of the fork at right angles to it.

○ Moving anti-clockwise round the table, place yourself behind the next guest. Holding your left hand (and the first guest's empty plate) behind the guest, lean forward and pick up the second used plate and its cutlery.
(Up to this point the technique has been exactly the same as for the two-plate method.)

○ Place the second plate in the crease of the palm of your left hand under the edge of the first plate, supporting it by your ring and little fingers. Place the fork alongside the fork on the first plate, and using the knife, move the scrap items from the first plate down onto the second plate. Place the knife alongside the knife on the first plate.

○ Moving anti-clockwise round the table, pick up the next guest's used plate.

○ Place the third plate so that it sits on the flat of your forearm and the rim of the second plate. Place the fork alongside the forks on the first plate and use the knife to move the scraps onto the second plate. Place the knife alongside the other knives on the first plate.

○ Continue anti-clockwise, collecting the plates, stacking the additional plates on the third plate, transferring the scraps onto the second plate and placing the knives and forks neatly on the first plate.

○ When you have collected as many plates as you can confidently manage, take them to the station (or the dish-washing area).

9.5 *CLEARING SIDEPLATES*

Clearing sideplates at the same time as dinner plates

If there are only three or four guests at the table, the side-plates may be collected at the same time as the used dinner plates, using the two-plate or the three-plate technique. Continue anti-clockwise round the table a second time, collecting the sideplates and knives. If using the two-plate technique the procedure is:

- Collect the sideplates and knives from the guests' left using your right hand.
- Transfer the sideplate to the pile of empty plates supported by your left hand and arm, holding your left hand well away from the table.
- Use the knife to move scrap items to the front of the first dinner plate.
- Place the knife on the first plate beside the other knives.
- Continue until all the sideplates have been collected and stacked on dinner plates.

If the three-plate clearing technique is used collect the knives and forks on the first plate and the scraps on the second plate, piling the sideplates on the cleared main course plates which are stacked on the third plate position.

9.6 *Clearing sideplates separately from dinner plates*

If there are more than four guests at the table, you will not be able to collect the sideplates at the same time as the dinner plates, but will have to collect them separately, using the two-plate method.

- Take a dinner plate to the table. It will provide you with a conveniently larger working surface than a sideplate.
- Treat this plate as if it were the first dinner plate collected, and use it as the receptacle for scraps and the side knives.
- Proceed round the table anti-clockwise, collecting the sideplates and knives from the guests' left, as described above.

Clearing sideplates with dinner plates; two-plate technique

Three-plate technique

Clearing sideplates separately from dinner plates

Clearing unusually-shaped items

9.7 *SOUP BOWLS, COUPES, AND ODD-SHAPED SERVING DISHES*

Untypical and relatively difficult items like soup bowls, coupes, oval pasta dishes, etc. will usually have been served on an underliner (see 7.7). As clean underliners are usually re-used they need not be stacked with the dirty dishes. They should therefore not be stacked but held separately from the used dishes, using the two-plate or three-plate carrying methods (9.3 and 9.4).

10

OTHER FORMS OF SERVICE

10.1 Apart from the basic table-service procedures — plate service and silver service — a waiter may encounter and be expected to be proficient in other specialist forms of service. Some of these are described in this chapter.

On completion of this chapter you will have a basic understanding of the techniques and procedures of:

- Soup service from a tureen or individual soup cup
- Guéridon service
- Family service
- Smorgasbord service
- Buffet service
- Cafeteria service.

10.2 *SOUP SERVICE FROM A SOUP CUP OR TUREEN*

A tureen is a deep bowl with a lid to keep the contents warm. Individual soup cups or, for a number of people, one large tureen may be used as an alternative to the plate service of (pre-filled) soup bowls. Individual soup cups (occasionally with covers) may be offered in a silver service procedure, while service from a large tureen is best performed at a guéridon.

The use of a tureen ensures that the soup stays hot until it is served at table.

10.3 *Individual soup cups*

- Place a hot empty soup bowl positioned on an under-plate for each guest from the guest's right.
- Carry a full individual soup cup on a service plate held on the flat of your left hand to the guest.
- Pour the soup from the cup into the guest's soup bowl, pouring away from the guest.

No wonder the guests get confused at a buffet or smorgasbord when the staff can't understand what they should be offering.

Silver service of soup from individual soup cups

○ If the soup contains items which cannot easily be poured, for example vegetables or noodles, carry a dessert spoon on the service plate and use it to spoon them into the soup.

10.4 *Large tureens*

○ Set a guéridon with hot soup bowls, underliners and a soup ladle, and place it near the table (see 10.5).

○ Take the lid off the tureen and present the soup to the host.

○ When the soup has been approved, place the open tureen on the guéridon.

○ Hold a soup bowl on an underliner in the left hand, and use the right hand to ladle soup from the tureen into the bowl.

○ Scoop the soup from the bottom of the tureen to ensure an even consistency.

○ Place the soup bowls in front of the guests from each guest's right, using the usual plate service procedure.

○ If the soup requires extra garnishing, serve the garnish from the left of the guest, using silver service procedure.

10.5 *GUÉRIDON SERVICE*

The term *guéridon* means a trolley (or side table) used for the service or preparation of foods in the dining environment.

Guéridon *service* specifically refers to the transfer of food from a serving dish to the plate on a guéridon. Guéridon *preparation* is the preparing or finishing of foods on the guéridon, for example table-cooking or the tossing of salads.

This section is concerned with guéridon service only. Guéridon preparation is dealt with in chapter 12.

10.6 *Guéridon service technique*

- ○ Set the guéridon with the appropriate mise-en-place for the service or preparation to be performed. It is essential that the mise-en-place is complete with all items before service begins. You should not leave the guéridon during service.
- ○ Place clean hot plates on the guéridon.
- ○ Present serving dishes containing the food prepared in the kitchen to the guests, and then place them on the guéridon.
- ○ At the guéridon use both hands to manage the service gear, holding the serving spoon in your right hand and the fork in your left.
- ○ Hold the spoon below the fork as you collect the food.
- ○ Position the main item to the front of the plate, with the vegetables around and behind it, allowing some space between the different food items, as in silver service (see 8.5).
- ○ Sauces may be served at the guéridon or may be served at table, using the silver service technique.
- ○ Place the plated meals in front of the guests from their right, using the usual plate-service technique.

Hold the spoon below the fork as you collect the food.

10.7 *FAMILY SERVICE*

Family service is a simple method of service in which serving dishes are placed on the dining table, allowing the guests to select and serve themselves. This style of service enables the guests to select only what they require and in appropriate portions.

Family service is often offered in addition to plate service. For example, the main item may be plate-served, and the guests left to help themselves to vegetables or salad.

10.8 *Family service technique*

- Before serving plates are placed on the table you must make room on the table for them.
- Using a service cloth, place clean hot plates from a stack in front of the guests from the guests' right.
- Place the serving dishes on the table, each with a set of serving gear resting on the sides of the dishes.
- The serving gear should be placed so that the handles face the nearest guest.
- The serving dishes may be removed when they are empty at any time during the meal.

10.9 *SMORGASBORD SERVICE*

In smorgasbord service guests select from a presentation of food items, hot or cold, serving themselves directly onto their plates without the help of service staff.

It is usual practice for the guests to select only one course at a time, returning to the smorgasbord to help themselves to later courses.

The waiter should maintain the arrangement of the food on the platters throughout service to ensure that the food is always attractively presented.

10.10 *BUFFET SERVICE*

In buffet service, like smorgasbord service, guests select what they want from a presentation of food items, hot or cold. The difference is that in buffet service staff serve the guests with the food they have selected, whereas in smorgasbord service the guests help themselves.

Service staff positioned behind the buffet assist the guests by plating their food for them as they select it.

Service staff use silver service technique to plate the guests' food. Hold the guest's clean plate in your left hand and, using a serving spoon and fork held in your right hand, transfer the food items selected from the service plates to the guest's plate.

As in silver service at table you must carefully place the selected items on the plate so that it is visually well-balanced and convenient for the guest.

10.11 *CAFETERIA SERVICE*

In cafeteria service guests collect their own meals on a tray as they select food items from the race. Modern food-hall operations often use this basic service technique.

Buffet, smorgasbord and cafeteria waiting staff, like all other waiters, must have a good knowledge of the items they are serving.

11

OTHER FOOD SERVICE PROCEDURES

11.1 At various stages of the meal the waiter may be required
- To crumb (or brush) down the table
- To serve hot or cold towels
- To change ashtrays.

The necessary techniques and procedures for these services are detailed in this chapter.

11.2 *CRUMBING/BRUSHING DOWN*

Tables are usually crumbed down after the main course and sideplates have been cleared.

Although a variety of brush and pan sets are available for this purpose, the most commonly used equipment is a dinner plate and a folded service cloth. This basic equipment is, of course, readily available in all styles of establishment.

11.3 *Use of service plate and cloth*

- Make sure the sideplates, cruets, and other items no longer required have been removed.
- Hold the plate on the flat of your left hand with your hand under the centre of the plate.
- Brush down from the guests' left (from where their sideplates were before they were cleared).
- Hold the plate just under the edge of the table with your left hand.
- Brush the crumbs onto the plate using a folded service cloth held in your right hand.

The little touches make the difference.

Crumbing down

○ Do not flick the crumbs, but brush them steadily towards you with the folded service cloth.
○ Move anti-clockwise round the table crumbing down each guest's place as required, finishing with the host.

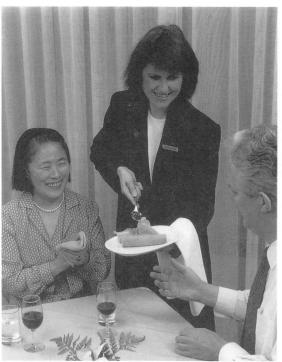

Offering a towel using service gear

Offering a cold towel using tongs

11.4 *SERVICE OF HOT OR COLD TOWELS*

Hot or cold towels or flannels are sometimes offered to the guests for them to refresh themselves either before or after the meal. The towels are moistened and lightly sprayed with a cologne.

Whether the towels are hot or cold is likely to depend on the climatic conditions. Moistened and slightly scented towels, either hot or cold, provide a refreshing start or finish to the dining experience.

11.5 *The technique of serving towels*

○ Stack the towels (rolled) on a serving tray together with a set of tongs or service gear for service.
○ Carry the tray of towels on the flat of your left hand.
○ Offer the towels from the guests' right.

- Holding the tongs or service gear in your right hand, use them to grip the edge of the towel so that it will open as you offer it to the guest.
- Move anti-clockwise round the table offering towels to each of the guests, with the host last.
- Place the serving tray on the centre of the table so that the guests can put their towels on it after they have finished with them.
- Remove the tray with the used towels on it.

11.6 *ASHTRAYS*

Many restaurants now have smoking and non-smoking areas, and in some no smoking is allowed. The correct procedure for laying and handling ashtrays will therefore depend on the rules of the establishment.

In some establishments ashtrays are not placed on the tables before service begins as part of the mise-en-place but are only brought when they are requested by guests. When this is so the waiter must be observant so that ashtrays are brought immediately they are required.

It is the responsibility of all waiting staff to ensure that used ashtrays are removed and cleaned frequently and that clean ashtrays are always available to smokers.

11.7 *Changing ashtrays*

Waiting staff should make regular rounds of the service area, clearing used ashtrays and replacing them with clean ones. Never remove an ashtray unless a clean one is available to replace the one removed.

The procedure for changing ashtrays is the same whether serving at table or at the bar. When clearing a used ashtray it must first be covered to avoid the possibility of spilling ash on the table or the bar. When the dirty ashtray has been covered and removed, replace it immediately with a clean one.

- Hold a clean ashtray in your right hand and place it over the dirty ashtray.
- Remove the two ashtrays together using the one hand.
- Transfer the dirty ashtray to your left hand.
- Use your right hand to place a clean ashtray the right way up where the dirty one was.

Dirty ashtrays should be held in the left hand or on a service tray well away from the guests.

Changing ashtrays

12

THE USE OF THE GUERIDON

Is there any reason why the term guéridon should suggest 'Big Bucks' to guests? Or why the term should suggest a lot of extra work and extraordinary skills to waiters?

In fact the guéridon can be used effectively in a simple way and without much expense to give guests a 'visual' of the fare. A guéridon allows waiters to demonstrate a greater versatility in their service style.

12.1 Most people imagine that the term *guéridon* refers to table cooking as demonstrated in fine dining-rooms. In fact the guéridon is simply a piece of equipment on which we serve or prepare food in the dining environment.

In this chapter we shall show the basic uses of the guéridon as a simple means of offering appropriate services to guests, and greater profitability to the establishment.

On completion of this chapter you should have a basic understanding of:

○ The definition of the guéridon and the uses to which it is put
○ The use of the guéridon as an aid to making sales
○ The selection of food for the guéridon
○ Guéridon mise-en-place
○ Guéridon food preparation techniques — tossing, cooking, boning, carving
○ Guéridon preparation of liqueur coffees.

12.2 *THE GUERIDON AND ITS USES*

A guéridon is simply a trolley or side table used for the service or preparation of food in the dining-room.

A guéridon can be an elaborate piece of moveable furniture on castors made from exquisite timbers and provided with expensive built-in cooking equipment and silver fittings. Or it can simply be an ordinary small dining table.

As we have seen, guéridon *service* means no more than the transfer of food from a serving dish to a plate on a side table or trolley in the presence of the guests (see 10.5 and 10.6).

Guéridon *preparation* is the preparing or finishing of food on the guéridon.

12.3 THE GUÉRIDON AS A SALES AID

The guéridon can be used most effectively as an aid to sales. The display of food on a guéridon and the preparation of food in the presence of guests, rightly used, can be powerful generators of extra sales. At its simplest the guéridon can be used to display or to prepare:

- hors d'oeuvres
- salads
- bakery items
- desserts
- fresh fruit.

12.4 FOOD SELECTION AND PRESENTATION

Food selection

When selecting food for display or preparation on the guéridon remember that the foodstuffs chosen should:

- be fresh and visually attractive
- not discolour or break down easily
- be simple to prepare and require a minimum of cooking time
- maintain their quality in spite of the limited preparation or cooking time
- not produce unpleasant smells or other offensive effects when they are prepared or cooked.

12.5 Salads

Some key points to consider when preparing salads on the guéridon are:

- Thoroughly clean salad items and drain them in the kitchen before they are brought to the guéridon.
- Prepare items in bite-size portions.
- Keep items chilled until they are needed for use.
- The salad dressing may be prepared either in the kitchen or on the guéridon.
- Salad items and the dressing should be tossed at the guéridon at the time of service.

12.6 Meat items

Key points when selecting and preparing meat items for the guéridon are:

- Select a product of premium quality.
- Remove all fat and sinews.
- Trim portions, allowing for one-minute cooking time.
- Keep prepared items chilled, ready for use.
- Seal meat items to maintain the juices.
- Complete the cooking in the minimum amount of time.

12.7 *Fruit*

Key points for consideration when preparing fruit for the guéridon are:
- Clean and portion the fruit.
- Take special care that fruits which may become discoloured when peeled or cut are kept in an appropriate juice to discourage discoloration.
- Keep prepared fruit chilled until it is needed for use.
- Avoid cooking fruit beyond the point at which it breaks down, taking special care of berries and soft fruit which break down easily.

12.8 *GUERIDON MISE-EN-PLACE*

To avoid any delay or confusion when preparing dishes at the guéridon in front of guests it is essential that the preparation (mise-en-place) of the guéridon should be complete.

The mise-en-place includes both the equipment used to prepare the food and the equipment needed to serve it, as well as the products required to create the item.

12.9 *VARIATION OF RECIPES*

The recipes used in cooking at the guéridon may vary in detail from one establishment to another, but the essentials of the classic recipes must be maintained to ensure that they are clearly identifiable to the guest. For example, a Caesar salad always includes lettuce, eggs, anchovies, crisp diced bacon, and croûtons, but Parmesan cheese is optional, and the eggs may or may not be cooked.

New dishes can be created for preparation at the guéridon to suit the establishment's menu, but they must of course follow the basic rules for the selection and preparation of foods.

12.10 *GUERIDON FOOD PREPARATION TECHNIQUES*

The following food preparation procedures are appropriate for use at the guéridon, and will enhance guests' enjoyment of their meals and tempt others to try the same items.

12.11 *Tossing*

Salads, seafoods and fruit are often suitable for tossing in front of the guests as they can be simply prepared and will tempt others to order some for themselves.

The main ingredient may be displayed in its natural state and then tossed with previously prepared sauces, dressings or liqueurs.

If the sauces or dressings are prepared at the guéridon then their preparation must be completed before the main item is added and tossed.

12.12 *Cooking*

Major considerations when cooking on the guéridon are:
- choosing the appropriate cooking medium, for example clarified butter or cooking oil
- the length of cooking time
- the ability to create the appropriate flavours in a minimum of time.

The majority of items cooked on the guéridon lend themselves to the additional effect of flaming (*flambé* work).

Table cooking no longer requires expensive cooking lamps, or guéridons with inbuilt cooking equipment, as a range of good but inexpensive table-top gas-cylinder cookers is now available.

An inexpensive modern cooking lamp

12.13 *Flambé work*

Flambé work involves lighting liquor (usually a spirit or liqueur) in a pan at the guéridon.

The procedure is:
- Light the cooking lamp.
- Pour the required quantity of the liquor into the pan.
- Cover the lamp's flame completely with the pan.
- Leave the liquor to warm in the pan while you place the bottle of liquor well away from the flame.
- Move the pan back towards you, tilting it *away* from you until the liquor just comes into contact with the flame and ignites.
- As soon as the liquor is alight, lift the pan slightly and move it gently in a circular motion so that the flames move around the pan.
- When igniting the liquor hold your body upright. Do not bend your head and shoulders over the pan — flames can flare up unexpectedly.

Pour the liquor into the pan

12.14 *Safety in guéridon cooking*

Cooking at the guéridon, particularly flambé work, obviously has its dangers because it involves naked flames in the dining-room, and fuel for those flames. Special precautions are therefore necessary.
- Regular checks of the cooking lamps and gas bottles will ensure that potential faults, in particular loose fittings or leaks, will be detected before the faults become dangerous.

Tilt the pan away from you

○ A fire blanket and a small hand-held extinguisher should be kept easily accessible, in a place well-known to all the waiting staff.

○ When preparing to use the guéridon, position it at a sufficient distance from the guests' table to make sure that there can be no danger to the guests. The guéridon should be at least its own width away from the table. This has the added advantage that service can take place round the table without the guéridon getting in the way of the waiters.

12.15 *Boning*

If there is a side table or trolley the waiter can use it for de-boning items for guests in their presence. Fine dining-rooms, employing staff with the necessary skills, are often able to offer a range of menu items requiring this form of guéridon technique.

The technique is most commonly used when guests are offered the service of having their (already-cooked) fish de-boned for them (see pages 94-5).

12.16 *Carving*

The carving of the joint, poultry or game at the table was for centuries a traditional part of the dining experience. Nowadays, in restaurants when the carving is done in the presence of the guests, it is usually performed at a special carvery or, where there is one, on an elaborate beef trolley , rather than on an ordinary guéridon.

Carving trolley

Carving at the trolley

12.17 *Liqueur coffee*

Liqueur coffees are often prepared in front of guests on a
guéridon because the process is visually interesting and
provides an exciting finale to the dining experience. The
technique of preparing liqueur coffees is explained later
(15.24 and 15.25).

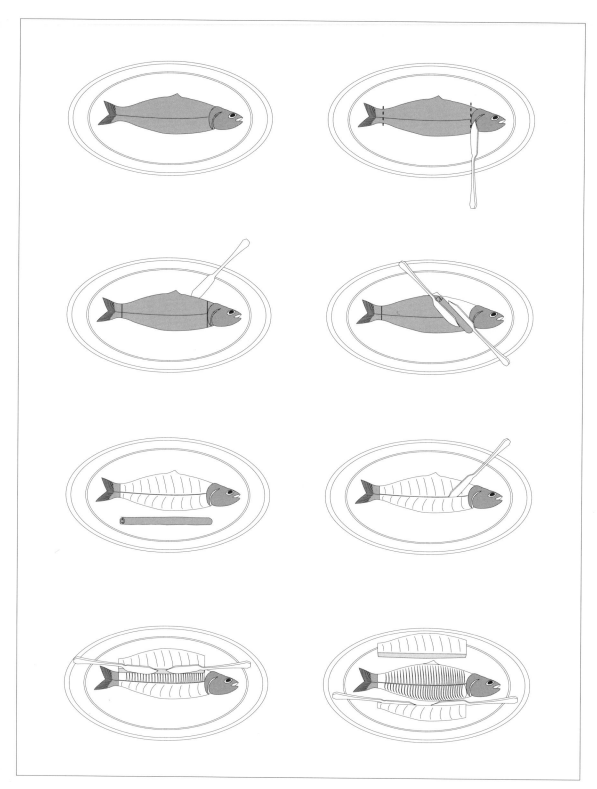

Boning fish

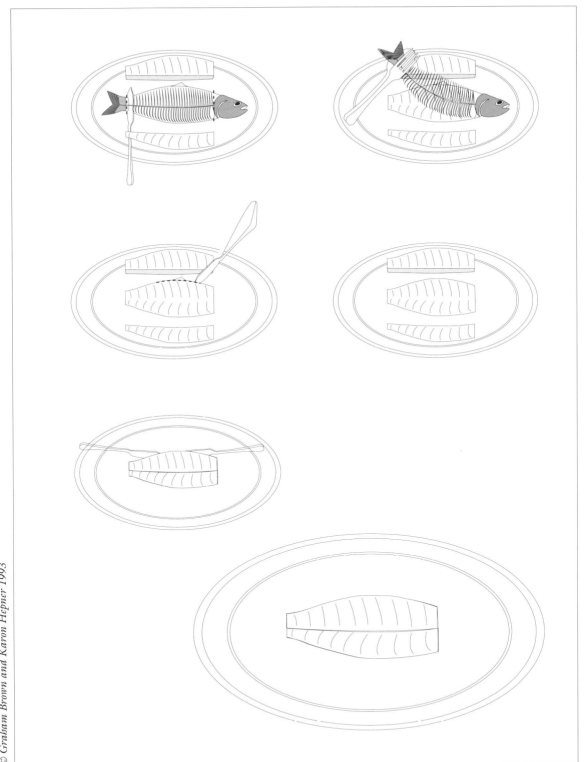

13

BEVERAGE EQUIPMENT AND SERVICE KNOWLEDGE

13.1 Beverages are as important as the food in the dining experience, and they should therefore be given as careful attention as the food when they are being prepared and served.

On completion of this chapter you should have a basic understanding of the following:

○ Beverage equipment identification
○ Equipment preparation and maintenance
○ Beverage lists
○ The handling and placement of equipment
○ The co-ordination of food and beverage service.

13.2 BEVERAGE EQUIPMENT IDENTIFICATION

The service of beverages requires a wide range of equipment. The types of equipment used will vary depending on the tasks to be performed and the type of establishment. A waiter should be familiar with the full range of commonly-used equipment, including all the equipment described in this chapter.

Our guests come expecting a pleasant and satisfying dining experience. All too often the expectations built up by an exciting menu, and all the good work of the chef in the preparation and presentation of the food and the good service of the food by the waiter, are thrown away by a lack of professionalism in the preparation and service of the drinks.

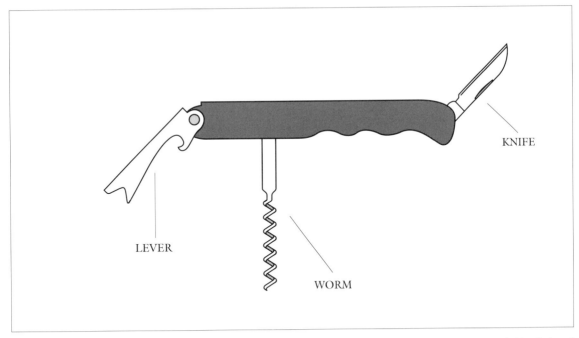

LEVER

WORM

KNIFE

Waiter's friend (open)

13.3 *Glassware*

There is now an enormous range of commercial glassware available so that food outlets from the simplest to the most traditional and expensive can choose glassware to suit all their particular needs.

When selecting glassware, management will take various factors into account, such as size, shape, ease of handling and washing, durability, and price. The glassware selected should, of course, be appropriate to the style of the establishment and its menu.

While the designs of the glassware available vary considerably from manufacturer to manufacturer, there are standard basic shapes which identify the glasses as belonging to the various classical types (see pages 98-9).

13.4 *Service equipment*

Many specialist devices and types of equipment have been produced over the years to help the waiter with the extraction of corks, the carrying of drinks, and the cooling of beverages. The 'waiter's friend' is the recognized device used by waiters to extract corks.

How these pieces of equipment are used is explained in Chapter 15.

Standard glassware

Paris

Red wine

White wine

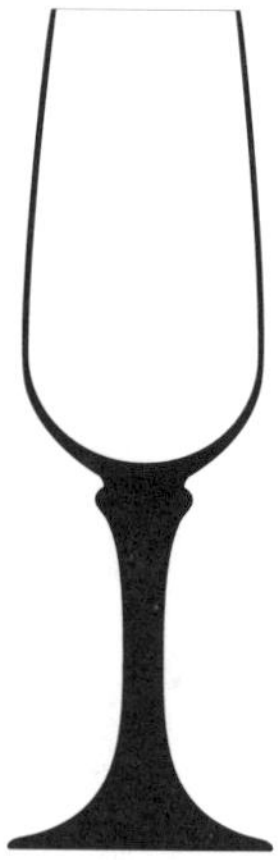

Champagne flute

Champagne saucer

Tumbler

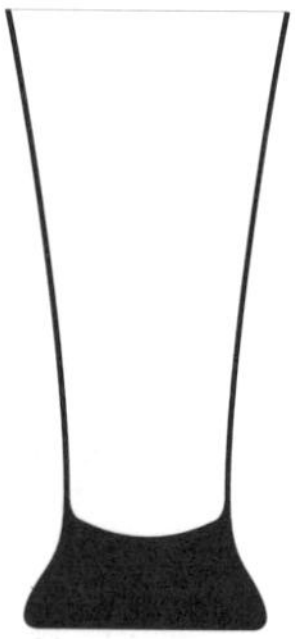

Standard beer glass (200 mL)

Pot/Middy (285 mL)

Pilsner

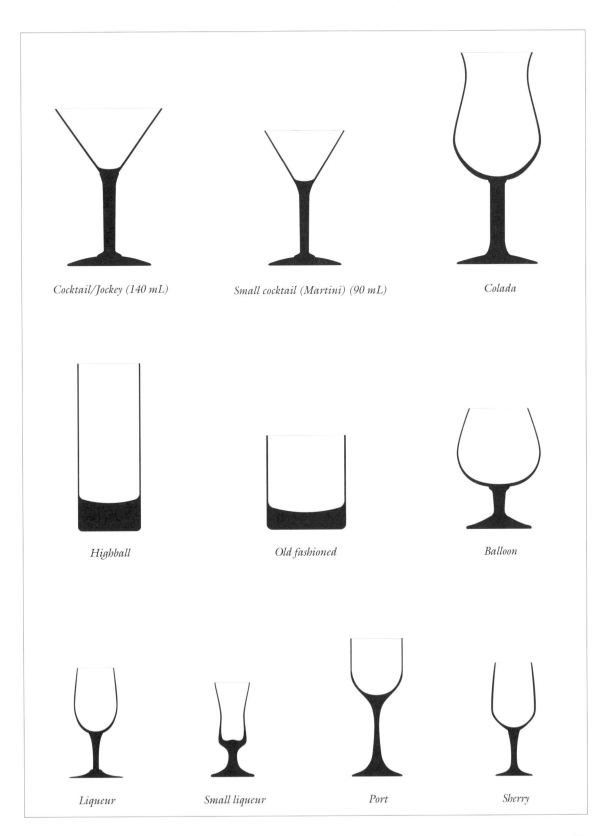

Cocktail/Jockey (140 mL)   Small cocktail (Martini) (90 mL)   Colada

Highball   Old fashioned   Balloon

Liqueur   Small liqueur   Port   Sherry

13.5 PREPARATION AND MAINTENANCE OF EQUIPMENT

The exact procedures to be adopted for the service of beverages will depend on the type of establishment, the styles of service offered, and the availability of service station areas.

Pre-service duties will include cleaning and polishing the necessary glassware, service station mise-en-place, preparation of ice buckets, and the handling and placing of equipment.

13.6 Cleaning and polishing glassware

Although glasses are hygienically washed and sterilized by the high temperatures of the washing cycle in a commercial dishwasher, it is still necessary to polish all glassware by hand before it is placed on the table or used to serve drinks. A lint-free polishing cloth should be used to polish glasses and make sure they are spotlessly clear.

13.7 Service station mise-en-place

Efficient service requires careful prior preparation of the service equipment. In some establishments this is done on a special piece of furniture in the dining-room known as the drink waiter's station. Often space does not allow this and a service station must be established behind the scenes; commonly the bar is used.

Here is a check-list of supplies and equipment that may be required for beverage service:
- additional glassware
- drinks trays
- wine lists
- table-napkins
- straws
- toothpicks
- matches
- ashtrays
- service cloths
- docket book
- wine coolers
- ice buckets.

13.8 Wine coolers and ice buckets

Ice buckets are used to keep white and sparkling wines cool in more formal and usually more expensive restaurants, while simple insulated wine coolers, sometimes placed on the table, are used in less formal establishments.

Ice buckets, when required for use, should be half filled with a mixture of crushed ice (two-thirds) and cold water (one-third). The water allows the bottle to sink into the ice instead of balancing on top of it. The bucket may be placed in a tripod stand.

13.9 *BEVERAGE LISTS*

Beverage lists come in many different formats. Sometimes a so-called 'wine list' will contain the entire range of beverages available. This format can be extremely confusing for the guest. A better solution is to divide the various different types of beverage into separate lists. This helps guests to find and select the beverages they require more speedily. Possible lists may include:

○ Cocktail list
○ Drinks list (includes apéritifs, beers, spirits and non-alcoholic drinks)
○ Wine list
○ After-dinner drinks list (liqueurs, ports, brandies)
○ Liqueur coffee list.

13.10 *The wine list*

Wine lists are usually divided into wines of different types, for example:

○ White table wines
○ Red table wines
○ Champagnes and sparkling wines
○ Dessert wines

See pages 102-3 and 14.3-14.6.

13.11 *HANDLING AND PLACEMENT OF EQUIPMENT*

For both hygienic reasons and presentation it is essential that all glassware should be handled by the stem or base of the glass. When glasses are being moved in the presence of guests they should always be carried on a beverage tray. Before the guests' arrival, when the tables are being laid, several glasses may be held upside down in one hand with their stems between one's fingers.

Carrying glasses in the presence of guests

13.12 *Placing of glasses*

If a single glass is being laid it should be placed 2.5cm above the main knife. If more than one glass is placed on the table, the glasses are positioned in a line at an angle of 45° in the order in which they will be required. See 4.11 and 4.14.

Carrying glasses before the guests' arrival

Wine and beverage lists

13.13 *FOOD AND BEVERAGE CO-ORDINATION*

Regardless of whether the establishment has decided to employ a specialist wine waiter, or to make all its waiters responsible for both food and beverage service, it is essential that the service of the food and the beverages should be co-ordinated.

The food waiter and the wine waiter must communicate if they are to provide a co-ordinated sequential service. The sequence of service requires both food and beverages to be served at the appropriate times throughout the meal without interfering with each other.

13.14 *Key points in food and beverage service co-ordination*

- Before the menu is presented guests are offered an apéritif (pre-dinner drink) to stimulate the appetite.
- Because the wines are selected to complement the food chosen, the wine list is usually presented after the food order has been taken.
- The wine selected to accompany each course is served just prior to the food in that course. It is usual to serve white wines before red, dry wines before sweet, young wines before old — but what wines are chosen and in what order is, of course, up to the guest; the 'right' wine is what the guest wants.
- Remind guests that dessert wines are available when the desserts are being ordered. Dessert wines are sweet, and complement sweet dishes.
- Orders for after-dinner alcoholic beverages are taken before coffee is served. This allows the coffee and other after-dinner drinks, such as port, cognac or liqueurs, to be served at the same time.

13.15 *BYO restaurants*

BYO restaurants, though more common in some states than in others, are an accepted part of our industry. While in BYO establishments we do not take responsibility for the sale of alcoholic beverages, we are responsible for serving them as professionally as in a fully-licensed restaurant.

BEVERAGE PRODUCT KNOWLEDGE

14.1 You cannot be a competent drinks waiter without a basic knowledge of the products you are selling and serving. This chapter lists and defines the various categories of beverages.

On completion of this chapter you should have a basic understanding of the following:

- Apéritifs
- Table wines
- Dessert wines
- Fortified wines
- Champagnes and sparkling wines
- Spirits
- Beers
- Liqueurs
- Cocktails
- Non-alcoholic beverages
- Aerated waters.

More information on particular beverage items may be found in the Glossary.

14.2 *APERITIFS*

An apéritif is a pre-dinner drink taken to stimulate the appetite. Most apéritifs are dry in style because dry beverages stimulate the appetite, while sweet drinks tend to dull the appetite. In spite of this some guests may prefer to drink a sweet drink before a meal as an apéritif.

A good waiter will never make guests feel uncomfortable because of the drinks they have chosen, no matter how

You may think that a bright personality and the ability to open a bottle of wine or beer is enough to make you a good drinks waiter, but without a basic knowledge of products, the job can only be half done.

Guests rely on us to assist them in making their selections and in educating them in their appreciation of wine and other beverages.

inappropriate they may seem. Popular apéritifs include:

- ○ dry champagne
- ○ pre-dinner cocktails (acidic or dry rather than creamy)
- ○ dry sherry
- ○ dry ('French') vermouth
- ○ a proprietary apéritif (for example, Campari, Fernet Branca, Dubonnet, or Rosso Antico).

14.3 *TABLE WINES*

The term 'wine' indicates a type of beverage made from fermented fruit. Wine may be made from a variety of fruits, but wine as we generally know it is made from the fermented juice of grapes. When another fruit is used to produce the wine, the name of the fruit used is included on the label, for example 'strawberry wine'.

As a general rule red wine is made from 'black' (actually purple) grapes, while white wine is made from 'white' (actually green) grapes. Rosé wine, which is pink (rosy), is made from black grapes, but the skins of the grapes are removed early in the process of fermentation.

In the early days of the Australian wine industry most wines were given generic labels, that is they were described as wines of a particular type, for example, moselle, hock, chablis, burgundy, riesling, or claret. Many of these are the names of districts in France or Germany famous for producing a particular kind of wine

Nowadays bottled wines usually carry a varietal label, that is the label tells you the variety of the grapes from which the wines are made. Common white varietal wines include chardonnay, Rhine riesling, sauvignon blanc, and gewürztraminer. Cabernet sauvignon, pinot noir, and shiraz (sometimes called hermitage) are red varietal wines. Often two or more varieties are blended, for instance traminer-riesling or cabernet-shiraz.

The different varietal wines have distinct characters. For example chardonnay is a fruity, dry, strongly-flavoured wine, Rhine riesling, also a dry wine, has a lighter taste, and gewürztraminer is distinctly spicy. Similarly among the reds, cabernet sauvignon wines are dark red, and have a strong flavour with an astringent edge to it; pinot noir wines, on the other hand, are light and velvety.

In addition to the varietal description, wine labels often state the district the grapes used to make the wine came from, for example Coonawarra, Hunter Valley, Margaret River, Barossa Valley, Goulburn Valley, and Yarra Valley.

As a general rule red wines should be served at 'room temperature' (about 18°C) and white wines should be served mildly chilled (about 6°C).

Some table wines

14.4 *DESSERT WINES*

Dessert wines are rich and sweet. They are designed to be consumed with sweet food items. Sauternes is a famous white dessert wine. Spätleses and ausleses are German styles of dessert wine.

14.5 *FORTIFIED WINES*

A fortified wine is a wine strengthened with the addition of spirit. The spirit also preserves the wine for longer periods after the bottle is opened. Fortified wines include sherry, vermouth, muscat and port.

There are various different styles of sherry, ranging from very sweet sherries to extremely dry. The sherries taken with a meal are usually dry. They are used as apéritifs or taken with soup.

Vermouths come in three main styles: rosso, bianco and dry. Rosso vermouth, sometimes called 'Italian', is light red, sweet and strong-tasting. Bianco is light golden, medium sweet, and spicy. Dry or 'French' vermouth is almost colourless and has a delicate flavour.

Australian muscats are rich, sweet, fortified wines. They can be red ('brown') or white ('orange'). Because they are often made from a variety of grape called muscat de Frontignan, these wines are sometimes called frontignacs. Rutherglen in Victoria is famous for its muscats.

Ports come in several styles: ruby, tawny, and vintage. Ruby ports are the youngest and least rich. Vintage ports mature in the bottle and develop a sediment. They should therefore be decanted before they are served. Almost all ports are red wines, but there are white ports.

14.6 *CHAMPAGNE AND OTHER SPARKLING WINES*

Sparkling wines get their sparkle or effervescence from carbon dioxide. Carbon dioxide is produced naturally in the process of fermentation and can be retained to produce a sparkling wine.

Champagne is a region of France renowned for its sparkling wine, known as champagne. Champagne is made by a complex process called the *méthode champenoise* or champagne method. The most important feature of the méthode champenoise is that fermentation takes place in the bottle. Some other sparkling wines ferment in vats and are bottled later.

French champagnes are made from a blend of grapes, usually pinot noir (black) and chardonnay (white) grapes. Meunier, a grape variety similar to pinot noir, is also used.

In Europe only champagnes produced in the Champagne district by the méthode champenoise can be called champagne. In Australia sparkling wine can only be described as 'champagne' if it is fermented in the bottle. There is a move to restrict the use of the word 'champagne' to imported French champagne. If natural fermentation in a vat produces the sparkle, it can be called a 'sparkling wine' but if the carbon dioxide is injected into the wine it becomes a 'carbonated wine'.

The styles of sparkling wine include:

- brut   dry
- sec   medium dry
- demi-sec   medium sweet
- doux   sweet

The dry styles are much more popular than the sweet.

Champagne is sold in a variety of bottle sizes, each with a special name. The most common are:

- Magnum   two ordinary bottles
- Jeroboam   four ordinary bottles

The other large bottle sizes are listed in the Glossary (see champagne bottle sizes).

14.7 SPIRITS

Spirits are distilled alcoholic beverages. Distillation is the process of converting liquid into vapour by heating, and then condensing the vapour back to liquid form. Almost any fruit or vegetable can be crushed to liquid, fermented, and then distilled to make a spirit.

These are the most popular spirits, and their base ingredients:

Spirit	Base
Whisky	Grain (barley, wheat and maize)
Gin	Neutral spirit made from grain and then flavoured with juniper berries
Rum	Sugar cane
Vodka	Potatoes or grain
Brandy	Grapes

Scotch is the most popular kind of whisky. Bourbon is an American whiskey made from maize. Cognac and armagnac are high-quality French brandies.

14.8 BEER

Beer is made from fermented grain by the process called brewing. The traditional ingredients are malt (barley soaked to germinate and then dried), yeast, hops and water. Beer is the general term for ales, lagers and stout. Ales and lagers are made by different techniques of fermentation: ales are top-fermented whereas lagers are bottom-fermented. In general lagers are paler and more highly-carbonated than ales. Most Australian beers are lagers. Stout is a dark heavy beer. Guinness is a kind of stout. 'Draught' beer is beer drawn from a keg, rather than bottled or canned.

Australian beers often carry confusing labels, for example a lager can be described as 'ale' and a bottled or canned beer may be described as 'genuine draught'!

14.9 *LIQUEURS*

Liqueurs are spirit-based (or sometimes wine-based) liquors, sweetened and flavoured. They have been made for centuries and new ones are being devised all the time.

Some liqueurs are generic, that is they are liqueurs of a particular type, which anyone may make. Advocaat, crème de menthe and curaçao are popular generic liqueurs. Other liqueurs are proprietary, that is they may only be made by a single distiller who owns the right to make the liqueur of that name. Bénédictine, Cointreau, Drambuie and Grand Marnier are examples of proprietary liqueurs.

Liqueurs are often taken with the coffee at the end of a meal. They are usually served neat (without any mixer) in a liqueur glass. They may also be taken in black coffee, as a liqueur coffee (see 14.13 under 'coffee', and 15.24-15.25).

Liqueurs are also frequently used in cocktails.

14.10 *COCKTAILS*

Cocktails are mixed drinks. Two or more ingredients are mixed by one of the following methods:
- Shake and strain (in a cocktail shaker, with ice)
- Stir and strain (in a mixing glass, with ice)
- Blend (in an electric blender, with the quantity of ice specified in the recipe)
- Build (prepared directly in the glass).

Cocktails fall into three broad types:
- Pre-dinner cocktails. These are usually acidic or dry and make good apéritifs. A Dry Martini is a classic pre-dinner cocktail.
- After-dinner cocktails. These tend to be richer, often creamy and sweet. A Brandy Alexander is an example.
- Long drink cocktails. These often contain fruit juices, soft drinks or milk in addition to their alcoholic base. A Tom Collins is an example.

Most cocktails are served with a garnish, which may be as simple as a slice of lemon or a cherry. The garnish should be appropriate to the contents of the cocktail. Many classic cocktails are served with a standard garnish. For example a Dry Martini is served with an olive or a twist of lemon, whereas a Gibson, which otherwise has the same ingredients, is served with a pearl onion. The garnish is as much part of the cocktail as its liquid ingredients.

Most classic cocktails have a spirit base, but this is not necessary. Some cocktails contain no alcoholic component at all, in which case they are called virgin cocktails or mocktails.

14.11 NON-ALCOHOLIC DRINKS

The term non-alcoholic drinks includes a wide variety of beverage items, from cold to hot and from the simple to the exotic. Some are served from the kitchen/still area and some are dispensed from the bar.

Non-alcoholic drinks served from the kitchen/still area

14.12 Tea

A growing demand for a variety of specialist teas has made it necessary for establishments to expand the range of teas they offer.

The majority of teas are prepared using tea-bags, but some teas are prepared from loose leaves. When tea is served guests pour for themselves. The waiting staff provide the prepared tea, additional hot water, milk, lemon, and the appropriate sweeteners. Types of tea commonly requested include English Breakfast, Earl Grey, Darjeeling, China, and herbal tea.

14.13 Coffee

Good quality coffee can be a key issue in ensuring a good dining experience, a visit to a brasserie or bar, and the guests' decision on whether or not to come back. In a restaurant coffee is generally the last product consumed. In bars and brasseries it is either the last product consumed on a meal visit or it may be the whole purpose of the visit. The correct preparation and serving of coffee is of more and more importance to customers (see also 15.21 and 15.22).

Coffee is available in many blends, and is prepared in many styles. It can be instant, or prepared using a filter/drip, a percolator, a plunger, or in an espresso machine. Styles of coffee frequently requested are:
○ **Long black**. Freshly percolated coffee served without milk or cream in a large (tea) cup.

- **Short black**. Usually an espresso, served in a small coffee-cup or demi-tasse.
- **Café au lait** or white coffee is coffee served with milk. Café au lait is usually made with hot milk (*au lait* is French for 'with milk'), whereas ordinary white coffee has cold milk added. Sometimes cream is used instead of milk.
- **Espresso** coffee (literally 'pressed out' coffee) is made in a machine which uses steam pressure. An 'espresso' (without qualification) usually means a 'short black' made using an espresso machine. Espresso coffee should have a creamy golden froth. This is a the mark of a well-maintained machine, freshly-ground coffee, and the right quantity of coffee used in the process.
- **Cappuccino** coffee is made using an espresso machine, and has frothed milk added. It should be strong and milky with a creamy frothed crest. It is usually garnished with a sprinkling of chocolate or cocoa. Cappuccino coffee is so called because its appearance is reminiscent of the white on brown *cappuccio* or cowl worn by Capuchin friars.
- **Caffè latte** is also made using an espresso machine, but with a higher proportion of milk than a cappuccino. (*Latte* is Italian for milk.) The milk is not frothed. Caffè latte is the Italian version of the French café au lait. A popular breakfast coffee. Caffè latte is frequently served in a glass rather than a cup.
- **Macchiato** coffee is an extra-strong espresso served long or short in a glass with a dash of cold milk. *Macchiare* means to stain in Italian. A macchiato is a very strong coffee just 'stained' with a little milk, barely enough to change its colour.
- **Vienna coffee** is topped with thickened cream, very rich.
- **Turkish** or **Greek** coffee is strong, dark and sweet. It is made from a fine powder of pulverized coffee beans. Unlike other coffees, the water is not passed through ground coffee beans, rather the coffee and the water are 'cooked' together. Sugar is added during the preparation, rather than after it, since stirring the coffee would disturb the sediment which forms in the cups.
- **Decaffeinated** coffee is real coffee with the stimulant caffeine extracted. Some people prefer coffee substitutes, such as Caro, which are not made from coffee beans.
- **Liqueur** coffees are those served with a spirit or liqueur. Irish coffee is the obvious example. Irish whiskey is added to hot sugared black coffee which is then topped

with cold, fresh cream. A number of different liqueurs, for example Tia Maria or Galliano, are commonly served with coffee in the same way under a variety of names, for example 'Jamaican Coffee' or 'Roman Coffee'. (Liqueur coffees are, of course, alcoholic, but for convenience are described here with the other coffee variations. See also 15.24 and 15.25.)

14.14 Hot chocolate

Nowadays chocolate is almost always made from pre-prepared (instant) powder. The quality of the chocolate used is the essential factor in the end product — the better the brand, the better the result. If good chocolate is to be served you must use a good product, Suchard for example. The chocolate powder is mixed with hot (but not boiled) milk before service, usually in the cups in which it is to be served (see 15.23).

Non-alcoholic drinks dispensed from the bar

14.15 Aerated waters

Aerated water is simply water charged with gas, usually carbon dioxide, to make it effervescent. They often contain a syrup for taste and colour. Soda water is a colourless and tasteless aerated water. Bitter lemon, Indian tonic, and dry ginger are flavoured aerated waters.

14.16 Fruit juices

Commercially-packaged brands (canned or bottled) may be used or, for some varieties of fruit such as oranges, lemons and grapefruit, the juices may be prepared fresh. Serve chilled.

14.17 Squashes

These are preparations of fruit juices or syrups with sugar, water and other ingredients, usually described by the manu-facturers as 'cordials'. Some use mineral water instead of ordinary tap water.

14.18 Mineral waters

Mineral waters are so-called because of the minerals they contain and which are said to be good for health. They may be still or sparkling (effervescent). If they come unadulterated from a natural spring they are 'natural' mineral waters, and if their effervescence is also natural, rather than added by the injection of carbon dioxide, they are 'naturally sparkling'. Many mineral waters are not 'natural' but are simply tap water with minerals and aerated by the manufacturer. Aerated mineral waters are made from purified waters with carbon dioxide added.

Natural mineral waters are often named after the place from which they come. Evian, Perrier and Vichy are natural mineral waters from France (Evian is still, while Perrier and Vichy are naturally sparkling). Appollinaris is a naturally sparkling variety from Germany. There are a number of Australian mineral waters, such as Hepburn Spa and Deep Spring. Bisleri is an Italian brand, made under licence in Australia. Sometimes mineral waters are flavoured with fruit juices.

Mineral waters can be used as mixers or appreciated as refreshing, cleansing beverages.

14.19 *Non-alcoholic wines*

These are prepared from a fruit juice base, and can be still or aerated, with no alcohol content.

14.20 *Non-alcoholic cocktails (virgin cocktails or mocktails)*

Current trends towards responsible drink-driving habits have led to an increase in the availability of non-alcoholic drinks, including many non-alcoholic mixed drinks or cocktails. Often these are simply 'virgin' versions of an already popular cocktail, i.e. ones with the alcoholic ingredient left out or with some other ingredient substituted for it. A Virgin Mary, for example, is a non-alcoholic variation of the Bloody Mary with the vodka omitted. Responsible beverage servers are now very conscious of the need to offer a good variety of non-alcoholic drinks.

15

BEVERAGE SERVICE PROCEDURES

Do patrons purchase drinks simply to quench their thirst? Or do they really come to enjoy a total hospitality experience — the company, the atmosphere of the venue, and the service — as well as the food they eat and the beverages they drink?

15.1 Beverages may be served as an individual item of service (for example in bar or lounge service), or their service may be carefully co-ordinated with the service of the food so that the beverages complement the food, enhancing the guests' enjoyment of both.

The style of beverage service offered will depend on the character of the establishment and the type of beverages being served. The methods of service explained in this chapter reflect a common-sense approach to beverage service, but some establishments may require variations on these procedures.

On completion of this chapter you should have a basic understanding of the following:

- Selling beverages
- Taking beverage orders
- Handling glassware
- Tray carrying and service
- Beer service
- Wine service
- Champagne service
- Liqueur, port and brandy service
- Coffee and tea service
- Changing glassware.

15.2 *SELLING BEVERAGES*

The way beverages are sold is a key part of the hospitality experience. Bar and beverage service staff must not only understand the products they are selling, but they must know how to serve them, from both technical and psychological points of view.

15.3 *Venues offering beverage service*

Venues offering beverage service include:
- Bars (both public and specialized)
- Lounges
- Restaurants
- Function facilities.

15.4 *Bars*

The traditional names for the various bars suggest different types of customers, products, and skills in the bar staff. For example, the traditional public bar was a male domain, and most people drank beer there. Public bar staff needed few technical skills beyond knowing how to pull a beer and how to mix basic spirits. Things have changed. Today's public bar attracts both sexes; it may offer entertainment, and a complete range of beverages including premium beers, cocktails, and wines. Staff in public bars, saloon bars, and cocktail bars must now be equipped with the skills of mixing cocktails and serving wines, and must know how to sell them.

Techniques and vehicles for selling beverages in bars include verbal recommendations, promotional displays, board listings, and the availability of a drinks list.

15.5 *Lounges*

Lounge services are offered in a wide diversity of types of venues, including pubs, hotels, restaurants, lounge bars, discos and clubs. Guests can sit away from the bar in a relaxed environment and may be served by floor staff.

In the lounge sales are made by verbal recommendation, or by using sales tools like tent cards, or cocktail/beverage lists.

15.6 *Restaurants*

When beverages are sold and served in a restaurant consideration has to be given to the integration of food and beverage service so that they enhance each other.

The methods used to sell beverages in restaurants vary to suit the type of establishment but they commonly include verbal recommendation, tent cards, cocktail/beverage lists, 'wine lists', and liqueur coffee lists.

15.7 *Functions*

The beverages served at a function are usually pre-arranged by the function host with the venue operator rather than sold at the function itself. The venue manager may make verbal recommendations or may offer a beverage list from which the host selects the drinks to be served. Should the host request a beverage not on the standard list, it may be purchased by the venue especially for the function.

15.8 *General points on selling beverages*

When selling beverages
○ Do not dictate your personal preferences.
○ Offer a diversity of recommendations so that guests are prompted to choose what they personally prefer.
○ Suggest beverages that complement the occasion, but do not convey any sense of disapproval if something 'unsuitable' is chosen. Guests have the right to drink whatever they choose, and have come to enjoy themselves, not to be 'corrected'. Your job is to make them feel comfortable and relaxed.

15.9 *TAKING BEVERAGE ORDERS*

Beverage orders should be taken as soon as guests are comfortably settled, be it at a bar, lounge, or at a table in a restaurant. Remember the following points:
○ When taking the orders (verbally or in writing) make sure you clearly understand them and that they are precise, so that the guests receive what they have ordered. If you are not quite clear what has been ordered, do not hesitate to confirm it with the guest.
○ If there are several guests write the orders down in logical order (as the guests are seated, or with some other clear identification) so that you place the drinks correctly when they are served (see 6.9 and 6.10).
○ Avoid the use of abbreviations; they can easily cause confusion.
○ Different venues have different methods for recording sales. Whatever the system in use — hand-written dockets, a cash register, or a computer system — it is essential that you record all items sold in the appropriate way.
○ In a restaurant the wine order is usually taken after the guests have selected their food. Additional orders for wine may be taken throughout the meal; indeed, if the guests' glasses look nearly empty, discreetly ask the host whether another bottle of wine should be brought.

○ The order for after-dinner beverage items (such as port, brandy or liqueurs) should be taken prior to the service of coffee, so that the drinks can be served with the coffee.

15.10 *GLASSWARE AND DRINKS TRAYS*

All glassware, whether clean or used, should be carried upright on a drinks tray, except that wine glasses may be carried upside down by their stems, held between the fingers of the left hand, when setting covers before guests arrive (see 13.11).

All glassware (clean or used) must always be held only by the stem or base of the glass, never by the rim.

15.11 *Tray service*

A drinks tray is carried on a slightly cupped hand on the pads of the fingers. This allows the waiter to adjust the balance of the tray as glasses are removed or added to the tray. When serving drinks to seated guests from a tray hold the tray behind the guest's head, and use your right hand to place the drink from the guest's right (see also 5.9 and 13.11).

Tray service

Carrying the drinks tray

15.12 *BEER SERVICE*

Beers, in particular the increasingly popular premium and imported beers, are often served at the table from individual small bottles. The traditional large bottles of beer are now most commonly used for functions. Different procedures are used for large and small bottles.

15.13 *Small beer bottles*

The procedure for serving small bottles of beer at table is:

- Carry a clean cold beer glass and an open bottle to the table on a service tray.
- Hold the tray behind the head of the guest to be served.
- Pick up the glass at its base and place it to the guest's right.
- Take the bottle in your right hand with the label clearly showing to the guest.
- Pour the beer into the glass on the table so that the flow is directed to the inside opposite edge of the glass. Pour slowly so that a head can form.
- Continue pouring until the glass is full, with a well-rounded head.
- If the bottle still contains some beer, place it on the table to the right of the glass, with the label facing the guest.

15.14 *Large bottles of beer*

Do not carry large beer bottles on a tray. Take the glasses to the table on a tray and place them, as described above. Then go back and bring an open bottle of beer to the table. Hold it so that the label faces the guest. Pour the beer in the same way as for small bottles.

As large bottles are usually served at functions where several guests are drinking the same kind of beer, it is unlikely that any beer will remain in the bottle. If possible avoid leaving large beer bottles on the table.

Beer glasses, left to right:
Standard beer glass; Pot/middy;
Pilsner

Serving beer at the table

*Paris wine glass
(red or white)*

White wine glass

Red wine glass

15.15 *WINE SERVICE PROCEDURES*

The service of wine whether it be over a bar or at table is a sequence of tasks involving basic skills. At table, in licensed restaurants of all types, the correct procedure does not vary. There may be some modification of the procedure, however, in BYO restaurants and in busy bars.

15.16 *Service of table wines*

○ Present the wine which the host has selected on a service cloth held on the flat of your left hand, with the label directed to the host so that it can easily be read. Identify the wine verbally, mentioning the company, variety and vintage, so that the host can confirm that the correct wine has been brought — 'Hankin Cabernet Shiraz Malbec 1989, Sir?' Do not open the bottle until the host has confirmed that the wine is the correct one.

○ When the host has confirmed the wine is correct, take the bottle firmly in your left hand, holding it at a 45° angle at waist height. Cut the foil with the blade of the waiter's friend just above the raised ridge about 5mm below the top of the bottle. Ease off the top of the foil with the point of the blade. Note that the foil should always be cut in this way even if a perforated pull-tab has been built into the foil; a clean cut prevents the wine from catching in the perforations and dripping when poured.

○ Close the blade of the waiter's friend and open the spiral (corkscrew). Hold the neck of the bottle firmly in the left hand. Insert the sharp tip of the spiral into the centre of the cork. Slowly turn the spiral in a clockwise direction, keeping it in line with the core of the cork. Stop turning the spiral when the last turn of the spiral is still visible to prevent the spiral from piercing the base of the cork.

○ Tilt the arm of the waiter's friend so that the lever rests on the lip of the bottle. Hold the lever in place using the side of your index finger. Now extract the cork by raising the opposite end of the body of the waiter's friend, exerting leverage on the lip of the bottle until the cork starts to bend.

○ Now cease the lifting action and place your thumb and index finger at the base of the cork. Twist the cork gently onto its side to remove it from the bottle. This technique will prevent the cork from breaking and will allow the cork to be extracted without any distracting popping sound.

○ Remove the cork from the spiral and return the waiter's friend to the pocket.

Wine service procedure

○ In some establishments the cork is then presented to the host for inspection, particularly when fine red wines are being served. If it is the custom of the establishment to present the cork, a suitable small plate should be placed on the table in advance to accommodate it. If the cork has the name of the winery printed on it, the cork should be placed so that the writing can easily be read by the host.

○ Wipe the lip of the bottle with a service cloth.

○ The bottle is then held firmly in the right hand with the label directed toward the host. Pour about 30mL of wine into the host's glass for approval. The wine should be poured into the centre of the glass with the bottle held above and not touching the glass. (Note: If the table is laid with more than one style of wine glass, the smaller glasses should be used for white wine and the larger for red.)

○ After the host has approved the wine, fill the guests' glasses (no more than two-thirds full) starting with the guest immediately to the right of the host. At table the wine is poured from the guests' right. Moving anticlockwise round the table, complete the service by topping up the host's glass.

○ When all the glasses have been filled, bottles of white wine are placed in a cooler or ice bucket (if available), or placed on the table if the guests so request. Bottles of red wine should be placed on the waiter's station (if there is one) or placed on the table (if there is not, or if the guests request it).

○ Bottles of red wine may be collared with a napkin to improve their presentation. White wine bottles, if placed in an ice bucket, may have a napkin draped over them.

Service of table wine

○ The discarded cap, foil and cork must not be left at the table or dropped into the ice bucket. Put them in your pocket and dispose of them at the bar.

○ Keep an eye on the guests' glasses. When they are only one-third full top them up.

○ When the bottle is empty, ask the host whether they require another bottle of the same wine, or whether you should bring the wine list for them to select another. If another bottle of the same type of wine is ordered it is not necessary to change the glasses unless you are asked by the host to do so. Nor, in most establish-ments, is it necessary to repeat the tasting procedure. Simply open the bottle, and continue to top up the guests' glasses as before. If a different wine is selected, the glasses must be changed (see 15.26), and the tasting and opening pro-cedures are repeated in the same way as they were performed for the original bottle.

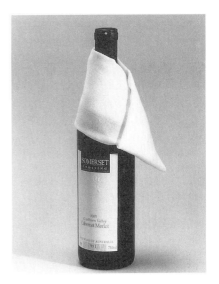

Bottles of red wine may be collared to improve their presentation

15.17 *CHAMPAGNE AND OTHER SPARKLING WINE*

Except that the technique of opening a bottle is different, the procedure for serving a sparkling wine is essentially the same as that for a still white table wine.

○ If a sparkling wine is selected place suitable glasses (narrow 'champagne flutes') in position.

○ Present the bottle on a service cloth held on the flat of your left hand, with the label directed to the host so that is can easily be read. Identify the wine verbally so that the host can confirm that the correct wine has been brought — 'Your Domain Chandon, Sir?'

○ When the host has confirmed that the wine is the correct one, proceed to open the bottle. Extraordinary pressure can build up in a bottle of sparkling wine, especially if it is shaken. People can be injured by the cork exploding violently out of the bottle, so opening must be undertaken with care. Never allow the bottle to point at your face or at anyone else; make sure it is pointing at the ceiling. During the opening procedure hold the bottle at an angle rather than straight up. This reduces the pressure on the cork.

○ Take the bottle firmly in your left hand, holding it at a 45° angle at waist height. With your right hand locate the wire ring on the muselet (muzzle or cage), and untwist it.

○ Remove foil and the cage, holding the cork in place with the thumb of your left hand as an extra precaution.

○ Take a service cloth in the palm of the right hand and with it cover and firmly hold the cork. Hold the base of the bottle with your left hand and twist it to loosen the cork. Ease the cork gently out of the bottle into the palm of your right hand.

○ Wipe the lip of the bottle with the service cloth.

○ Hold the bottle in the right hand so that the label faces the host, and pour about 30mL of the wine into the glass for approval.

○ Alternatively, the bottle may be held with the thumb in the punt (the indentation at the base) with the fingers spread out to support the body of the bottle.

○ When the host has approved the wine, fill the guests' glasses (no more than two-thirds full), starting with the guest immediately to the host's right and moving anti-clockwise round the table. Complete the service by topping up the host's glass. You may have to pause while pouring to allow the bubbles to settle.

Serving a sparkling wine

Alternatively, the bottle may be held with the thumb in the punt

- Place the bottle in an ice bucket unless the host requests otherwise. The bottle may be collared with a napkin to enhance its presentation.
- Top up the guests' glasses, and offer an additional bottle, as for ordinary table wines.

The bottle may be collared with a napkin

15.18 *LIQUEURS, PORT AND BRANDY*

Liqueurs, port and fine brandies (usually cognac, but sometimes armagnac or old Australian brandy) are commonly served with coffee at the conclusion of a meal. The waiter may suggest them verbally or offer the drinks list after the sweets or desserts. Glasses are usually pre-poured and served at table off a tray, but in some establishments the bottle is presented at the table and then poured for the guest or served from a beverage trolley.

The normal measure for brandy or liqueurs is 30mL, and for port or other fortified wines it is 60mL.

Fine brandies are served in wide-bottomed glasses (balloons). It is usual for guests to warm their own brandy glasses in the palms of their hands but the waiter may be requested to warm the glasses before the brandy is served. Some establishments have special warming lamps for this purpose. Note that the glass is empty when warmed on a lamp, the brandy itself is not warmed for the guest.

Brandy balloon

15.19 *COFFEE AND TEA*

The exact procedure for serving coffee and tea at table will vary, depending on the venue, the style of service and the equipment available.

The preparatory steps for coffee and tea service are the same. They are:

- Take the order.
- Place the accompanying items (milk, sugar, and, if required, cream and lemon) on the table. An underliner may be used to present these items. Make sure the sugar bowl has a clean spoon with it.
- Place a cup and saucer, and a teaspoon from each guest's right. If coffee or tea are being served with cheese or dessert, or for afternoon tea, the cup and saucer are placed to the right of the cover.
- If tea or coffee are being served at the end of a meal after the table has been cleared, the cup and saucer should be placed near the centre of the cover.
- The handle of the cup should be to its right, and the teaspoon should be placed at a 45° angle on the saucer just behind the handle.

15.20 *Tea*

The ritual for serving tea allows the guests to pour for themselves. Present the teapot and its accompanying hot water pot on an underplate with a tea-strainer, and a small napkin.

The strainer and the napkin may not be provided in all establishments. A strainer is unnecessary if tea-bags have been used, but one still may be asked for by guests. If tea-bags have been used they should not be 'jigglers'; pots should not be served with tea-bag strings and labels hanging out. The napkin is to assist the guest to hold the hot pots while pouring.

Place the underplate to the right of the guest, with the handles of the teapot and hot water pot directed to the guest.

15.21 *COFFEE*

The way in which coffee is prepared and served depends on which kind of coffee it is. The many different kinds of coffee were described in the previous chapter (14.13). Regardless of which kind of coffee is being served there are no points to be won by serving insipid, thin coffee. Most people prefer rich and flavoursome coffee, with only a minority preferring their coffee weak. Most people who drink black coffee, particularly short black espresso, want quality, rich and strong coffee. Coffee can always be diluted if it is too strong. However, unless it is made with a plunger, it cannot be strengthened if it has been made too weak. The amount of water pushed through the coffee determines its strength, without (up to a point) compromising its richness and aroma. The less water, the richer and stronger the coffee.

Good coffee is essential in modern brasseries and café-bars. It is usually prepared on an espresso machine. Different machines work in rather different ways but the keys to successful espresso coffees are:

- fresh coffee
- hot cups
- a well-serviced machine
- an understanding of what makes good coffee good.

Espresso coffee, especially when served as a short black, should have a creamy golden-brown froth. This is a sign of a well-maintained machine, freshly ground coffee and the right quantity of coffee used in the process. There are two styles of **short black** espresso coffee, the French and the Italian. The French style is slightly weaker, and the small cup or demitasse is filled somewhere between half and completely full, depending on the size of the cup. The Italian style is extremely strong and the small cup is less than half filled.

It is the ratio of coffee to milk which distinguishes a **caffè latte** from a cappuccino. A caffè latte has more milk and less coffee. This is achieved by putting a little less coffee in the espresso 'arm' than you would for a cappuccino, and by filling only a quarter of the cup or glass with coffee, and then filling it up with hot milk. A caffè latte is often served in a glass rather than a cup.

A **cappuccino** also requires the correct ratio of coffee to milk. Fill the 'arm' of the espresso machine according to the instructions, or as advised by your colleagues. About a third of the coffee cup is then filled with coffee, and the rest with frothed milk. The key to a good cappuccino is not the crest of froth but the coffee/milk ratio. A cappuccino should be strong and milky with a creamy frothed crest.

An important point to remember is that hot milk does not froth. Frothing is achieved by forcing hot air through cold milk, boiling it in the process. To achieve well-frothed milk only add enough milk for the coffees you are making.

A cappuccino is usually served in a cup, but it is some-times served in a glass like a caffè latte. The chocolate sprinkled on top as a garnish is an option, not an essential part of a good cappuccino.

15.22 *Service of coffee*

Except when guests have ordered a full pot of coffee, or when espresso coffee is being served, coffee is normally poured for them at table.

Coffee is served from the right of the guest. If the coffee pot has a short spout (e.g. a Cona pot) pick up the cup and bring it up to the pot to fill it. If the pot has a long spout enabling you to direct the flow accurately, you should pour the coffee straight into the cup on the table.

In formal silver service present the coffee pot and milk jug on an underliner and then pour both coffee and milk for the guests.

Coffee and tea can both be prepared on and served from a guéridon. If speciality coffees and teas are served, the guéridon enables you to make the most of their presentation (see 10.5, 10.6 and chapter 12). Liqueur coffees are particularly suited to preparation on the guéridon (see 15.24 and 15.25 below).

Serving coffee from a coffee pot with a long spout

15.23 HOT CHOCOLATE

Hot chocolate is usually served in cups prepared in the still area rather than poured from a pot at the table. The cups are served from the guests' right. For chocolate preparation see 14.14.

15.24 LIQUEUR COFFEE

Liqueur coffees can provide an additional highlight to the dining experience. When prepared and served correctly they will not only impress the guests but encourage them to order more. The simplicity of the technique involved, and its impressive visual effect, make liqueur coffees particularly appropriate for preparation in front of guests, either on a guéridon or at the bar.

The preparation of a perfect liqueur coffee is a simple process in which fresh, cold, pouring cream is floated on hot liqueured coffee. The result should be a dramatic visual contrast of white on black.

A liqueur coffee is not only enjoyed for its eye appeal, aroma and for its taste; there is also the special sensation of drinking the hot liqueured coffee through the layer of cold, fresh, cream. If a liqueur coffee is to be fully appreciated it is therefore essential that the cream should not be semi-whipped, whipped, or dispensed from a pressure-pack can.

Although different establishments may make minor variations to the recipes, and may use their own names for the various liqueur coffees they offer, the simple technique used to create the perfect liqueur coffee should not be altered.

15.25 *Liqueur coffee preparation*

To prepare a perfect liqueur coffee:
- Choose an appropriate glass, preferably one made of clear, toughened glass, with a stem or with a handle.
- Pour 30mL of the selected spirit or liqueur into the glass.
- For additional visual effect, the spirit or liqueur can be warmed and flamed in a spirit warmer before it is poured into the glass.
- Add sugar, if required.
- Pour hot, black, percolated or filtered coffee into the glass, filling the glass up to 1.5cm from its top.
- Stir.
- Lightly aerate the cream by shaking it in a closed container for about three seconds.
- Pour the cold, aerated cream into the bowl of a spoon placed at the level of the top of the coffee. Continue until the cream is about 1cm deep.
- Remove the spoon, and serve.

Pouring from a spirit warmer

15.26 *CHANGING GLASSWARE*

The original glassware may be used if additional bottles of the same type of wine as was originally ordered are required, unless a change of glasses is requested. If wine of a different style or type is ordered then fresh glasses must be placed before the new wine is served.

Select the style of glassware appropriate to the style of wine chosen (for example, champagne flutes for a sparkling wine), and take the glasses to the table on a drinks tray. Place the glasses a little further away from the guests than the original glasses and at an angle of 45° to right of them.

Remove the original glasses when the guests have finished the wine in them.

Remember that the glasses should be handled by their stems whether they are being placed or removed.

After-dinner drinks (liqueurs, ports and after-dinner cocktails) should be served in fresh glasses for each new order.

Add aerated pouring cream

15.27 *ASHTRAYS*

The drinks waiter must see that guests' ashtrays are clean and, if necessary, frequently replaced. For the technique of changing ashtrays see 11.6 and 11.7.

16
END-OF-SERVICE PROCEDURES

'First-rate meal, well served, but if we could only find a waiter to give us our bill we would be able to leave. The show begins in ten minutes.'

16.1 We have already stressed the importance of greeting and receiving guests warmly and professionally and ensuring that effective and efficient meal service takes place. However the total experience for the guest does not end there; an equal emphasis must be placed on the end-of-service procedures.

When you have read this chapter you should have a basic understanding of the correct ways to deal with:
○ Preparing and presenting a bill
○ Payment procedures and methods
○ Tips (gratuities)
○ Farewelling guests
○ Tidying, cleaning and resetting after service.

16.2 PREPARING AND PRESENTING A BILL

The methods in which bills are prepared and processed vary from one establishment to another. They range from hand-written dockets to high-tech computerized systems.

The two purposes of a guest's bill are to inform the guest of the amount to be paid (giving details of what is charged for), and to act as a control system for the establishment. To make sure that their control systems operate effectively establishments must make sure that their new service staff understand how the billing system works before they begin to serve guests.

Guests' bills may be presented at the table, at the bar, or at a cashier's desk. No matter where it is presented, the bill should be kept up to date at all times. Where possible, the bill should be kept ready for presentation as soon as the guest requires it. This may not always be possible, particularly when beverages are being served right up to the time of the guests' departure.

16.3 *Presenting the bill*

It is essential that you should be alert to signs that guests may want their bill. Nothing is more irritating to guests than to be kept waiting while they try to attract the attention of a waiter to ask for their bill (or 'check' as the Americans call it). This is particularly so for busy business-people at lunchtime. Many a promising restaurant has failed because it earned a reputation for slow service, and the fatal slowness may well have been in the bringing of the bill rather than in the actual food service.

Generally speaking, bills should not be presented until they are asked for, but some establishments, which specialize in quick service and a high turnover of guests, place the bill on the table before the end of the meal.

When a bill is presented at table it is placed in front of the host (probably the person who has asked for the bill) on a small plate from the right. Either the bill is folded so that the amount to be paid cannot be seen by the other guests, or it is placed in a billfold which serves the same purpose. If there is no obvious host you may place the bill in the centre of the table.

Bills presented at bars should be presented on a plate, folded, or in a billfold.

If the establishment requires guests to pay at a cashier's desk as they are leaving, make this clear to the guests to avoid confusion and delay.

Do not hover around waiting for your guests to pay; leave them alone to pay in their own time. Remain alert though, so that when they have paid (or signed) for their meal, there is no unnecessary delay while they are kept waiting for you to collect the payment.

16.4 *METHODS AND PROCEDURES FOR PAYMENT*

Common payment methods include cash, credit cards, cheques, vouchers, and charge accounts. You must be familiar with the procedures for these various methods of payment and know which methods of payment are acceptable to the establishment.

Cash payments are very simple, only requiring the settling of the bill and the tendering of the guest's change.

Credit cards The precise procedures for use with credit cards will vary from establishment to establishment. When the card is placed on the bill you should collect it and, before processing it, check

- that the establishment accepts the kind of card presented,
- its expiry date, and
- that it has been signed.

It is also wise to check the number against the current warning bulletin.

Credit card companies set a 'floor limit' for the 'merchants' accepting their cards. Any card transaction for a sum above the floor limit must be approved by the company. If the amount of bill to be settled is above the floor limit then either the waiter or the cashier must telephone through to the credit-card company for approval. You must therefore know the floor limit of the establishment.

When phoning for approval you must have the card with you so that you can quote its number and expiry date. You will also be asked for your establishment's 'merchant number' so you must have that at hand also.

Processing credit cards involves either the traditional manual completion of a voucher for signature by the guest, or for the card to be run through an electronic imprinter which will produce a transaction slip for the guest to sign. When vouchers are prepared it is usual not to complete the Total line so that the guests can confirm the amount signed for and add a tip if they so wish (see 16.5 below).

After you have checked that the guest has clearly completed the Total line on the voucher with the sum due (or more), and you have checked that the signature on the voucher is the same as that on the card, the card should be returned to the guest along with the customer's copy of the voucher. The guest's voucher should either be returned upside down or (better) in the billfold which was used to present the bill.

Cheques are not accepted in many establishments. Those which do accept cheques will usually require some other identification from the customer, or prior authorization. It is essential that you adhere to house policy when cheques are offered.

Vouchers may be used for pre-paid transactions. They may be gift vouchers for example, or parts of a package, or through a complimentary offer. The voucher takes the place of money payment, but it must be accounted for like any other form of payment.

Charge accounts Before a guest can be allowed to charge the cost of a meal (or drink) to a charge account the transaction must have been authorized by management. It may be necessary to check the guests' signatures against a charge record or, if it is in a hotel, the guest's name against a room number. Procedures for recording information on charge account transactions vary from establishment to establishment. You must, of course, strictly follow house procedures.

16.5 *TIPS (GRATUITIES)*

Tips are a bonus for especially satisfying service and should not be thought of as a right. There are no hard-and-fast rules on the amount of the tip or, indeed, on whether one is left or not. Never expect or anticipate a tip. If the guest has paid in cash always place the full change on the table unless the guest has very clearly indicated that the excess payment is intended as a gratuity.

Never ever allow guests to leave with the humiliating impression that you think they should have tipped you, or that their tip could have been more generous. If you do, they will not come back. Remember, the waiter has absolutely no right to a tip.

In some establishments it is house policy that all tips should be pooled and distributed among all the staff. This is called the 'trunk system'. Where this system is in place it must be very strictly adhered to or there will be bitter disputes. In other establishments individual waiters keep the tips they have been given.

16.6 *FAREWELLING THE GUESTS*

The last impression guests are given as they leave after a meal is as important as their first impression on arrival. The farewell should be warm and friendly, and as personal as possible. If you are not too busy serving other guests, assist those departing by moving their chairs for them, collecting their personal belongings (not forgetting coats, hats, and BYO bags!), and offering to call for a taxi.

If it is not physically possible to assist your guests to leave because you are busy serving others, at least acknowledge their departure with a nod and a smile. If you can, wish them "Good evening" and thank them for coming. You should have taken the trouble to note their names (the credit card is an invaluable reminder for names); if you know the name, use it: "Good night, Mrs Hill. We look forward to seeing you again soon".

16.7 *TIDYING, CLEARING AND RESETTING*

The waiter's responsibilities do not end with the departure of the guests. When the guests have left, the tables and service areas must be cleared of used and soiled items and the tables prepared for use again.

The procedure for resetting the tables and work areas will vary from one establishment to another. In some establishments each table is reset for the same meal service as soon as the guests sitting at that table have left. This allows the table to be used again, increasing the number of covers served in that meal service. In other less hurried establishments, after the guests from one meal service have left the tables are reset for the next service — for example, when one set of guests has finished their lunch the table may be reset for dinner.

16.8 *Procedure for clearing and re-setting*

- Remove coffee cups and centre items, glassware and ashtrays. (If you have kept the table tidy throughout the service of the meal, these should be the only items left on the table when the guests depart.)

  The cups and saucers should be carried using either the two- or the three-plate carrying technique (see 7.5 and 7.6). Do not stack the cups. Glassware should be removed on a drinks tray. The remaining centre items are removed by hand.

- If tablecloths are used in the establishment, the table must be reclothed. If the table is reclothed after service (when the restaurant is empty) use the clothing procedure described in 4.6. If the table is reclothed during service, follow the procedure in 4.7. If tablecloths are not used, all tables must be carefully wiped down.

- Whether the table is reset or not, ensure that all the chairs are returned to their original positions round the table. Do not forget to check the chairs for crumbs.

- The procedures for setting or resetting covers are described in chapter 4, particularly in 4.10-4.16.

- In most establishments workstations are restocked with cleaned, polished equipment immediately after the completion of service in preparation for the next service. See Station Mise-en-Place, 4.8.

17

FUNCTION OPERATIONS

17.1 Functions offer people who lack formal training their greatest opportunity to gain part-time employment and establish themselves in the hospitality industry. The relatively simple skills required of a waiter for a specific function can easily be demonstrated by the employer, and working at the function will ensure that those skills are practised repeatedly over a short period.

By the end of this chapter you will have a basic understanding of:

○ Styles of functions
○ The variation of function covers
○ Food and beverage service in function operations
○ Function staff organization.

17.2 STYLES OF FUNCTION

Function catering can involve anything from the simple service of sandwiches and coffee or tea to gala banquets, and the functions can take place anywhere, indoors or out-of-doors, from the garden of a private home to a grand ballroom.

The precise tasks required of service staff at functions requiring food-and-beverage service are defined by:

○ the customer's needs
○ the occasion
○ the types of food and beverages to be served
○ the amount the customer is prepared to spend.

Within these constraints the only limits to the diversity of function operations and what services are provided are the physical facilities available and the imagination of the caterer.

How often do we attend a function where the standard of service is not only unsatisfactory for the guests but an embarrassment to the staff employed to provide it?

Far too often function staff are left to survive as best they can when prior knowledge of the simplest of skills would have given them a sense of pride, and the service expectations of the guests would have been fulfilled.

135

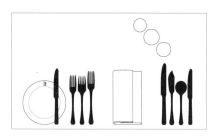

A possible function cover

Set menu cover with dessert gear

17.3 FUNCTION COVERS

The cover for a function is dictated by the menu items to be served. Functions usually have set menus and the cutlery items are set in the order in which they will be used (see 4.10 and 4.12).

17.4 Dessert covers

Dessert cutlery presents special problems for which there is more than one acceptable solution. At functions it is very likely that there will be pressure on space on the table, which adds to the advantages of bringing the dessert cutlery to the table only when it is needed for the sweet course (see 4.13). If the dessert cutlery has been laid with the original cover it will have to be corrected. For the procedure for correcting dessert covers see 6.13.

17.5 Glassware

At functions, there may also not be room to place all the glasses in a single line in order of their probable use. If there are more than two glasses they may have to be arranged in a triangle (see 4.14).

17.6 Cups and saucers

If cups and saucers are required when the cover is laid they are placed above and slightly to the right of the main knife, with the handle of the cup turned to the right so that it may be conveniently grasped by the guest without any need to turn it. Alternatively (and more usually for dinner functions) cups and saucers may be placed immediately before they are required for use (see 15.19).

17.7 FUNCTION SERVICE

The basic styles of service offered at functions are no different from those in restaurants — plate service, silver service, etc. The skills required for each style of service have been described in previous chapters (see chapter 7 for plate service and chapter 8 for silver service).

17.8 Function service skills

The basic skills required for function service are:
- Providing hospitality (see 1.3, 1.4)
- Setting tables (4.10, 4.12, etc.)
- Carrying a tray or platter (5.9, 13.11, 15.11)
- Use of a service cloth (7.4)
- Carrying or clearing plates (7.2-7.6, 9.2-9.7)
- Pouring wine (15.16, 15.17)

17.9 *Function staff organization*

The number and organization of the staff at a function will depend on the particular requirements of different functions. Different styles of functions demand different staff arrangements and procedures. In some circumstances the waiting staff work as a team serving all of the guests at a number of tables, in others they have particular stations allocated to them and they are responsible for serving a set number of guests.

In most circumstances the team organization best satisfies the needs and expectations of the guests and lightens the load on individual serving staff.

17.10 *Team operations*

At large functions, to preserve a smooth and quick level of service, the service staff is often divided into teams.

Each team is made up of the number of staff needed to handle the service of a complete table. For example, tables seating ten guests may require a team of five staff. The team of five is itself divided into two groups with different functions — a serving group of three and a 'running' group of two.

The runners are responsible for the picking up of plated items from the kitchen and their transfer to a service area within the dining-room. The serving group collects the plates (or other items) from the service area and serves them directly to the guests.

When one table has been served, the whole team — servers and runners — moves on to another table.

Clearing is done in the same way. The serving group clears the table and carries the used items to the service area, and the runners remove them from the service area to the washing-up area.

The number of tables a service team can handle depends on the complexity of the menu, the style of service and the facilities at the venue. A food-service team of five, plate-serving an 'average' three-course dinner, might be expected to serve up to twenty tables of ten guests, i.e. up to 200 guests.

17.11 *Beverage service at functions*

Responsibility for beverage service is normally pre-arranged by a station drinks waiter. The precise duties involved will depend on the selection of beverages and the way they are to be served. They may range from serving a variety of beverages from a tray to table service of apéritifs (15.11), table wines (15.16), sparkling wines (15.17), after-dinner drinks (15.18), and coffee (15.19, 15.21).

If food and beverage service at functions is to be co-ordinated, the beverages must be served alternately with the food. The beverages for each course should usually be served before that course.

At functions there will usually be separate teams responsible for serving the beverages, alternating at the tables with the food-service teams. Even if there are not, and the same waiters are responsible for serving both food and beverages, the beverages and the food are not served simultaneously but separately, to avoid confusion.

GLOSSARY

This glossary is not simply an explanation of the technical words used in the text of *The Waiter's Handbook*. It also covers a large number of the terms used in food and beverage service and which are frequently used in menus in the *descriptions* of the dishes on offer. It therefore covers much of the food product knowledge with which every waiter should be equipped.

The headwords are in **bold** type. After the headword, if it comes from a language other than English, its language of origin is given in brackets in abbreviated form in *italics*, e.g. (*Fr.*) for French. Most of these are obvious enough, but some are a little rare, e.g. (*Heb.*) for Hebrew or (*Yid.*) for Yiddish. Occasionally the reference is to a culture rather than to a particular language, e.g. (*Ind.*) for Indian (which is not the name of a language).

For words of non-English origin, especially the many French words, there follows in square brackets a simple pronunciation guide. This is not as simple as it may seem because some languages make use of sounds for which there is no equivalent in English, for example the nasal **in** in the commonly-used French word *vin* (wine) which we have tried to indicate by using brackets: [vi(n)]. There is also the problem of the soft **j** sound in French which we have indicated by

-zj, as in *jus* [zjoo] (meat juice) or *aubergine* [oh-bear-zjeen] (eggplant).

All French nouns have a gender — masculine or feminine — as well as a number — singular or plural. Adjectives used to describe nouns have to agree with them in both gender and number, the adjective following the noun, as in *marrons glacés* (candied chestnuts). Most plurals are easy, just add **s**, but some are less obvious as in *gâteaux* (cakes). When the plural is not obvious we have included it after the headword, therefore **gâteau(x)**.

Because French words are so common in food service, and because French adjectives have to agree with their nouns, we include the gender when a French noun is explained, for example — **crème** (*Fr.*) (fem.). Because *crème* is feminine any qualifying adjective must also be feminine, as in **crème brulée**.

As French adjectives have both masculine and feminine forms we have included both when you are likely to encounter them. In most cases all the feminine form requires is to add **e** to the masculine form. We have indicated this by putting the additional **e** for the feminine form in brackets, for example **gratiné(e)**.

Most words used in definitions which are themselves defined in this glossary are printed in **bold** type.

---

abalone [aba-lony] Large mollusc (genus *Haliotis*) in rough ear-shaped shell.

abalone mushroom **Oyster mushroom**; large white mushroom with a slight taste of **seafood**.

abats (*Fr.*) (masc. pl.) [a-ba] Offal (always referred to in the plural — **les** *abats*). (*See also* **sweetbreads**.)

accompaniment **Condiment** offered by the waiter to add relish to the dishes served. Many condiments are traditional, e.g. red currant jelly with lamb or **Parmesan** cheese with **pasta**.

acidity Wine-tasting term indicating tartness.

advocaat **Liqueur** of egg yolks, sugar, and brandy; egg nog. (In Dutch 'advocate' or 'lawyer'.)

aflatoxin Food poison (toxin) derived from the yellow mould *Aspergillus flavus*.

agneau (*Fr.*) (masc.) [anyo] Lamb.

ail (*Fr.*) (masc.) [ahyuh] **Garlic**.

aïloli/ailloli (*Fr.*) (masc.) [ahyuh-oh-lee] **Provençal garlic mayonnaise**. (From *ail* 'garlic' and provençal dialect *oli* 'oil'.)

à la (*Fr.*) [ah lah] With, in the manner of, when referring to a feminine noun, e.g. *à la carte* (*see* **carte, à la**), *à la russe* (*see* **russe, à la**) etc. (*A la* is the feminine equivalent of **au**).

al dente (*Ital.*) [al dentay] Cooked so as to be firm not soft, when bitten, esp. referring to **pasta**. (*Dente* means 'tooth'.)

ale Top-fermented **beer**. (*See* 14.8.)

alfalfa sprouts [al-fal-fa] Lucerne; fine hairy sprouts used in salads and sandwiches.

almond paste *See* **marzipan**.

à maison *See* **maison**.

amande (*Fr.*) (fem.) [amah(n)d] Almond.

amandine (*Fr.*) [amah(n)deen] With almonds.

amaretto (*Ital.*) (1) Bitter almond-flavoured **liqueur**. (2) Small almond biscuit or **macaroon** served at the end of the meal or with desserts.

amino acid Fatty acid derived from ammonia.

amontillado (*Span.*) [amon-till-ahdoh] Medium-dry style of **sherry**.

ananas (*Fr.*) (masc. sing.) [a-nah-na] Pineapple.

anchovy Small very strongly-flavoured fish, usually preserved in salt.

anglaise, à l' (*Fr.*) [ah longl-ayz] English-style; means different things with different items, but is most commonly applied to boiled vegetables served simply with chopped parsley and a knob of butter. (*See also* **crème anglaise**.)

Angostura Bitters **Proprietary** brand of aromatic bitters used as a flavouring, by the addition of a few drops only, in drinks, e.g. **Pink Gin** or **champagne cocktail**, and in cooking. (Angostura is the former name of Cuidad Bolívar, Venezuelan town where first made.)

Anna *See* **pommes Anna**.

antipasto (*Ital.*) (*pl.* **antipasti**) Selection of **appetizers** served prior to eating. Italian equivalent of **hors d'oeuvre**. (Literally 'before' (*anti*) 'the meal' (*pasto*).)

apéritif (*Fr.*) (masc.) [apay-rit-eef] A drink served before a meal to stimulate the appetite. (*See* 14.2.)

à point *See* **point, à**.

appetizer/appetiser Food served before a meal to stimulate the appetite.

apple/apricot Danish *See* **Danish pastry**.

Appolinaris Brand of mineral water. (*See* 14.18.)

arborio rice Italian rice used for **risotto**.

armagnac (*Fr.*) (masc.) [ar-man-yak] Fine **brandy** made in the Armagnac district, S. France. (*See* 14.7.)

aroma (1) Fragrance, smell. (2) Wine-tasting term. Scent of the grapes in a young wine. As wine matures the aroma decreases and the **bouquet** increases. (*See also* **nose**.)

aromatic Fragrant, sweet-smelling.

artichoke Two quite different vegetables: (1) **globe artichoke** Thistle-like plant with a large flower. The 'heart' and the base of the scaly leaves of the immature flower are eaten, usually with **vinaigrette**. (French *artichaut* [arti-show].) (2) **Jerusalem artichoke** Vegetable used in soups, stews, etc. It looks like a knobbly potato or piece of fresh **ginger**. (The name has nothing to do with Jerusalem but is a corruption of *girasole*, Italian for sunflower. French *topinambour* [topi(n)-am-bore].)

aspic Savoury jelly (natural **gelatine**) made from meat **stock**. Used for setting cold fish or meat in a mould with vegetables, and for garnishing.

assiette (*Fr.*) (fem.) [assy-ett] Plate, e.g. *une assiette de viandes*.

au (*Fr.*) (masc.) [oh] With, in the manner of, when referring to a masculine noun, e.g. *au beurre* (*see* **beurre, au**), *au poivre* (*see* **poivre, au**), etc. (*Au* is the feminine equivalent of **à la**.)

aubergine [oh-bear-zjeen] Eggplant.

auslese (*Ger.*) [ows-layz-uh] Sweet dessert wine made from selected late-picked **riesling** grapes. (*Auslese* means 'selected'.) (*See also* **spätlese**.)

aux (*Fr.*) (plural) [oh] With. (Plural of **au** and **à la**, e.g. **feuilleté** *aux* **pommes**, **soupe glacée** *aux* **moules**.)

B and B **Cocktail** of **brandy** and **Bénédictine**.

baba (*Fr.* from *Polish*) [baa-baa] Small light yeast cake, usually containing raisins. *Babas au rhum* (**rum babas**) are soaked in **rum** syrup.

Bacardi **Proprietary** brand of white **rum**.

back of house The parts of the **establishment** not seen by the guests; the kitchen, **stillroom** and accounts department as opposed to the dining room. (*See also* **front of house**.)

bacteria Plural of bacterium. Tiny single-celled organisms often dangerous to health, but sometimes useful, e.g. in cheese-making.

bagel (*Yid.*) [bay-gul] Ring or doughnut-shaped hard bread roll.

bagna cauda (*Ital.*) [banya cowda] Hot **anchovy** dip. (Literally 'hot bath', from Piemont in N. Italy.) (*See also* **crudités**.)

baguette (*Fr.*) (fem.) [bag-ett] French bread stick.

bain-marie (*Fr.*) (masc.) [ba(n) maree] Large open dish partly filled with hot water, in which pans stand so that their contents are kept hot without overcooking. (Literally, 'bath of Mary'.)

baklava/baclava (*Grk. & Turk.*) **Filo** pastry cake containing almonds and spices and dipped in honey. Traditionally it is cut into triangular shapes.

ballottine (*Fr.*) (fem.) [ba-yot-teen] Meat or fish boned, stuffed, rolled and served cold with an **aspic** glaze, or in a **chaudfroid**. A ballottine may also be served hot, **glazed** in its own **reduced** juices. (*Ballot* means 'bundle'.)

Balmain bug *See* **bug**.

balsamic vinegar Fragrant, matured, sweet, wine **vinegar** with intense flavour used in **vinaigrette** dressings and to enhance the flavour of fruit, e.g. strawberries. (*See also* **malt vinegar**, **rice vinegar**, *and* **wine vinegar**.)

balthazar Very large bottle of **sparkling wine**, the equivalent of 16 standard 750mL bottles. (Balthazar was one of the three wise men who visited the infant Jesus.) (*See also* **champagne bottle sizes**.)

baron of beef   Very large joint of beef, including **loin** and rump, often spit-roasted.

barquette (*Fr.*) (fem.) [bar-ket]   Small boat-shaped pastry which can be filled with various ingredients. (Literally, 'little boat', 'little barque'.)

basil   Pungent, sweet leaves from related plants (species *Ocimum*) used as flavouring herb, esp. in Italian and SE Asian cookery. (*See also* **pesto** *and* **pistou**.)

basmati rice [bass-mutee]   Long-grain rice used in Indian cuisine, esp. **pilau** and **biryani**.

batter   Fluid dough of flour and water or milk, usually with egg, used in cooking. It may be poured, e.g. to make **pancakes**, **waffles**, or **Yorkshire pudding**, or it may be used as a coating, e.g. to make **fritters** or deep-fried fish.

bavarois (*Fr.*) (masc.) [bavah-rwah]   Dessert of custard stiffened with **gelatine**, mixed with whipped **cream**, shaped in a mould and served cold. (*Bavarois* means 'Bavarian', from Bavaria, state in S. Germany.)

bay leaf   Leaves of the bay tree used, fresh or dried, to give flavour to **casseroles**, **stocks** and **marinades**. They are also used in a traditional **bouquet garni**.

bean curd   Bland curd made from **soya beans** and rich in minerals and protein. (*See also* **tofu**.)

béarnaise (*Fr.*) [bay-air-nayze]   Sauce made of beaten egg yolks and **reduced wine vinegar** mixed with butter and served warm, usually with fish or grilled meat. (The French is *sauce béarnaise*. Béarn is a province in SW France.)

beaujolais (*Fr.*) [bow-zjol-lay]   French wine from the Beaujolais region of E. France, or a **generic** wine in that style. The wine is red, fruity and light, and drunk while still young. (*See below*.)

beaujolais nouveau (*Fr.*) [bow-zjol-lay noo-voh]   Beaujolais wine from the latest **vintage**. Australia has borrowed from the French tradition of racing the new vintage to particular restaurants as soon as it is bottled to see who can serve it first.

beef olive   *See* **paupiette**.

beef bourguignon   *See* **boeuf bourguignon**.

beef Stroganov   *See* **boeuf Stroganov**.

beef Wellington   Beef **fillet**, liver **pâté** and mushroom **duxelles** baked in **puff pastry**. (Named in honour of the Duke of Wellington, 1769-1852, British general and Prime Minister.) (*See also* **croûte, en**.)

béchamel (*Fr.*) (fem.) [bay-sha-mel]   Sauce made by adding milk to a **roux**; it is the foundation of many other sauces. (Attributed to Louis de Béchameil, Lord Steward to Louis XVI.)

beef rendang   *See* **rendang daging**.

beer   Alcoholic beverage made from **fermented** malted barley (sometimes wheat) flavoured with hops; general term for **ales**, **lagers** and **stouts**. (See 13.8.)

beignet (*Fr.*) (masc.) [bay-nyay]   **Fritter**.

Belgian endive   *See* **chicory**.

Bénédictine (*Fr.*) [benny-dick-teen]   **Proprietary liqueur**, very sweet and spicy, from Normandy (N. France). (*See also* **B and B**.)

bergamot   Orange-scented herb (*Monarda didyma*) used in savoury and sweet dishes. It gives a distinctive flavour to **Earl Grey tea**.

beurre (*Fr.*) (masc.) [burr]   Butter.

beurre, au (*Fr.*) [oh burr]   Cooked in butter.

beurre blanc (*Fr.*) (masc.) [burr blo(n)]   Smooth sauce made by whipping butter into a **reduced** mixture of white wine, **wine vinegar** and finely chopped onions. (*Blanc* means 'white'.)

beurre fondu (*Fr.*) (masc.) [burr fon-doo]   Butter melted slowly with lemon juice, white **pepper** and salt, often served with boiled or steamed vegetables and poached fish. (*Fondu* means 'melted'.)

beurre maître d'hôtel (*Fr.*) (masc.) [burr may-truh doh-tell]   Softened butter added to mushroom **duxelles**, chopped parsley and lemon juice. Usually served with fish or grilled meat. (*See* **maître d'hôtel**.)

beurre meunière (*Fr.*) (masc.) [burr murn-ee-yair]   **Beurre noisette** with lemon juice added. (*See also* **meunière, à la**.)

beurre noisette (*Fr.*) (masc.) [burr nwa-zet]   Sauce of butter heated until brown (nutty) and served very hot. (*Noisette* is French for 'hazelnut'.)

bianco (*Ital.*) [bee-yan-ko]   Golden medium-sweet style of **vermouth**. (Literally, 'white'.)

bien cuit (*Fr.*) (masc.) [bee-an cwee]   Over-cooked (steak). (Literally, 'well cooked'.) (*See also* **bleu, point (à)**, *and* **saignant**.)

bifteck (*Fr.*) (masc.) [biff-tek]   Beef steak, e.g. *bifteck au* **poivre**, '**pepper** steak'. (*Bifteck* is a French corruption of the English words 'beef steak'.)

billfold (*USA*)   Wallet or folder used for presenting bills, change, etc. (See 16.3.)

bill of fare [fair]   **Menu**.

biryani/biriani (*Ind.*) [birry-ahnee]   **Pilau**, usually spiced and coloured yellow with **saffron** and garnished with hard-boiled egg.

bisque (*Fr.*) (fem.) [beesk]   Thick creamy soup, usually based on **seafood**, e.g. prawn bisque. (*See also* **chowder** *and* **potage**.)

bistro/bistrot (*Fr.*) [beess-troh]   Small informal restaurant or licensed café.

bitters   Flavoured alcoholic spirits of varying strengths. Different brands have very different characters and uses. (*See* **Angostura Bitters**, **Campari**, **Fernet Branca**, *and* **Underberg**.)

black bean   Salted **soya bean** available dried or bottled. (*See also* **black bean sauce** *below*.)

black bean sauce   Sauce made from fermented **soya beans** used in Chinese cooking.

black pepper *See* **pepper, peppercorn**.

black pudding (*UK*) Savoury pork sausage stuffed with oatmeal, blood, seasoned meat, etc. The French equivalent is **boudin noir**.

blanc(he) (*Fr.*) [bla(n)/blah(n)sh] White.

blanch To place briefly in boiling water and then drain to remove excess salt, bitterness, etc. before normal cooking. (Literally, to whiten.)

blanquette (*Fr.*) (fem.) [blahn-ket] Delicate but creamy stew of **veal**, lamb or chicken with vegetables, e.g. *blanquette de* **veau**. (From *blanc*, 'white'.)

blend To mix, usually in an electric blender. Common technique for mixing **cocktails**. (*See* 14.10.)

bleu (*Fr.*) [bluh] Extremely **rare** (steak, etc.). (Literally, 'blue'.) (*See also* **bien cuit, point** (**à**), *and* **saignant**. *See also below*.)

bleu, au (*Fr.*) [oh bluh] Way of cooking freshly-killed fish, particularly trout, so that skin has a bluish tinge. (*Bleu* means 'blue'.)

blini (*Russ.*) [blee-nee] Small thick savoury **pancake**, in Russia traditionally served with **soured cream** to accompany **caviare**.

blintz (*Yid.*) Small savoury **pancake** like a **blini**, but often filled with cheese, etc.

Bloody Mary **Cocktail** of **vodka** in **tomato juice**, flavoured with lemon juice, **Tabasco**, and **Worcestershire sauce**.

blue Extremely **rare** (steak, etc.). (*See also* **bleu**.)

blue vein Blue mould in blue or green cheese. (*See* **Gippsland blue, gorgonzola, roquefort,** *and* **stilton**.)

bocconcini (*Ital.*) [bokon-cheenee] Small balls of fresh white **mozzarella** preserved in **whey** to retain moisture. Bocconcini are often served as part of the **antipasto** or in salads. (Literally 'little mouthfuls'.)

body As wine-tasting term describes the consistency or 'thickness' of the wine.

boeuf (*Fr.*) (masc.) [burf] Beef. (*See also* **bifteck**.)

boeuf à la ficelle (*Fr.*) [burf ah lah fee-sel] Beef **fillet** tied with string to keep its shape, and cooked in **stock**. (*Ficelle* means 'string'.)

boeuf bourguignon (*Fr.*) [burf boor-gee-nyo(n)] Beef bourguignon. A **casserole** made with braising steak and red wine. (*Bourguignon* is French for 'Burgundian' or 'from **Burgundy**'.)

boeuf en daube (*Fr.*) [burf o(n) dobe] Beef **braised** in a red wine **stock**. (*See also* **daube, en**.)

boeuf Stroganov/Stroganoff Strips of beef in a creamy sauce garnished with mushrooms. (The Stroganovs were a wealthy merchant family ennobled by Peter the Great of Russia.)

bok choy (*Chin.*) White cabbage with fleshy white stems and light green leaves.

bolognais(e) (*Fr.*) [bol-on-ayz] With a thick meat-and-tomato sauce; properly *à la bolognaise* in French, meaning 'in the style of Bologna' (city in NE Italy).

bolognese (*Ital.*) [bolon-ayz-ay] Italian for **bolognaise**. (In Italy a bolognaise sauce is usually called *ragu*.)

bombe (*Fr.*) (fem.) [bombuh] Frozen dessert (*bombe glacée*) made in a spherical mould (or one with a rounded top) lined with ice-cream and various fillings. (*Bombe* is French for 'bomb', or 'spherical container'.)

bon appétit! (*Fr.*) [bo(n) apay-tee] Enjoy your meal! (Literally, 'good appetite'.)

bonne femme (*Fr.*) [bon fam] Simply cooked; home-style, with potato, e.g. **potage** *bonne femme*. (Literally, 'good woman'.)

bordelaise, à la (*Fr.*) [ah lah bord-eh-layz] In the style of Bordeaux (town in SW France); cooked with **shallots** and wine, e.g. *poulet sauté à la bordelaise*.

bortsch/borsh (*Russ.*) [borsch] Beetroot soup served with **soured cream**.

botrytis Fungus or mould (*Botrytis cinera*), sometimes called **noble rot**, which shrivels late-picked grapes and makes them intensely sweet. Botrytis-affected grapes are used to make many excellent sweet **dessert wines**. (*See* 14.4.)

bottomless cup System used for **coffee**, etc. whereby customers may have their cups refilled as often as they like at no additional charge.

botulism Food poisoning found principally in canned food and sausages caused by the bacterium *Clostridium botulinum*. (*Botulus* is Latin for 'sausage'.)

bouchée (*Fr.*) (fem.) [boo-shay] Small **savoury** consisting of a round **puff pastry** with various fillings. (Literally, a 'mouthful'; *bouche* means 'mouth'.)

boudin (*Cajun*) [booda(n)] Sausage made of pork liver, cooked pork, rice, and seasonings.

boudin noir (*Fr.*) [booda(n) nwa] **Black pudding**; sausage made from pig's blood, **cream**, fat, and seasonings. (*Noir* means 'black'.)

bouillabaisse (*Fr.*) (fem.) [boo-ya-bayss] Rich **provençal** stew of fish, mussels, etc. simmered with **herbs**. (*See also* **gumbo** *and* **pochouse**.)

bouillon (*Fr.*) (masc.) [boo-y-o(n)] Plain unclarified meat or vegetable **broth** used as **stock** in cooking. (*See also* **consommé, julienne, potage,** *and* **soupe**.)

bouquet (*Fr.*) (masc.) [boo-kay] Wine-tasting term. The smell of a maturing wine (as opposed to the **aroma** of the grapes). (*See also* **nose**.)

bouquet garni (*Fr.*) (masc.) [boo-kay gar-nee] Bunch of herbs, traditionally consisting of **thyme, marjoram**, parsley and **bay leaves**, used for flavouring sauces, **stock**, etc.

bourbon [burbun] American **whiskey** made principally from fermented maize grain. (Originally from Bourbon County, Kentucky.)

bourguignon *See* **boeuf bourguignon**.

braise To stew meat etc. slowly in very little liquid in a closed pan.

brandy Distilled **spirit** made from fermented grapes. (*See* **armagnac, cognac** *and* 14.7; *see also* **calvados** *and* **cherry brandy**.)

Brandy Alexander **Cocktail** of brandy, brown **crème de cacao**, and cream.

brandy snap Golden-brown lacy biscuit flavoured with **ginger** and rolled into a cylindrical shape; they are sometimes made to form a basket in which to serve ice-cream desserts.

brasserie Café selling alcoholic beverages, especially beer, as well as coffee and food. The word originally meant a brewery. (*Brasser* is French for 'to brew'.)

bratwurst (*Ger.*) [brat-voorst] Uncooked highly-seasoned sausage made from pork and **veal**. (Literally, 'frying sausage'.)

brawn Pieces of meat, esp. calf's or pig's head, cooked and set in **aspic**, shaped into a loaf and served cold. (*See also* **galantine**.)

bread and butter pudding (*UK*) Sweet **pudding** of bread layered with sultanas, candied (mixed) peel and sugar, cooked in egg custard.

breathe Wine-tasting term. To allow a wine to 'breathe' is to allow it to come into contact with air by removing the cork from the bottle some time before the wine is drunk in order to enhance the **bouquet**.

brie (*Fr.*) [bree] Soft creamy cows'-milk cheese with a soft edible crust. (Brie is a small town near Paris.) (*See also* **camembert, chèvre**, *and* **King Island**.)

brine Solution of salt and water usually used as a preservative. (*See also* **cure, pickle**, *and* **smoke**.)

brioche (*Fr.*) (fem.) [bree-osh] Light soft roll, often in the shape of a ring, made from yeast dough with eggs and butter.

brochette (*Fr.*) (fem.) [bro-shett] Skewer on which pieces of meat, etc. are cooked, as for **kebabs**.

brodo (*Ital.*) [brohdoh] **Clear soup**; **stock**. (*See also* **minestra** *and* **zuppa**.)

broil To grill.

broiler Young chicken bred for broiling.

broth Meat, fish, or vegetable **stock**.

brunch Substantial late-morning meal, replacing breakfast and lunch. (*Compare* **yum cha**.)

brunoise (*Fr.*) (fem.) [broon-warze] **Diced** vegetables, often **braised** in butter, used as a **garnish** for soups, sauces, etc. (*Brun* means 'brown'.)

bruschetta (*Ital.*) Baked or toasted slices of bread, oiled and sprinkled with herbs and served as an **appetizer**. **Tomato** and **garlic** are sometimes added. (*See also* **canapé** *and* **crostino**.)

brush down To remove crumbs, etc. from tables or tablecloths prior to service of next course, also called

crumbing down. (*See* 11.2.)

brut (*Fr.*) [broot] Very dry (**champagne**).

bubble and squeak (*UK*) Mashed potatoes mixed with cooked cabbage and fried. (*See also* **réchauffé**.)

buckwheat Not strictly speaking a **cereal**, but the round plump seeds of an annual plant (*Fagopyrum esculentum*) used in a similar way. It has a strong, distinctive taste and is much used in Chinese, E. European, and Jewish cuisine. Buckwheat flour is used to make **blini** and **piroshki**.

buffet [boof-ay] (1) Meal consisting of a number of dishes set out so that guests can select what they want for themselves. (*See* 10.10 and **smorgasbord**.) (2) Room or counter where snacks or light meals may be bought.

buffet froid (*Fr.*) (masc.) [boof-ay fwah] Cold meats or shellfish; one of the later courses of the **classic menu**, following the salads and preceding the sweets (**entremets**).

buffet, turkey *See* **turkey buffet**.

bug Shellfish with flesh similar to **rock lobster** but without long legs and feelers. There are two common varieties: Balmain bug and Moreton Bay bug.

build Cocktail-mixing term. To add ingredients one to the other in the glass in which they will be served. (*See* 14.10.)

bunya nut Fruit of Australian tree, *Araucaria bidwillii* with a thin woody shell or cone about the size of an almond and similarly shaped.

burghul (*Mid. East & Grk.*) Style of **cracked wheat**, whereby the grains are hulled (removed from their husks), steamed and cracked. (*See also* **kibbeh**.)

burgundy Smooth, soft red wine from Burgundy (province in W. France) or similar in style. There are also white burgundies, always so-called. (*See also* **boeuf bourguignon, chablis, pinot noir**, *and* 14.3.)

bus (*USA*) To perform general clearing duties in a food-or-beverage service area.

busboy/busgirl (*USA*) Person who clears crockery, glassware, etc. from a food-and-beverage service area.

bush food/tucker (*Austral.*) Native food of Australia; food available in the wild.

bush tomato/bush raisin (*Austral.*) Yellow fruit of *Solanum centrale* , and light brown when dried. Bush-tomato **chutney** is available commercially .

butterfly (~ied) Cut of meat or fish, esp. prawns, split so that one side remains intact while it is opened flat on the barbecue or grill.

BYO Bring Your Own (**liquor**); restaurant to which you can bring your own liquor.

cabernet sauvignon [cab-air-nay so-vee-nyon] Grape variety used to make red wines, especially **claret**.

Called simply 'cabernet' when blended with other varieties, e.g. cabernet-**malbec**.

cacciatore/cacciatora (*Ital.*) [cat-cha-toray] Cooked with **tomatoes**, **mushrooms**, herbs and, usually, wine, e.g. *pollo alla cacciatora*, chicken cacciatora. (*Cacciatore* means 'hunter'.) (*See also* **chasseur**.)

Caesar salad Salad consisting of **cos** lettuce, dressing, almost raw eggs, **Parmesan** cheese, diced crisp bacon, **anchovy fillets** and **croûtons**, often served as a substantial first course. (*See also* 12.9.) (Devised by Caesar Cardini, chef in Tijuana, Mexico *c.* 1925.)

café au lait (*Fr.*) (masc.) [caffay oh lay] White **coffee**; coffee with hot milk or **cream** added. (*See* 14.13.)

caffeine [caf-feen] Mild stimulant found in **coffee** and **tea**.

caffè latte (*Ital.*) [caffay lahtay] White **coffee** made in an **espresso** machine with milk but not frothy like **cappuccino**. (*See* 14.13, 15.21.)

Cajun/Cajan [kay-jun] **Cuisine** developed by **creole** French-speakers in Louisiana (state in S. USA). The key ingredients are **capsicum**, onion, and celery with plenty of **pepper**. (*See also* **gumbo**.)

calamari (*Ital.*) (pl.) [kal-a-maar-ee] Squid. (The anglicized spelling *calamary* appears in English dictionaries but is very rarely found in menus.)

calcium Mineral, found esp. in cheese and milk, necessary for the building of bones and teeth.

call away/call up To request the kitchen to plate up the next **course**.

Calorie Obsolescent measure of the energy in food. Short for kilocalorie. 1 Calorie = 4.2 **kilojoules**.

calvados Apple **brandy** made in Normandy (province in N. France famous for apples). (*See* **normande**.)

calzone (*Ital.*) [kal-zohny] Savoury pasty made with **pizza** dough.

camembert (*Fr.*) [cam-embear] Soft cheese made from cows' milk with a downy skin. (Camembert is a village in Normandy, N. France.) (*See also* **brie**, **chèvre**, *and* **King Island**.)

Campari Brand of Italian **bitters**. Bright red, it is often served as an **apéritif** mixed with **soda**.

canapé (*Fr.*) (masc.) [can-a-pay] Small piece of bread (usually toasted) or biscuit, garnished with **caviare**, cheese, **pâté**, **smoked** salmon, etc. Cold canapés are usually served as savoury **appetizers** with drinks before a meal; hot canapés are sometimes served as **entrées** in the meal itself. (*See also* **bruschetta**, **crostino**, *and* **Melba toast**.)

canard (*Fr.*) (masc.) [can-ar] Duck. (*See also* **caneton**.)

cane spirit Clear spirit distilled from sugar, often used in **cocktails**.

caneton (*Fr.*) (masc.) [can-uh-to(n)] Duckling. (*See also* **canard**.)

cannelloni (*Ital.*) (pl.) Form of **pasta** in large tubular rolls filled with cheese or meat, etc. and baked.

cantaloup/cantaloupe Rock melon.

Cantonese One of the five main styles of Chinese cuisine; *Cantonese* cuisine is the style usually encountered in Westernized restaurants. (*See also* **Fukien**, **Honan**, **Peking**, *and* **Szechwan**.) (Canton is a city in S. China near Hong Kong, now called Guangzhou.)

caper **Pickled** bud or young berry of a Mediterranean shrub (*Capparis spinosa*) used as a **garnish** or seasoning.

capon [kay-pon] Neutered male chicken, prized for tenderness.

caponata (*Sicily*) [capon-ahtah] Dish of eggplant, tomatoes, and celery flavoured with **capers**, **anchovies** and **olives** fried together in olive oil but served cold, usually as an **hors d'oeuvre**.

cappuccino (*Ital.*) [cap-poo-chee-no] Popular style of **espresso coffee** served with frothy milk. (*See* **coffee**, 14.13 *and* 15.21.)

capretto (*Ital.*) [kap-rettoh] Milk-fed kid (young goat).

capricciosa (*Ital.*) [caprit-chosa] Sauce containing **tomato**, cheese, ham, mushrooms, **olives**, and usually **anchovies** commonly served as **pizza** topping. (*Capriccioso* means 'naughty' or 'capricious'.)

capsicum Family of plants otherwise called **peppers**, including **chillies** and **sweet** (or bell) **peppers**. The word, used alone, usually refers to the latter.

carafe (*Fr.*) (fem.) [ca-raaf] Glass bottle or spoutless jug used for water or wine.

caramel Melted sugar heated slowly until it is brown.

caramelize (1) To turn sugar into **caramel** by heating. (2) To pour melted sugar over food to brown it.

carbohydrate Essential energy-giving **nutrient**; an organic compound of carbon, hydrogen and oxygen. (Starch, sugar, and cellulose are groups of carbohydrates.)

carbonara (*Ital.*) Bacon-and-**cream** sauce served on **pasta**.

carbonated wine Wine made effervescent (bubbly) by pumping carbon dioxide into it. (*See* 14.6 *and* **sparkling wine**.)

Caro Trade name of a naturally **caffeine**-free instant **cereal** and **chicory** beverage often used as a substitute for **coffee**.

carob Pod of *Ceratonia siliqua* (locust bean) used ground as a sugar or chocolate substitute.

carpaccio (*Ital.*) [car-patchy-o] Thin slice of raw beef (or tuna) with a **vinaigrette** sauce, served cold.

carré (*Fr.*) (masc.) [caray] Cut of meat, e.g. *carré d'agneau* (**rack** of lamb), *carré de veau* (neck of veal).

carte, à la (*Fr.*) [ah lah kart] Type of **menu** which offers a choice of items which are individually priced and cooked to order. (*See* 2.10.)

carte du jour (*Fr.*) (fem.) [cart doo joor] **Menu** of the day. (*See* 2.13.)

cassata (*Ital.*) [kass-ahta] Layers of different ice-creams, one of which is flavoured with **liqueur** and contains **glacé** fruits. (Literally 'little case' because of its traditional brick shape.)

casserole (1) Pan with a lid for cooking stews. (2) Stew cooked in a casserole.

cassis (*Fr.*) (masc.) [cass-eece] (1) Blackcurrant. (2) Blackcurrant **liqueur**.

cassoulet (*Fr.*) (masc.) [cass-oo-lay] **Râgout** of **haricot** beans and meat with a **gratin** topping.

catsup *See* **ketchup**.

caviare/caviar Salted sturgeon's eggs. Other fish **roe**, esp. **lump-fish**, is often used as a substitute.

cayenne pepper Hot spice made from dried, ground red **chillies**, sometimes placed on the table in a small **cruet**. Also called 'red pepper' or 'chilli powder'. (Originally from Cayenne, city in French Guyana.)

cep [sep] Kind of edible mushroom with thick stalk (*Boletus edulis*). (French *cèpe* [saip].) (*See also* **morel**, **oyster mushroom**, **pine mushroom**, *and* **truffle**.)

cereal [seerial] (1) Any grain used as food; corn: wheat, barley, maize, oats, rye, etc. (2) Packaged pre-cooked breakfast food made from such grain. (Ceres was the Roman goddess of corn crops.)

cervelles (*Fr.*) (fem. pl.) [sur-vel] Brains.

cevapcici (*Serb.*) [sevap-chee-chee] Skinless spicy sausage or meatball made of several different meats minced with **capsicum** and **garlic**.

chablis [shablee] Dry white **table wine** made in the northern **Burgundy** district of France, or a **generic** wine in that style.

chafing dish [chay-fing dish] (1) Portable pan with a source of heat used for cooking at table, or on a **guéridon**. (2) Hotplate for keeping dishes warm; a **réchaud**. (*See* 3.6.)

cha gio (*Viet.*) [chah zo] **Spring rolls**; small **pancake** parcel filled with minced crab, pork, and mushroom deep-fried and wrapped in a lettuce leaf with **Vietnamese mint** and dipped in **nuoc cham**.

champagne (1) **Sparkling wine** from the Champagne region (N. France). (2) (*Austral.*) Wine fermented in the bottle in the same style. (*See* 14.6.)

champagne bottle sizes Champagne and other sparkling wines are often available in extra large bottles, the different sizes have these traditional names: **magnum** (2 bottles), **jeroboam** (4 bottles), **rehoboam** (6 bottles), **methuselah** (8 bottles), **salmanazar** (12 bottles), **balthazar** (16 bottles), and **nebuchadnezzar** (20 bottles). (The 'bottles' are multiples of the standard 750 mL bottle.)

champagne cocktail Cocktail of **champagne** with a small measure of **brandy**, a sugar cube and a few drops of **Angostura Bitters**.

champignon (*Fr.*) (masc.) [shom-pee-nyo(n)] Mushroom.

chantilly *See* **crème chantilly**.

chapati/chupatty (*Ind.*) Thin unleavened bread; **roti**.

charcoal grill To grill food over a 'natural' heat source of burning charcoal. (*See also* **char grill**.)

charcuterie (*Fr.*) (fem.) [shar-coot-er-ee] (1) Pork butchery. (2) Cooked meats, e.g. **terrines**, **smoked** ham, **salamis**, etc., made primarily from pork. (*See also* **smallgoods**.)

charcutière, à la (*Fr.*) [ah lah shar-coot-ee-air] Served with a **demi-glace** containing wine and thin strips of **dill pickle**.

chard, rainbow *See* **silverbeet**.

chardonnay [shar-don-ay] Grape variety used to make white wines, e.g. white **burgundy**.

char grill To cook food on a grill which has coke or coals over an 'artificial' electric or gas heat source. (*See also* **charcoal grill**.)

charlotte (*Fr.*) (fem.) [sharl-ot] Hot baked dessert of **puréed** fruit cased in or layered with bread or sponge-cake, cooked in a mould. (Named in honour of Queen Charlotte, consort of George III.)

charlotte russe [sharl-ot rooss] Cold dessert of custard prepared in a **charlotte** mould lined with jelly and sponge fingers. (*Russe* means 'Russian'.)

Chartreuse Old French **proprietary liqueur** with very complex flavours. There are two styles: green and yellow. The green is stronger and less sweet.

chasseur (*Fr.*) (masc.) [shass-ur] Cooked with white wine, **shallots**, mushrooms, and tomatoes, e.g. **tournedos** *chasseur*. (*Chasseur* means 'hunter'.)

châteaubriand (*Fr.*) (masc.) [shat-oh-bree-ond] Tender thick **fillet** steak, usually served with a **béarnaise** sauce. (Devised by the chef to the Vicomte de Châteaubriand, 1768-1848, French diplomat, writer, and gourmet.)

chaud (*Fr.*) [show] Hot.

chaudfroid (*Fr.*) (masc.) [show-frwah] Cold dish of fish or meat served in a solidified coating of **gelatine** (aspic) sauce; cooked hot and served cold. (*Chaud* is French for 'hot' and *froid* is French for 'cold', so literally 'hot-cold'.)

chawarma/shwarma (*Leb.*) [sha-warma] *See* **döner kebab**.

cheddar   The most popular kind of tasty cheese, jocularly known as 'mousetrap' (originally made in the village of Cheddar in Somerset, England).

chef (*Fr.*) (masc.) [shef]   Senior or head cook. (*Chef* is French for 'chief' or 'head'.)

chef de rang (*Fr.*) (masc.) [shef duh rung]   Traditional term for a senior waiter; the waiter immediately under the station head waiter in an **establishment** with a full service brigade. (*See* **rang** *and* 1.6.)

cherry brandy   Cherry-flavoured **liqueur**, usually made by **macerating** cherries in neutral spirit. (*See also* **kirsch**.)

cherry tomato   *See* **tomato**.

chervil   Small plant with parsley-like leaves used as a herb for seasoning, esp. in French cuisine; one of the ingredients of **fines herbes**.

chèvre (*Fr.*) (fem.) [shevruh]   (1) She-goat. (2) Goat's cheese.

chevreuil, en (*Fr.*) [ahn shev-ruyee]   Cooked to taste like **venison**; **marinated** meat served with *sauce* **poivrade** or *sauce* **venaison**. (*Un chevreuil* is a roe-deer.) (*See also* **salmis**.)

chiboust   *See* **crème chiboust**.

chick-pea   Seed of the **legume** *Cicer arietinum*. It is a staple of Middle Eastern cooking, and is used in dishes such as **hummus** and **falafel**.

chicory   (1) Belgian or white **endive** (*Cichorium intybus*), also called **witloof**; vegetable with tightly-wrapped white leaves which may be thinly sliced and served raw in salad or cooked by steaming or boiling. Its roots are ground and mixed with **coffee** and it is used in coffee substitutes like **Caro**. (2) (*UK*) Curly **endive** (Cichorium endivia); sharply-flavoured spinach-like vegetable. (Italian *cicoria*; Greek *rathikia*.)

chiffonnade (*Fr.*) (fem.) [shiffon-ard]   Leaves of salad vegetables (lettuce, **chicory**, etc.) cut or shredded into thin strips, used as a **garnish**.

chilli   Pod and seeds of varieties of the **capsicum** plant used as a very hot spice, particularly in SE Asian, Indian and Mexican food. Chillies are red or green. When dried and powdered red chillies become **cayenne pepper**. (*See also* **pepper** *and* **sweet pepper**.)

chilli con carne (*Mex.*) [chilly con car-nay]   Stew of **chillies**, **minced meat** and beans. (*Con carne* is Spanish for 'with meat'.)

China tea   Green **tea**, often served without milk. (*See also* **jasmine tea**.)

Chinese parsley   *See* **coriander**.

chipolata [chipoh-lahta]   Very small sausage.

chives   Thin green flavouring **herb** related to onion and **garlic**, but without a distinct 'bulb'; it is one of the ingredients of **fines herbes**.

chlorophyll   Substance which makes plants green.

(Literally, 'green leaf' in Greek.)

choi   *See* **choy**.

cholesterol [kolesterol]   Fatty substance found only in animals, high levels of which are associated with heart attacks.

chop suey (*Chin./USA*) [chop sooee]   Shredded meat cooked with vegetables.

chorizo (*Span. & Mex.*) [koreet-soh]   Spicy pork sausage usually eaten cooked, esp. with **paella**.

chou (*Fr.*) (masc.) [shoo]   Cabbage. (*See also* **choy**.)

choux (*Fr.*) (masc. pl.) [shoo]   Small light buns made of **choux pastry**. Choux are served either cold as a **sweet** with a **cream** filling, or with a savoury stuffing as **hors d'oeuvres**.

choux pastry [shoo]   Very light pastry used to make **choux**, **éclairs**, **profiteroles**, etc.; **pâte à choux**.

chowder (*USA*)   Stew or thick soup, usually milk-based and made with **seafood**, e.g. clam chowder. (*See also* **bisque**.)

chow mein (*Chin./USA*) [chow meen]   Fried **noodles** with green vegetables and, usually, meat.

choy (*Chin.*)   Cabbage. (*See also* **bok choy** *and* **choy sum** *below*.)

choy sum (*Chin.*)   Pretty variety of cabbage with long stem and yellow flowers. The stems are particularly tasty, with a mildly bitter flavour.

Christmas pudding (*UK*)   Rich steamed pudding containing dried, fresh, and **glacé** fruits, spices, nuts, eggs, **suet**, and **brandy**. It is made months in advance and reheated on Christmas Day.

chutney (*Anglo-Ind.*)   Thick mixture of fruits and vegetables preserved in **vinegar**, sugar and spices, served as a **condiment**.

citronelle   *See* **lemon grass**.

citrus   Fruit from any citrus tree — lemon, lime, orange, grapefruit, cumquat, etc.

clafoutis (*Fr.*) [claff-ootee]   Baked **pudding** of **batter** spread thickly on a base of fruit, esp. black **morello** cherries, and served warm.

claret   Red wine either from the Bordeaux region of SW France or of similar type. Clarets are medium-bodied and have a distinctively astringent aftertaste because of their high **tannin** content. (The English word 'claret' comes from the French word *clairet* meaning 'clear, bright' (wine).) (*See also* **cabernet sauvignon**.)

clarify   To make clear; to remove the impurities from **stocks**, etc. so that they are no longer cloudy. **Stocks** may be clarified by boiling egg whites in them which coagulate and trap the particles to be removed. (*See also* **ghee**.)

classic menu   The full traditional banquet menu as it developed in France in the nineteenth century, with courses offered as follows: (1) **hors d'oeuvre**

(2) soups (**potages**) (3) egg dishes (**oeufs**) (4) **pasta** and rice dishes (**farinaceous** dishes) (5) fish (**poissons**) (6) **entrées** (meaning small, preliminary meat dishes, the first of the meat courses, *see* 2.2) (7) **sorbets** (8) **relevés** (9) roasts (**rôtis**) (10) vegetables (**légumes**) (11) salads (12) cold buffet (**buffet froid**) (13) sweets (**entremets**) (14) **savouries** (15) cheeses (**fromages**) (16) desserts (in the sense of fresh fruit and nuts, *see* 2.2) (17) beverages (coffee, tea, etc. — not, strictly speaking, a course).

clear soup Consommé. (*See also* **brodo, julienne, marmite petite, steamboat,** *and* **tom yam.**)

cloche Dish cover, usually metal, often semi-spherical with a handle at top, serving to keep food warm. A cheese cloche (to protect from flies, etc.) is usually made of glass or transparent plastic. (*See* 3.5.)

clotted cream *See* **cream, clotted.**

cocktail Mixed drink, almost always alcoholic, often with a **spirit** base. (*See* 14.10.)

coconut Edible flesh of the fruit of the coconut palm. It can be **desiccated** (dried), shredded and used in **curries,** cakes, **puddings** and confectionary.

coconut cream Thick mixture of processed **coconut** flesh and **coconut milk** used in **curries** and Asian dishes.

coconut milk (1) Liquid from inside the **coconut.** (2) Processed milky mixture of **coconut** flesh with **coconut milk** used as a drink or in Asian cooking.

cocotte (*Fr.*) (fem.) [cock-ot] Small round or oval ovenproof cooking dish in which food may be both cooked and served. (*See below.*)

cocotte, en (*Fr.*) [ahn cock-ot] Cooked and served in a small **cocotte** dish (e.g. **oeufs** *en* **cocottes**).

coeur à la crème (*Fr.*) [cur ah lah crem] Dessert of **fromage blanc,** drained and set in a perforated heart-shaped mould and turned out to serve with fresh fruit or a **coulis.**

coffee Drink made from the ground beans of the coffee (*Coffea*) plant, usually served after a meal. There are many ways of serving it. (*See* 14.13, 15.21 *and* 15.22; *see also* **café au lait, caffè latte, cappuccino, Cona, decaffeinated, espresso, Greek, iced, liqueur, macchiato, mocha, Turkish,** *and* **Vienna coffee.**)

cognac (*Fr.*) (masc.) [con-yak] Fine **brandy** from the Cognac region of SW France.

Cointreau (*Fr.*) [kwi(n)-troh] Popular **proprietary** French **triple sec curaçao liqueur.**

Colada One of a group of **blended** long-drink **cocktails,** all including white **rum, coconut cream,** pineapple juice and cream.

com chien (*Viet.*) [kom chin] Fried rice.

commis (*Fr.*) (masc.) [commie] Assistant or trainee.

Short for commis cook or **commis de rang.**

commis de rang (*Fr.*) (masc.) [commie duh rung] Assistant or trainee waiter, below the **chef de rang** in the traditional service brigade. (*See* 1.7.)

commis waiter [commie] Ordinary assistant waiter or trainee waiter. (*See* **commis** *and* **commis de rang.**)

compote (*Fr.*) (fem.) [kompot] Fruit cooked in syrup; stewed fruit.

com tam (*Viet.*) [kom tum] 'Broken' rice topped with pork. (*Com* is 'rice', *tam* 'crushed'.)

Cona coffee Method of making **coffee** by vacuum **infusion,** similar in principle to the percolator method. The equipment consists of two bowls which are placed one above the other. Water is boiled so that it rises from the lower bowl through a tube into the upper bowl where it passes through ground coffee and a filter before returning to the lower bowl from which it is served. Cona is a trade name. (*See* 3.5.)

Condé (*Fr.*) [conday] Various dishes dedicated to the Prince de Condé, great French general, 1621-86 or his descendants. A Condé is usually a cold dessert of poached fruit, esp. apricots, arranged in and around a ring of sweet, creamy rice and served cold.

condiment Seasoning (e.g. **mustard, soya sauce,** or **pickle**) used to give relish to food, usually added to the food after it has been served at table.

confit (*Fr.*) (masc.) [con-fee] Piece of almost boneless meat, usually duck, goose, or **game,** cooked in its own fat and juice and sealed in a pot, immersed in the same fat, for preservation, e.g. *confit d'oie.*

consommé (*Fr.*) (masc.) [con-som-ay] Thin soup made from a pure beef **stock.** It is usually served hot but may be chilled in which case it will be jelly-like but not solid. (*See also* **bisque, bouillon, garbure, julienne, marmite petite, pistou, potage, soupe,** *and* **vichyssoise.**)

contaminate (verb) hence **contamination** (noun) (1) To pollute or infect. (2) To blend different mixtures thus spoiling both. This often occurs when one utensil is re-used in the preparation of different dishes.

continental breakfast Light breakfast of fruit juice, **croissants** or toast with butter, preserves and coffee.

coq au vin (*Fr.*) [cock oh va(n)] Chicken **casseroled** with bacon, onion, **garlic** and **mushrooms** in **brandy** and red wine. (Literally 'cock in wine'.)

coquille (*Fr.*) (fem.) [coh-kee] Shell (of fish etc.).

coquilles Saint (St) Jacques (*Fr.*) [coh-kee san zjak] **Scallops** served cooked in a creamy sauce and presented in a scallop shell with mashed potato **piped** around the edge. (The scallop shell was the symbol of the pilgrims who visited the tomb of St Jacques — St James — of Compostella, N. Spain.)

cordial (1) Any stimulating beverage.
(2) Concentrated fruit squash, e.g. lemon cordial.
(3) (*USA*) **Liqueur**.

coriander Fragrant herb or spice with a bitter flavour, also called **Chinese parsley**. Both the leaves and seeds are commonly used in S and SE Asian **cuisine**.

corkage Charge made by an **establishment** for opening bottles brought by customers.

corked/corky wine Wine which has been spoiled because the bottle has a faulty and mouldy cork. Seriously corked wine becomes bitter and foul-smelling but mild corking may be difficult to detect. The word has nothing to do with pieces of cork which may fall into the wine when the bottle is opened.

corn (**on the cob**)/**sweet corn**/**Indian corn**/**maize** Cluster of small yellow grains on a central core or cob covered with fine silky threads and a green sheath. If served whole a **fingerbowl** is required. Miniature baby corn is used whole esp. in Chinese dishes. (In French *maïs*.) (*See also* **polenta**.)

corn chip Thin crisp wafer made from maize (**corn**) flour and served with **nachos** or eaten as a snack.

cos [koz] Lettuce with crisp, long leaves.

côte (*Fr.*) (fem.) [coat] Rib, e.g. *côtes de* **veau**.

coulibiac (*Fr.*) [cooly-bee-ahkee] French adaptation of a Russian fish pie, traditionally layered salmon, rice, and chopped hard-boiled eggs rolled in pastry.

coulis (*Fr.*) (masc.) [coo-lee] Thin **purée** of fruit, seasoned cooked vegetables, or fish.

coupe (*Fr.*) (fem.) [coop] (1) Stemmed bowl, usually made of glass. (*See* 3.5.)
(2) Dessert served in such a bowl (*coupe* **d'**ananas, *coupes* glacées).

courgette (*Fr.*) (fem.) [koor-zjet] **Zucchini**.

course Stages of a meal, e.g. **entrée**, main course, **dessert**. (*See* 2.3 *and* **classic menu**.)

court-bouillon (*Fr.*) (masc.) [coar bwee-yon] **Broth** of white wine, herbs, and vegetables in which fish is simmered; a seasoned fish **stock**.

couscous (*Arab.*) [koos koos] N. African dish of steamed **semolina** served with meat or vegetables.

cover (1) Place setting for one guest.
(2) The number of guests at a **function** or **establishment**. (*See* 4.10.)

cracked wheat Whole wheat grains cracked and broken open by crushing to produce a coarse meal. (*See also* **burghul** *and* **kibbeh**.)

crackling Crisp baked skin or rind of pork, usually served sliced.

crayfish/crawfish/(informal) **cray** Southern **rock lobster** (*Jasus novae-hollandiae*); large salt-water **crustacean** without large claws; in Australia commonly (and somewhat misleadingly) referred to

simply as '**lobster**'. The French for the salt-water crayfish is **langouste**. There are also other varieties of freshwater crayfish (French **écrivisse**), e.g. **marrons** and **yabbies**. (*See also* **langoustine**.)

cream (1) Thick fatty part of milk. Light or reduced cream has a lower fat content. Thickened cream has a thickening agent (e.g. **gelatine**) added to enhance whipping.
(2) Food resembling pure cream in consistency; dessert containing cream; creamed soup, e.g. butter cream, custard cream, cream of mushroom soup. (*See also* **crème** *etc.*, *and below*.)

cream cheese Soft, spreadable cheese.

cream, clotted Cream, skimmed from **scalded** milk, cooled and traditionally served with **scones** and jam for cream tea. (*See also* **Devonshire tea**.)

cream, soured Thick **cream** to which a culture has been added to give a sharp taste. (It is not cream that has gone 'off'.)

crème (*Fr.*) (fem.) [crem] **Cream**, custard.

crème, à la (*Fr.*) (fem.) [ah lah crem] Cooked with **cream**, cream sauce, or custard.

crème anglaise (*Fr.*) [crem on-glaze] Custard of a pouring consistency cooked slowly over a **bain-marie**. (Literally, 'English cream'.)

crème brûlée (*Fr.*) [crem broo-lay] Thick, smooth custard covered with a thick crust of sugar which has been grilled until **caramelized** and crisp. (*Brûlée* means 'burnt'.)

crème caramel (*Fr.*) [crem cara-mel] Custard set in a mould containing a **caramel** sauce. Once turned out the sauce sits on top and slips down the sides.

crème chantilly (*Fr.*) [crem shahn-tee-yee] Fresh **cream** whipped and sweetened with **vanilla sugar**. (Chantilly is a town near Paris.)

crème chiboust (*Fr.*) [crem shiboost] Custard similar to **crème pâtissière** but with **gelatine** added. The eggs are separated and the whipped whites are added to the warm custard. (Chiboust was a pastry-cook in 19th-century Paris.)

crème d', de … (*Fr.*) [crem duh] Cream **liqueurs** (*crème d'*amandes, *crème de* cacao, *crème de* menthe).

crème de cacao [crem duh kakau] **Liqueur** made from **vanilla** and cocoa beans. There are white and brown styles. (*Cacao* is French for 'cocoa'.)

crème de menthe (*Fr.*) [crem duh mah(n)th] Peppermint-flavoured **generic liqueur**, usually bright green. (*Menthe* means '**mint**'.)

crème fouettée (*Fr.*) [crem foo-ettay] Whipped **cream**.

crème fraîche (*Fr.*) [crem fraysh] Thick **cream** to which a culture has been introduced resulting in a sharp taste and almost solid consistency. (Literally, 'fresh cream'.) (*See also* **mascarpone**.)

crème pâtissière (*Fr.*) [crem paht-ees-see-year] Thick

custard thickened with flour to which beaten egg white is added to provide a **mousse**-like texture which will hold its shape in cakes and desserts. (*Pâtissier* (fem. *~ière*) means 'pastry cook' or 'confectioner'.) (*See also* **crème chiboust**.)

creole [cree-yoal]   In the style of the West Indies. Typically savoury dishes contain **capsicums** or bananas, and sweet dishes contain sugar, **rum**, or bananas. (French, *créole* [cray-oal].) (*See* **Cajun**.)

crêpe (*Fr.*) (fem.) [krep]   Very thin **pancake** cooked on both sides, usually filled and rolled up when served. *Crêpes* can be sweet or savoury.

crêpes Suzette (*Fr.*) (fem. pl.) [krep soo-zet]   Sweet **crêpes** flavoured with orange juice and orange **liqueur** (e.g. **curaçao** or **Grand Marnier**). They are often cooked at the table in a **chafing dish** and served **flambé** in lighted **rum**. (Invented by chef Henri Charpentier *c*. 1900, and named in honour of a child dinner guest of the Prince of Wales.)

crépinette (*Fr.*) (fem.) [krep-in-ett]   Finely minced meat with seasonings cooked in a caul (thin membrane); a flat sausage.

cress   (1) Salad greens from the mustard family. (2) *Lepidium sativum*, a tiny green seedling with little black seeds commonly known as garden or mustard-and-cress. (*See also* **rocket** *and* **watercress**.) (French, *cresson*.)

croissant (*Fr.*) (masc.) [kwa-sahn]   Crescent-shaped sweet roll usually made of **puff pastry**, commonly served at breakfast with butter and jam or chocolate. (Literally 'crescent'.) (*See also* **pain au chocolat**.)

croquembouche (*Fr.*) [crockem-boosh]   Conical tower of small **choux** buns filled with custard or **cream** and coated with spun sugar, traditionally served at weddings. (Literally, 'crisp in the mouth'.)

croque-monsieur (*Fr.*) (masc.) [crock muss-yure]   Toasted sandwich, esp. one filled with ham and **gruyère** cheese. (*Croque-madame* has a fried egg on top.) (*Croquant(e)* means 'crunchy' from *croquer* 'to crunch', 'to devour'.)

croquette (*Fr.*) (fem.) [kro-ket]   Minced mixture, usually meat or fish, with vegetables and seasoning, prepared with a sauce to bind and shaped into a small ball, tube, or **patty**. It is rolled in egg and breadcrumbs before it is fried.

cross-contamination   Spoiling of food by germs passing from one organism to another.

crostino (*Ital.*) (*pl.* **crostini**) [cross-teeno/ee]   **Canapé** or small savoury toast served as an appetizer; a **croûton**.

croustade (*Fr.*) (fem.) [kroo-stahd]   Case of pastry, or deep-fried bread, mashed potato, or rice containing a savoury mixture in a cream sauce or a **purée**, e.g. *croustades à la* **marinière**. (*See also* **vol-au-vent**.)

croûte (*Fr.*) (fem.) [kroot]   (1) Pastry case. (2) Slice of fried bread on which **appetizers** are served. (*See also below.*)

croûte, en   Cooked in a pastry case (e.g. **pâté** *en croûte*, **poulet** *en croute*). (*See* **croûte** *above.*)

croûton (*Fr.*) (masc.) [kroo-ton]   Small cube of fried or toasted bread used to **garnish** soups and some salad and vegetable dishes. (*See also* **crostino**.)

crudités (*Fr.*) (fem. pl.) [kroo-di-tay]   Small pieces of vegetable served as an **appetizer** with an accompanying savoury dip. Typical vegetables include carrot, celery, mushroom, cauliflower, broccoli and **capsicum**. Many sauces are used: avocado dip, **mayonnaise**, **taramasalata** or any with a soft consistency.

cruets   Salt and **pepper** set, and (now rarely) containers for oil and **vinegar**.

crumb down   To brush the tablecloth between courses thus removing all debris. A table is usually crumbed down after the main course and before **dessert**. (*See* 11.3.)

crustacean(s)   Shellfish, including **crayfish**, **lobsters**, **scallops**, prawns, shrimps, and crabs. (French *les crustaces*.)

cuisine (*Fr.*) (fem.) [kwi-zeen]   (1) Kitchen or kitchen staff (**chef** *de cuisine*). (2) (Style of) cookery or food (e.g. French cuisine, Thai cuisine, **cuisine naturelle**).

cuisine minceur (*Fr.*) [kwi-zeen mansur]   Style of cooking using low-kilojoule ingredients and replacing the rich sauces of traditional French **cuisine** with vegetable **purée**, **fromage blanc**, or **crème fraîche**. (Created by Michel Guérard, *b*.1933; *minceur* means 'slenderness'.) (*See also* **cuisine naturelle**, **haute cuisine**, **nouvelle cuisine**, *and* **Pritikin**.)

cuisine naturelle (*Fr.*) [kwi-zeen natoor-ell]   Style of cooking using fresh ingredients prepared so that the natural flavour is evident. Fats, alcohol, salt, and sugar are used sparingly. (Created by Anton Mosimann, *b*. 1947, at the Dorchester Hotel in London.) (*See also* **cuisine minceur**, **haute cuisine**, **nouvelle cuisine**, *and* **Pritikin**.)

Cumberland sauce   Sweet-and-sour sauce made of orange and lemon juice and zest, red currant jelly and **port**, usually served cold with roast or **braised** strong-tasting meats like mutton, **venison** or duck. (From Cumberland, county in N. England.)

curaçao [cure-a-soh]   Orange **liqueur**, either white or blue in colour. (Originally made with oranges from Curaçao, W. Indian island.) (*See also* **triple sec**.)

curd   Rich creamy fattening part of milk which can be separated from the watery part or **whey**.

cure   To **preserve** food by drying, salting, **pickling**, or smoking. (*See also* **brine**.)

curry (*Anglo-Ind.*)   Dish of meat or vegetables prepared with spices, particularly **turmeric**; general term for Indian dishes. The English word curry comes from a Tamil (S. Indian) word meaning sauce, but the word is little used in Indian cookery.

custard apple   Soft fruit of W. Indian tree (*Anona reticulata*) shaped like large apple with flesh tasting like custard.

cutlet   (1) Thick slice of meat on the bone from the neck of lamb or **veal**. (*See also* **papillote**.)
(2) Thick slice of fish on the bone. (*See also* **darne** *and* **tronçon**.)

cuvée (*Fr.*) (fem.) [koo-vay]   Batch of wine or a blend of wines from different vats.

dahl/dal (*Ind.*) [dahl]   Thick **purée** of **lentils**. With **roti** it is the staple food of N. India.

daikon radish [dye-ko(n)]   Giant white radish which is **pickled** and served beautifully sliced or shredded as a **garnish** with many Japanese meals. (*See also* **horseradish** *and* **wasabi**.)

damper (*Austral.*)   Dough of flour and water traditionally baked in the ashes of an outdoor fire.

Danish pastry   Flaky yeast cake topped with icing, nuts and fruit and usually baked in a scroll shape. (Also known as Apple Danish, Apricot Danish etc.)

dariole (*Fr.*) (fem.) [da-ree-ole]   (1) Small steep-sided mould used in making small pastries and **puddings**.
(2) Food that is baked or set in a *dariole*.

Darjeeling tea   Fine black Indian **tea**. (Darjeeling is a hill town in the tea-growing area of NW India.)

darne (*Fr.*) (fem.) [darnuh]   Steak or **cutlet** of large round fish such as schnapper or cod, cut through the bone. (*See also* **tronçon**.)

daube, en (*Fr.*) [ahn dobe]   Cooked slowly in a pan; **braised**, e.g. **boeuf en daube**. (*Une daubière* is a stewpan.)

de (*Fr.*) (masc.) [duh]   Of, as in **côte** *de* **boeuf** ('side *of* beef'), **pâté** *de* **foie** ('pâté *of* liver'); spelt **d'** when next word starts with a vowel, as in **mignonnettes** *d'***agneau** ('mignonnettes *of* lamb').

decaffeinated coffee/tea   **Coffee** or tea from which **caffeine** has been extracted. (*See* 14.13.)

decant   To pour a **liquor**, especially wine, carefully without raising sediment from a bottle into a **decanter**, **carafe** or jug.

decanter   Narrow-necked glass jug, usually with a stopper, used for storing or serving wines or **spirits**.

deglaze   To remove fat from a pan in which meat has been cooked by pouring alcohol into the pan and boiling briskly. **Stock** or **cream** is then added to form a **jus** or sauce. (French *déglacer*.)

dégustation (*Fr.*) (fem.) [day-goo-stah-seeo(n)]
(1) Tasting; sampling food and drink.
(2) Wine-tasting.
See also **menu dégustation**.

de la (*Fr.*) (fem) [duh la]   Of the, when used with a feminine noun, as in *de la* **maison** ('*of the* house'). Note that **du** is the masculine form of *de la*, used with masculine nouns.

deli   Shop selling cheeses, cooked meats and groceries; casual restaurant. (Short for *delicatessen*, literally 'delicacies' in German.) (*See also* **charcuterie**.)

delicatessen   *See* **deli** *above*.

délice (*Fr.*) (masc.) [day-leece]   Trimmed and folded fillet of fish.

demi-glace (*Fr.*) (fem.) [demee gluss]   Rich brown sauce made by **reducing stock** to half its original volume. **Madeira**, **sherry**, or **brandy** is often added after the reduction. (Literally, 'half glaze'.)

demitasse [demee tass]   Very small **coffee** cup for after-dinner coffee. (*See also* **espresso**, **Greek**, **Turkish**, *and* 3.5.) (French, literally 'half cup'.)

des (*Fr.*) (pl.) [day]   Of, when used as a plural, e.g. **purée** *des* **marrons**.

desiccate   To preserve by drying, e.g. desiccated **coconut**.

dessert   (1) Final, **sweet** course of a meal.
(2) Fruit and nuts served at the end of a meal. (*See* 2.2 *and* **classic menu**.)

dessert wine   Sweet wine usually served with dessert. (*See* **auslese**, **muscat**, **spätlese**, **sauternes**, *and* 14.4.)

devilled   **Marinated** meat in a thick, slightly sweet, spicy sauce. A devil mixture usually contains one or all of the following: **mustard**, **Worcestershire sauce**, sugar, and **tomato** sauce. (*See* **diable**.)

Devonshire tea   Afternoon **tea** with **scones**, **clotted cream**, and jam. (From Devon, county in SW England.)

diable, à la (*Fr.*) [ah lah dee-ah-bluh]   **Devilled**, as in **boeuf** *à la* **diable**. (*Diable* means 'devil'.)

dice   To cut up into small even cubes. (*See also* **macédoine**.)

digestif (*Fr.*) (masc.) [dee-zjes-teef]   A digestive; an after-dinner drink, particularly a **liqueur**, said to aid digestion, whence the name.

Dijon (*Fr.*) [dee-zjo(n)]   **Mustard** which is prepared with verjuice (acid from unripened grapes) and white wine. (Dijon is a city in Central W. France.)

dill   Fragrant annual plant, the feathery leaves of which are used as a **garnish** and as a flavouring herb. The seeds are used in **pickles**. (*See* **dill pickle** *below*.)

dill pickle   Baby cucumber pickled with **dill** seeds.

dim sim/sum (*Chin./Austral.*)   Small savoury **dumpling** containing meat and cabbage wrapped in a **won ton** wrapper and steamed or deep fried.

distillation   Process used to make **spirits** from **fermented** 'wine'. (*See* 14.7.)

doily   Lace-like paper mat used to decorate plates, particularly under cakes, or on an **underliner**.

dolmas (*Grk.* & *Turk.*) [doll-mahth] (*pl.* **dolmades** [doll-mah-thess]) Vine (or cabbage) leaves stuffed with oily rice, sometimes with nuts, currants and minced lamb, etc. in the rice. Dolmades are often served with **meze**.

döner kebab (*Turk.*) [doaner kuhbahb] **Marinated** lamb, thinly sliced from a vertical **salamander**, rolled with salad, **tahini** and **hummus** in **pita** bread. (Lebanese equivalent is **chawarma**.)

Drambuie   Proprietary **liqueur** made from Scotch **whisky**, heather, honey, and herbs.

draught beer   Beer drawn from a barrel (keg) rather than bottled or canned.

dredge   To sprinkle with castor sugar, flour, etc.

dredger   Sugar castor, sugar shaker. (*See* 3.5.)

dressing   *See* **French dressing** *and* **vinaigrette**.

dry ginger (**ale**)   Non-alcoholic drink of carbonated water flavoured with **ginger** extract. Often called 'dry' as in '**brandy** and dry'. (*See* **ginger**.)

Dry Martini   **Cocktail** of gin with a little dry (French) **vermouth**, **garnished** with a green **olive** or a twist of lemon.

du (*Fr.*) (masc.) [doo]   Of the, when used with a masculine noun, as in **carte** *du* **jour** ('**menu** *of the* day'). Note that **de la** is the feminine form of **du** and **des** is the plural.

Dubonnet   French brand of aromatized wine or **vermouth** commonly served with **soda** or with ice as an **apéritif**.

duchesse   *See* **pommes duchesse**.

du jour (*Fr.*) (masc.) [doo zjoor]   Literally 'of the day', e.g. **poisson** *du jour* ('fish of the day').

dumpling   Ball of dough, either baked or simmered in a **casserole**; they may be sweet or savoury and flavoured with sugar, syrup, or herbs, etc. (*See also* **dim sim**, **gnocchi**, **quenelle**, *and* **won ton**.)

duxelles (*Fr.*) (fem. pl.) [dook-sel]   **Sautéed** mixture of finely chopped onions or **shallots** with mushrooms, seasoned and **reduced**. Duxelles are used as a **garnish** or stuffing. Such dishes are described as *à la duxelles* (as in **omelette** *à la duxelles*).

Earl Grey tea   Smoky-tasting blended **tea** flavoured with **bergamot**. (Earl Grey, 1764-1845, was a British statesman and reforming Prime Minister 1830-4.)

échalote (*Fr.*) (fem.) [ay-shallot]   **Shallot**.

éclair (*Fr.*) (masc.) [ay-clair]   Small cylindrical cake made from **choux** pastry, split and filled with **cream** and iced with chocolate icing.

écrivisse (*Fr.*) (fem.) [ay-cree-veece]   European freshwater crayfish, used also as the French word for **yabby**. (*See* **crayfish**.)

egg-nog/egg flip   Alcoholic drink of liquor mixed with eggs and milk served either just warm or cold.

eggs Benedict   Poached eggs with grilled ham served on a **muffin** or toast covered in **hollandaise**.

émincé (*Fr.*) (masc.) [ay-mah(n)-say]   Thin slice, esp. of meat; rasher (of bacon). (*Emincer* means 'to slice finely'.) (*See also* **émincés** *below*.)

émincés (*Fr.*) (masc. pl.) [ay-mah(n)-say]   Thin slices of left-over meat reheated in **jus** or sauce. (*See also* **émincé** *above, and* **réchauffé**.)

en (*Fr.*) [ahn]   In, as in *en* **cocotte**. (*See also* **chevreuil**, **cocotte**, **croûte**, **daube**, **gelée**, *and* **papillote**.)

enchilada (*Mex.*) [en-chill-ahda]   Fried **tortilla** filled with cheese and/or meat and rolled. Served with **chilli** sauce and, possibly, **guacamole**.

endive [en-dive]   (1) *Cichorium endivia*, sometimes referred to as curly endive, a bitter green-leaf vegetable used in salads.
(2) (esp. *USA*) Belgian endive, **chicory** (*Cichorium intybus*) or **witloof**, used in salads or as a cooked vegetable.
(Both meanings may be encountered in Australia but the first is more common.)

English Breakfast tea   Blended Indian and Ceylon (black) **teas**.

entrecôte (*Fr.*) (masc.) [ahn-truh-coat]   Rib steak of beef, often pounded and served as **minute steak**. (Literally, 'between the rib'.) (*See also* **filet mignon**, **porterhouse**, **rump**, **sirloin**, *and* **T-bone**.)

entrée (*Fr.*) (fem.) [ahn-tray]   In Australia the first **course** of a meal. In the USA (and often in the UK) it refers to the main dish of the meal. In the **classic menu** the entrée was the first (and smallest) of the meat courses, following the fish course. (Literally, 'entrance'.) (*See* 2.2.)

entremets (*Fr.*) (masc. pl.) [ahn-truh-may]   Sweet **course**. (*See* **classic menu**).

épinards (*Fr.*) (masc. pl.) [ay-peenard]   Spinach. (*See also* **silverbeet**.)

escalope (*Fr.*) (fem.) [ess-cal-op]   Thin slice of boneless meat, e.g. *escalope de veau*.

escargot (*Fr.*) (masc.) [ess-car-go]   Snail.

eschalot   *See* **échalote**.

espagnole (*Fr.*) [ess-pan-yol]   Spanish, as in **omelette farcie** *à la espagnole* ('Spanish omelette'). (*See also below*.)

espagnole, sauce (*Fr.*) (fem.) [sohs ess-pa(n)ol]   **Reduced** brown sauce flavoured with **tomatoes** and **sherry**. (*See also* **salmis**, **sauce**.)

espresso (*Ital.*) [ess-press-oh]   Strong black **coffee** made by forcing steam through ground coffee beans. (*Espresso* is Italian for 'pressed' or 'forced out' and, incidentally, for 'express' or 'fast'.) (*See* 14.13, 15.21, *and* 15.22.)

essence   Concentrated extract from fruit, flower, or nut used for flavouring, e.g. **vanilla essence**.

establishment   A business in the hospitality industry — restaurant, hotel, etc.; a hospitality operation.

Evian   Brand of **mineral water** (from Evian-les-Bains, spa town in French Alps). (*See* 14.18.)

extra virgin   *See* **virgin olive oil**.

falafel/felafel (*Arab.*) [fell-a-fell]   (1) **Chick-pea** ball flavoured with spices.
(2) Roll of **pita** bread filled with salad, **hummus**, and **chick-pea** balls.

farce (*Fr.*) (fem.) [farse]   Savoury stuffing; **forcemeat**.

farci(e) (*Fr.*) [farsee]   Stuffed; a stuffed dish. (*Farcir* means 'to stuff'.)

farinaceous [farin-ay-shus]   Consisting of cereals, beans, or pulses. (*Farina* is Latin for flour.)

felafel   *See* **falafel**.

fennel   (1) Large bulbous plant with a slightly aniseed taste. It is **braised** and served as a vegetable or can be sliced raw and mixed with salad greens.
(2) Feathery fronds of the fennel plant used as a herb or **garnish**, especially with fish.
(3) Fennel seeds, aromatic and used as a flavouring, especially in **pickled** foods.

fermentation   Process of converting a liquid containing sugar into alcohol by the action of yeast.

Fernet Branca [fair-nay brankah]   Brand of Italian **bitters**, usually served as an **apéritif** with **soda**.

feta/fetta (*Grk.*)   Cheese (traditionally made from ewes' milk, though Australian fetta is usually made from cows' milk) preserved in **brine**. It is a solid white cheese with a sharp and slightly salty taste. (*Fetes* means 'blocks' or 'slices', the curd being cut into blocks before being preserved.)

fettuccine (*Ital.*) (pl.) [fett-yu-cheeny]   Thin ribbons of **pasta** cut to a length of about 30 cm. Very similar to **tagliatelle**.

feuilleté (*Fr.*) [foo-ee-et-ay]   **Puff pastry** case, traditionally cut into a leaf shape or triangle, but now any shape. e.g. *feuilleté de* **coquilles**, scallops cooked in a puff pastry case. (*See also* **pâte feuilletée**.)

ficelle, boeuf à la   *See* **boeuf à la ficelle**.

filet (*Fr.*) (masc.) [fill-ay]   **Fillet**. (*Filet de* **boeuf** is 'fillet of beef').

filet mignon (*Fr.*) (masc.) [fill-ay mee-neeyon]   Small, round **fillet** steak. (*See also* **entrecôte**, **minute steak**, **porterhouse**, **rump**, **sirloin**, *and* T-**bone**.)

fillet   (1) (noun) Thick boneless piece of meat or fish, usually the prime cut (e.g. fillet steak).
(2) (verb) To remove from the bone.

filo pastry [feel-oh]   Very thin paper-like pastry, buttered, and cooked in layers.

fine champagne   Description of the finest kind of **cognac** (**brandy**, *not* **sparkling wine**).

fine dining (**room**)   High-class dining (room) with formal service, typically found in **five-star** hotels.

fines herbes (*Fr.*) (fem. pl.) [feen airb]   Herbs (**chervil**, parsley, **tarragon** and **chives**) chopped up and mixed together, used to flavour food, typically **omelettes**, meat, and various sauces.

fingerbowl   Small bowl filled with water (and perhaps a piece of lemon) placed on the table so that guests can clean their fingers.

finish   Wine-tasting term. The last taste impression from a mouthful of wine.

fino [fee-noh]   Style of Spanish **sherry**.

five-star   First class (of hotels); top of the market, offering the full range of facilities and services.

flambé(e) (*Fr.*) [flahm-bay]   Flamed. Food served *flambé* has had **spirits** poured over it and then been ignited. (*See* 12.13.)

flan   Open tart containing a filling (of custard, fruit, etc.) (*See also* **frangipane**.)

fleuron (*Fr.*) (masc.) [flur-o(n)]   Crescent- or flower-shaped decorative edible (e.g. a *fleuron* of **puff pastry**).

float   (1) (verb) Cocktail-mixing term; to place one liquid above another in the glass so that they do not mix but one 'floats' above the other.
(2) (noun) Change placed in the till before trading begins.

floating islands   Soft balls of **meringue** poached in milk and served in custard sauce. (In French, **oeufs à la neige**.)

florentine [flo-ren-teen]   Thin biscuit of **glacé** fruit and nuts coated on one side with chocolate, often served after dinner with coffee.

florentine, à la (*Fr.*) [ah lah flo-ren-teen]   In the style of Florence (Italian city). Cooked or served with spinach and (usually) **mornay** sauce, e.g. **suprêmes** of chicken *à la florentine*.

flute   (1) (noun) Narrow-stemmed glass used for serving **sparkling wines**. (*See* 13.3 *and* 15.17.)
(2) (noun) Long thin French roll.
(3) (noun) Groove made on the outside of a food item for decoration.
(4) (verb) To make grooves on the surface of a food item, such as a pie crust or a **mousse**.

focaccia (*Ital.*) [fok-ah-cheea]   Flat bread similar to a **pizza** base. It is often spread with **garlic**-herb butter and served warm with **antipasto**.

fondant   Soft mixture of flavoured sugar used as icing on cakes or served as a **sweetmeat**, sometimes coated with chocolate.

fondue (*Swiss*) (fem.) [fon-doo]   Dish cooked at table by dipping small pieces (usually of meat or bread) into a bowl containing hot oil or melted cheese. (*Fondu* is French for 'melted'.) (*See also* **raclette**.)

fool   Cold dessert made of **puréed** fruit and whipped **cream**.

forcemeat   Meat chopped and seasoned for use as a stuffing; a **farce**.

forestière, à la (*Fr.*) [ah lah foress-tee-air]   Served with **sautéed** mushrooms. (*Forestière* means 'forester's wife' or 'female forester'.)

fortified wine   Wine strengthened by the addition of some **spirit**. Fortified wines include **muscat**, **sherry**, and **port**. (*See* 14.5.)

four, au (*Fr.*) [oh foor]   Oven-baked; roasted. (*Four* means 'oven'.)

framboise (*Fr.*) (fem.) [frahm bwaz]   Raspberry.

française, à la (*Fr.*) [ah lah frahn-sez]   In the French style; usually served with **demi-glace** sauce. *Petits pois à la française* are cooked with lettuce and onion.

frangipane [fronzji-pahn]   Custard made with ground almonds or crushed **macaroons**. (In French *crème frangipane*.) (*See also* **crème pâtissière**.) (Named after an Italian marquis, Muzio Frangipani, who lived in Paris in the 16th century and devised a bitter-almond scent for sprinkling on gloves.)

frangipane tart/flan   Jam-lined pastry case filled with **frangipane** cream and decorated with fresh **cream** and **pistachio** nuts.

frankfurter   **Smoked** beef-and-pork-sausage usually simmered and served in a bread roll as a hot dog. Tiny **cocktail** frankfurters are served as **appetizers**. (Frankfurt is a city in central Germany.)

frappé (*Fr.*) [frappay]   Cocktail-mixing term; chilled with crushed ice, e.g. **crème de menthe** *frappé*. (Literally, 'crushed' or, more exactly, 'beaten'.)

French   Dry white **vermouth** (as in **gin**-and-**French**).

French dressing   Cold dressing for salad, etc. made with oil and **wine vinegar**, and seasonings like **pepper**, salt, **garlic** and **Dijon mustard**. Lemon juice is sometimes used instead of vinegar. (*See* **vinaigrette**.)

friandises (*Fr.*) (fem. pl.) [free-on-deez]   Dainties, e.g. fruits dipped in chocolate, or **petits fours**, often served at the end of a meal with the **coffee**.

fricassee [frik-a-see]   Pieces of meat, usually a white meat like chicken, cooked in **stock** and served in a white sauce. Fricassee has been adopted as an English word; the French is *fricassée* [frik-a-say]; so you should say 'chicken fricassee' (pronounced *see*) but *fricassée* (pronounced *say*) *de* **poulet**.

frite (*Fr.*) [freet]   Fried. (*See* **pommes frites**.)

frittata (*Ital.*) [frit-ahta]   **Omelette**; beaten eggs fried

on both sides to form a cake. Vegetables are sometimes beaten into the egg mix.

fritter   Food, either sweet or savoury, dipped in **batter** and deep-fried. (*See also* **pakora**.)

fritto misto (*Ital.*)   Mixed vegetables deep fried in **batter**. (Literally, 'fried mixed'.)

fritto misto de pesce (*Ital.*) [fritoh mistoh dee pescay]   Mixed **seafood** deep fried in **batter**. (Literally, 'fried mixture of the sea'.)

froid (*Fr.*) [fwah]   Cold, as in **buffet froid**.

fromage (*Fr.*) (masc.) [from-ahje]   Cheese.

fromage blanc (*Fr.*) [from-ahje bla(n)]   Low-fat fresh cheese made from skimmed milk. It is used in place of **cream**, or as an accompaniment to fruit. (*See also* **cuisine minceur**.)

frontignac [fron-ti-nyak]   Grape variety.   *See* **muscat**.

front of house   The part of the **establishment** seen by the guests; the dining room as opposed to the kitchen. (*See also* **back of house**.)

frost   (1) To cover with sugar, esp. a cake. Frosted fruit is first dipped in egg white or lemon juice. (*See also* **frosting**.)
(2) To garnish a glass by dipping the rim in lemon juice and sugar or salt.

frosting (*USA*)   Soft icing used to decorate cakes.

fruits de mer (*Fr.*) (masc. pl.) [frooee duh mair]   **Seafood**. (Literally, 'fruits of the sea'.)

fruity   Wine-tasting term. Pleasing taste of a young wine; description of its **aroma**.

Fukien [foo-kyen]   One of the five main styles of Chinese cuisine. Fukien cuisine is known for its **clear soups** and **seafood**. (Fukien, now called Fujian, is a coastal province of China.) (*See also* **Cantonese**, **Honan**, **Peking**, *and* **Szechwan**.)

fumé (*Fr.*) [foomay]   (1) **Smoked**.
(2) Style of white wine, usually a **sauvignon blanc**, cloudy and piquantly tasty, called fumé blanc.

function   Pre-arranged occasion (banquet, dinner, cocktail party, etc.) for a known number of guests.

funghi (*Ital.*) (pl.) (*sing.* **fungo**) [foon-gee]   Mushrooms, e.g. **risotto** *alla funghi*.

gado-gado (*Indon.*) [gahdo gahdo]   Vegetables cooked in peanut sauce with hard-boiled egg.

galantine [galan-teen]   Boned meat, usually stuffed with **forcemeat**, pressed into shape and covered in **aspic** jelly. It is served cold. (*See also* **brawn**.)

galette (*Fr.*) (fem.) [ga-let]   Flat cake; **pancake**; thick shortbread biscuit.

Galliano   Golden-yellow herb **liqueur** from Milan (city in N. Italy). (Named after Major Galliano, a hero of the Italian-Abyssinian war of 1896.)

game   All wild animals and birds which are hunted. (In French *gibier*.) (*See also* **venison**.)

gammon Ham, usually served hot as gammon steak.

garam masala (*Ind.*) [garram ma-sah-la] Ground spices used as a flavouring in Indian cooking. Different mixtures are used for different purposes. (*Garam* means 'hot'.) (*See also* **curry** *and* **masala**.)

garbure (*Fr.*) (fem.) [gar-boor] A very thick, hearty soup containing cabbage, beans, and **pickled** meat (typically **confit d'oie**), served ladled over wholemeal bread. (*See also* **potage** *and* **soupe**.)

garde-manger (*Fr.*) (masc.) [gard marnge-ay] Specialist cook in charge of cold items and decorative work in a large kitchen.

garlic Strong-smelling flavouring herb from the same family as onions. The garlic bulb consists of segments called cloves, the juice from which is used to flavour savoury foods.

garni (*Fr.*) (masc.) [gar-nee] Decorated. (*See also* **bouquet garni**.)

garnish (1) (noun) Items placed on or around a dish (or drink) for decoration or taste.
(2) (verb) To place such items on a dish or in a drink.

garniture Items in a **garnish**; the trimmings.

gastronome An expert on good eating and drinking; an epicure.

gastronomy Science or art of good eating and drinking.

gâteau(x) (*Fr.*) (masc.) [gah-toe] Cake(s).

ga xao sa ot (*Viet.*) [gah saow shah u(t)] Chicken with **lemon grass** and **chilli**. (*Ga* is 'chicken', *xao* means 'fried', *sa ot* is 'lemon grass'.)

gazpacho (*Span.*) [gaz-pah-cho] Cold soup of **puréed** tomatoes, cucumber, onions, **garlic** and **red pepper**, often garnished with **croûtons**.

gelatine/gelatin [jell-a-tin] Almost colourless, odourless, tasteless, soluble substance extracted from animal skin, bones and cartilage, etc. used to make jellies and various cold desserts. (*See also* **aspic**.)

gelato (*Ital.*) [jel-ahtoh] Whipped soft ice-cream.

gelée (*Fr.*) (fem.) [zjelay] Jelly.

gelée de cuisine [zjelay duh kwi-zeen] Aspic jelly.

gelée, en [ahn zjelay] In jelly, e.g. **oeufs poché** *en gelée*.

generic Of a general type (which anyone may make), as opposed to **proprietary** (particular brand, the exclusive property of a person or business); also as opposed to **varietal** in reference to wine. (*See* 14.3 *and* 14.9.)

genever [jenny-vur] Style of Dutch gin. (It has no connection with Geneva, the Swiss city, but is derived from the French word for 'juniper', *genièvre*.)

génoise (*Fr.*) (fem.) [gay-nwaz] Genoese sponge; light sponge cake.

Gentleman's Relish (*UK*) **Proprietary anchovy** paste usually spread on toast. (Also known as patum peperium, or patum for short.) (*See also* **relish**.)

gewürztraminer [geh-vurts-tram-eener] Variety of the **traminer** grape used to produce spicy white wine. (*Gewürtz* [gewoortz] is German for 'spicy'.)

ghee (*Ind.*) [gee] Clarified cow- or buffalo-milk butter used as a cooking medium, especially in Indian cookery. There is a much cheaper vegetable-oil ghee substitute, called *vanaspati* (vegetable) ghee.

gibier (*Fr.*) (masc.) [zjee-bee-ay] **Game** (wild animals and wildfowl). (*See also* **venison**.)

giblets [jib-lets] Innards of poultry and **game** birds, the edible portions of which are the liver, heart, etc.

Gibson **Cocktail** of gin with a little dry (French) **vermouth**, **garnished** with a pearl (cocktail) onion. (*Compare* **Dry Martini**.)

gigot (*Fr.*) (masc.) [zjee-go] Leg (of mutton or lamb).

gin **Spirit** made from grain alcohol distilled with selected herbs and fruit, in particular juniper berries. The most popular style, used in **cocktails**, is London Dry. The other main style, hollands (or **genever**) gin has a strongly distinctive flavour which makes it less suitable for mixing.

ginger The root of *Zingiber officinale*, used freshly grated in **curries**, dried and powdered as a sweet or savoury spice, or preserved in syrup and **glacéed**.

ginger ale *See* **dry ginger ale**.

ginger beer Slightly alcoholic, aerated drink made of **ginger**, **sugar syrup**, and yeast.

gingerbread Golden-brown soft biscuits or cake made into shapes and decorated with sweets (e.g. gingerbread man, gingerbread house).

Ginger Wine, Green *See* **Green Ginger Wine**.

Gippsland blue Fine **blue-veined** cheese from Gippsland in SE Victoria.

girella Boneless cut of lamb or veal from the top of the leg.

glace (*Fr.*) (fem.) [gluss] (1) Ice (cream); iced drink.
(2) **Glaze**, e.g. *glace de* **viande** ('meat glaze').

glacé(e) (*Fr.*) [gluss-ay] (1) Iced, icy.
(2) Glazed. Preserved in sugar (e.g. glacé fruits).

glaze To make shiny, usually by coating with beaten egg or with a **reduced stock**. (*See also* **miroir**.)

globe artichoke *See* **artichoke**.

glühwein (*Ger.*) [gloo-vine] Spicy **mulled wine**.

gluten Elastic protein substance found in wheat flour. Sticky when wet, it holds the dough together and traps the air bubbles produced by the **fermenting** yeast so helping the bread to rise.

gnocchi (*Ital.*) (pl.) [nee-o-kee] Small **pasta dumplings** made from potato or **semolina**.

goi cuon (*Viet.*) [goi kuon] Chewy, soft, transparent **rice-paper** rolls containing rice **noodles**, prawns, and pork. They are eaten cold dipped in a peanut and bean sauce. (*Goi* means 'raw food', *cuon* is a roll.) (*See also* **cha gio** *and* **spring roll**.)

gomme syrup Sugar syrup.

gorgonzola (*Ital.*) Moist, creamy **blue-veined** cheese made from cows' milk. (Gorgonzola is a village near Milan, N. Italy.) (*See also* **Gippsland blue**, **roquefort**, *and* **stilton**.)

gougère (*Fr.*) (fem.) [goo-zjair] Cheese-flavoured **choux** puff served warm. In **Burgundy** they are traditionally eaten cold when wine-tasting.

goujon (*Fr.*) (masc.) [goo-zjon] Thin strip of fillet of fish or chicken (a *goujon* is literally a gudgeon, a small freshwater fish).

goulash (*Hun.*) [goo-lash] Red stew of meat and onions seasoned with **paprika** and garnished with potatoes.

gourmand (*Fr.*) (masc.) [goor-mond] Lover of food; a glutton. (*Compare* **gourmet**.)

gourmet (*Fr.*) (masc.) [goor-may] Expert in food and wine; an epicure or **gastronome**. (*Compare* **gourmand**.)

Grand Marnier [gron marny-ay] **Proprietary liqueur**, **cognac**-based, with an orange flavour.

granita (*Ital.*) [gran-ee-tah] Crushed ice drink.

grappa (*Ital.*) Italian **spirit** made from the remnants of grapes (skins, stalks, pips, etc.) after the **fermented** juice or **wine** has been removed.

gras (*Fr.*) (adj.) [grah] Fat (as in **pâté de foie gras**).

gras, au (*Fr.*) [oh grah] With ham or bacon.

gratin, au (*Fr.*) [oh grat-i(n)] With a golden crust; sprinkled with breadcrumbs and/or grated cheese, and baked or grilled. (*See also* **gratiné(e)** *below*.)

gratiné(e) (*Fr.*) [grat-ee-nay] Cooked, usually with breadcrumbs and grated cheese, to form a golden crust. The word can be anglicized into 'gratinated'.

grazing Practice of eating modest snacks at different places instead of having substantial regular meals.

grecque, à la (*Fr.*) [ah lah grek] In the Greek manner; mushrooms and vegetables with **coriander** seeds cooked in olive oil, served cold.

Greek coffee Strong, dark, sweet **coffee** served in small cups; **Turkish** coffee. (*See* 14.13.)

Green Ginger Wine **Proprietary** fortified wine made from dried grapes and flavoured with **ginger**.

green pepper *See* **sweet pepper**.

green peppercorn *See* **peppercorn**.

grenadine [grenna-deen] Red pomegranate-flavoured **cordial**, used for sweetening or colouring drinks.

grissino (*Ital.*) (*pl.* **grissini**) [griss-eenoh] Long, thin, crisp bread-stick served with **antipasto**.

gros sel (*Fr.*) (masc.) [grow sell] Rock salt. (Literally 'coarse salt'.)

gruyère (*Swiss* & *Fr.*) [groo-yair] Cows'-milk cheese, firm and smooth in texture with small holes or eyes. The rind is not usually eaten. (Gruyère is a village in Switzerland.) (*See also* **raclette**.)

guacamole (*Mex.*) [gwah-kah-mo-lay] Spicy avocado sauce. (*See also* **enchilada** *and* **nacho**.)

guéridon [geri-don] Trolley or table on which food is prepared in the dining-room. (*See* 3.6 *and* 12.2.)

guéridon service Service from a **guéridon**. (*See* 10.5 *and* 10.6.)

Guinness Famous Irish **stout**, originally brewed in Dublin, but now also elsewhere including (under licence) Australia.

gumbo (*Creole* & *Cajun*) (1) **Okra** or **lady's fingers**. (2) Spicy **casserole** of **seafood** and vegetables (including **okra**). (*See also* **bouillabaisse** *and* **pochouse**.) (3) (*USA*) **Okra** soup, or other preparations made using okra.

hâché(e) (*Fr.*) [ah-shay] Minced; mashed, *e.g.* **bifteck** *hâché.*, **minced beef**, hamburger.

halal (*Arab.*) [ha-laal] Lawful for Muslims; meat killed and prepared according to Muslim law. (Muslim equivalent of the Jewish **kosher**.)

haldi (*Ind.*) **Turmeric**.

halva (*N. Africa* & *E. Medit.*) Light, crunchy **sweetmeat** of ground **sesame** seeds, sugar, almonds, etc.

haricot (*Fr.*) (masc.) [arry-coh] Bean, esp. the small white navy bean used, for example, in a **cassoulet** or for baked beans. (*See also* **haricot vert**.)

haricot vert (*Fr.*) (masc.) [arry-coh vair] French or string (runner) bean. (*Vert* means 'green'.)

hash browns (*USA*) Cake of **puréed** potato and onion, bound with egg, and fried.

haute cuisine (*Fr.*) (fem.) [ote kwiz-een] French cooking and service of a very high standard. (*Haute* means 'high'.) (*See also* **cuisine**.)

Hawthorn strainer Cocktail strainer; it has two prongs which fit over the side of the blender with a wire coil which fits inside the rim.

herb Aromatic plant used in cookery to flavour food, *e.g.* **chervil**, **tarragon**. (*See also* **fines herbes**.)

herbal tea An **infusion** or 'tea' made by adding boiling water to the leaves or flowers of various herbs. Most, but not all, herbal teas are **caffeine**-free. Also called **tisane**.

hermitage Grape variety. (*See* **shiraz**.)

highball (1) Any **spirit** mixed with ice and soda or ginger ale served in a highball glass, *e.g.* a **Whiskey** Highball. (2) A style of tall, straight-sided glass. (*See* p. 99.)

hock English name for German Rhine wine; **riesling**; **generic** wines made in that style. (From Hochheim, German town from which hocks were shipped.)

hoi sin sauce (*Chin.*) Sweet and spicy sauce made of **soya beans**, **garlic**, and spices and served as a **condiment**, esp. with **Peking duck** and pork dishes.

hollandaise [oll-and-ayz]   Rich sauce made from the careful **blending** of egg yolk, butter, and lemon juice or **vinegar**. The French term is *sauce hollandaise* [sohs oll-and ayz].

hollands   Dutch style of **gin**.

homard (*Fr.*) (masc.) [om-ahr]   **Lobster**. (*See also* **crayfish, langouste** *and* **rock lobster**.)

hommos   *See* **hummus**.

Honan [hoe-nan]   One of the five main styles of Chinese cuisine. **Sweet-and-sour** dishes are typical of spicy *Honan* cooking. (Honan, now called Henan, is a province in central China.) (*See also* **Cantonese, Fukien, Peking,** *and* **Szechwan**.)

hors d'oeuvre(s) (*Fr.*) (masc.) [or-durv]   **Appetizer** or small **savoury** served before or at the beginning of a meal. (Literally, 'before the work'.)

horseradish   Pungent root of the mustard family (*Cochlearia armoracia*), usually used grated. (*See also* **daikon, horseradish sauce,** *and* **wasabi**.)

horseradish sauce   Grated **horseradish** mixed with **cream, vinegar,** and seasonings and traditionally used as a **condiment** with roast beef, **smoked** trout and mackerel.

host(ess)   (1) Patrons who are entertaining their own guests in an **establishment** and who are responsible for paying. (*See* 5.4.)
(2) Person who greets the restaurant's patrons, takes their coats, and shows them to their table, 'mine host'.

house wine   Moderately priced wine usually bought in bulk by an **establishment** and often served from **carafes**. (*See* **vin ordinaire**.)

huître (*Fr.*) (fem.) [ooee-truh]   Oyster.

hummus/houmos (*Grk.* & *Arab.*) [hoomuss]   **Purée** of **chick-peas** and **sesame seed** paste, often served with **pita** bread as a **meze** or **hors d'oeuvre**.

iced coffee   Strong black **coffee** mixed with ice-cold milk, usually garnished with ice-cream.

iced tea   **Tea**, usually Indian, poured over ice and served cold garnished with slices of lemon or **mint** leaves.

Illawarra plum (*Austral.*)   Fruit of *Podocarpus elatum*, also known as the brown pine plum. The fruit is small and dark blue and is usually made into **preserve**. (From Illawarra district, SE NSW.)

Indian tonic water   *See* **tonic**.

infusion   (1) The immersion of vegetables, herbs, **tea** or **coffee** in boiling liquid or wine until the flavours have been absorbed, so producing an aromatic fluid.
(2) Method used to give **liqueurs** their flavour. (*See* 14.9.)
(3) Beverage given its flavour by infusion.

insalata (*Ital.*) [insal-ahta]   Salad.

insalata mista (*Ital.*) [insal-ahta mista]   Mixed salad.

Irish coffee   **Liqueur coffee** made using Irish whiskey. (*See* 14.13 *and* 15.24.)

jaffle   Toasted sandwich with sealed edges. (*Compare* **waffle**.)

jaggery (*Anglo-Ind.*)   Dark, crumbly sugar made from sugar-cane or the sugar palm and tasting of treacle. It is used in Indian cuisine. (*See also* **palm sugar**.)

jambon (*Fr.*) (masc.) [zjom-bo(n)]   Ham.

jardinière, à la (*Fr.*) [ah lah jar-danee-air]   Garnished with vegetables, esp. carrots, turnips, French beans, cauliflower, and peas. (A *jardinière* is a 'female gardener'.)

jasmine tea   **China tea** scented with jasmine flowers.

jeroboam (jerruh-boh-am)   Large bottle of **sparkling wine** (e.g. **champagne**) containing the equivalent of 4 standard (750mL) bottles. (Jeroboam was King of Israel, 931-910 BC.) (*See also* **champagne bottle sizes**.)

Jerusalem artichoke   *See* **artichoke**.

jugged hare (*UK*)   Jointed hare **casseroled** in its own blood with wine, vegetables and seasonings.

julienne (*Fr.*) (fem.) [zhoo-lee-en]   (1) Vegetables or meat cut into thin, evenly-sized strips for preparation in cooking, or for use as a **garnish**, especially for **consommés**. (Perhaps named after a French chef called Jean Julien. The word julienne has been used in cooking since the early 18th century.)
(2) Clear vegetable soup.

jus (*Fr.*) (masc.) [zjoo]   Meat juice, or unthickened pan juices, gravy, **stock**. (*See* **jus** (**au**) *and* **jus-lié,** *below*.)

jus, au (*Fr.*) [oh zjoo]   (Meat) dressed with its own juice.

jus-lié (*Fr.*) [zjoo lee-ay]   Thickened meat juice, gravy. (**Lié** means 'bound'.) (*See also* **jus** *above*.)

kabana/cabanossi (*Pol.*) [ka-bahna]   Long, thin **smoked** sausage made from pork and beef seasoned with herbs and served cold.

Kahlua   Proprietary Mexican **liqueur** based on cane spirit flavoured with coffee.

Kalamata olive   Large black **olive** from Greece. (Kalamata is a town in S. Greece.)

kartoffel (*Ger.*) [car-toff-ell]   Potato.

kassler/kasseler (*Ger.*) [kass-lair]   **Pickled, smoked** pork cutlets thinly sliced and served cold, or carved in thicker pieces and fried. (Named after a butcher from Berlin, named Kasel.)

kebab/kabab/kebob (*Turk.* & *Ind.*)   Small pieces of meat or fish, with vegetables, cooked on a skewer. (*See also* **brochette, döner kebab** *and* **shish kebab**.)

kedgeree (*Anglo-Ind.*)   Dish of cooked rice, **smoked** fish, hard-boiled egg, and parsley flavoured with **turmeric** or **saffron**, usually served for breakfast.

ketchup Sauce made from **tomatoes**, mushrooms, **vinegar** and spices and used as a **condiment**. (In USA known as 'catsup'.)

kibbeh (*Arab.*) General term for the many dishes made from **burghul** used in the Middle East, especially Lebanon.

kilojoule Metric measure of the energy in food (abbreviation kJ.)

Kilpatrick (*Austral.*) Sauce, the essential ingredients of which are bacon, **tomato sauce** and **Worcestershire sauce**, typically served hot (baked) on oysters as 'oysters Kilpatrick'.

kimchee (*Korea*) [kim-chee] Hot **pickled** cabbage served with almost all Korean meals.

King Island Island in Bass Strait noted for its dairy produce, e.g. King Island **cream**, **crème fraîche**, **cheddar**, and **cream cheeses** such as **brie** and **camembert**. Meats, e.g. herbed **salami** and bushman's bacon, are also prepared there.

kirsch [keersh] Style of **cherry brandy**. (*Kirsche* is German for 'cherry'.)

Kobe beef [kohbay] Fine grain-fed and milk-fattened beef prized in Japanese cuisine. (Kobe is a city near Osaka, S. Honshu.)

kohlrabi [coal rah-bee] Turnip-like vegetable with a swollen, edible stem.

korma (*Ind.*) [kor-mah] Spicy meat **casserole** cooked in a rich **coconut** sauce.

kosher (*Heb.*) [koh-sher] Lawful for Jews; meat killed or food prepared according to Jewish law. (*See also* **halal**.)

kumara (*NZ*) Sweet potato; yam.

kümmel [kewmel] Dutch **liqueur** flavoured with caraway seeds, ususally served on ice as a **digestif**.

kurrajong flour (*Austral.*) Flour made from the seeds of one of the varieties of kurrajong tree, e.g. the Illawarra flame tree (*Brachychiton acerifolium*). Kurrajong flour and pastry made from it has a delicate yeasty-cheese taste.

la (*Fr.*) (fem.) [lah] The, when used with a feminine noun, e.g. *la maison*. (*See also* **le** *and* **les**.)

ladyfinger Finger-shaped sponge cake. (In French *langues de chat*, literally 'cat's tongues'.)

lady fingers/lady's fingers (1) **Okra** *or* **gumbo**. (2) Small stubby bananas.

lager (*Ger.*) [laag-er] Bottom-fermented **beer**. Most Australian beers are lagers. (*See* 14.8.)

lait, au (*Fr.*) [oh lay] With milk, as in **café au lait**. (*Lait* means 'milk'.)

laksa (*Singa.*) Spicy **seafood** soup with rice **noodles**. (*See also* **tom yam kung**.)

langue (*Fr.*) (fem.) [lahn-guh] Tongue.

langouste (*Fr.*) (fem.) [lahn-goost] Salt-water crayfish or **rock lobster**. (*See also* **lobster** *and* **homard**.)

langoustine(s) (*Fr.*) (fem.) [lahn-goose-teen] **Scampi**.

lapin (*Fr.*) (masc.) [lapi(n)] Rabbit.

lardon (*Fr.*) (masc.) [lardo(n)] Strip of pork fat or bacon inserted into raw meat to enhance flavour while cooking or cooked and served as a garnish with salads and vegetables.

lasagne (*Ital.*) (pl.) [laz-an-yuh] Large flat pieces of **pasta**; the dish comprising layers of lasagne alternating with layers of meat sauce and cheese sauce.

layer Cocktail-mixing term. To pour the ingredients into the glass so that they do not mix but remain one above the other in clear layers.

le (*Fr.*) (masc.) [luh] The, when used with a masculine noun, e.g. *le jus*. (*See also* **la** *and* **les**.)

legume Vegetable with seeds in a pod, e.g. bean, **lentil**, and pea. (*See also* **légumes** *below*.)

légumes (*Fr.*) (masc. pl.) [lay-goom] Vegetables. (*See also* **classic menu** *and* **legume** *above*.)

lemon grass Bushy grass-like herb used to flavour food, esp. in Thai cooking. (In French *citronelle*.)

lentil Bean (*Lens esculenta*) rich in nutrients including **protein**, one of the earliest cultivated foods known to man; the basic ingredient of **dahl**.

les (*Fr.*) (pl.) [lay] The, when used with a plural noun, e.g. *les légumes*. (*See also* **la** *and* **le**.)

liaison (*Fr.*) (fem.) [lee-ay-zon] Mixture, typically egg yolks and **cream** or flour and butter, used for thickening sauces and soups.

lié (*Fr.*) [leeay] Thickened (as in **jus lié**). (*Lier* means 'to bind', 'to thicken'.)

Ligurian olive Tiny black Italian olive. (Liguria is a province in NW Italy.)

lilly-pilly/lillipilli (*Austral.*) Tree (genus *Syzgium*) whose berries are small and crisp in texture and range in colour from white through pink to purple. They are used to flavour desserts or to make jam or flavoured vinegar. The magenta lilly-pilly (*Syzgium paniculatum*) is the most common in SE Australia; its flavour is sweetly spicy.

linguini (*Ital.*) (pl.) [lingweenee] Type of **pasta** cut into long, very thin strips with square-cut edges.

liqueur [li-cure] **Spirit**- or wine-based **liquors** sweetened and flavoured with aromatic substances often served as **digestifs** (e.g. **Grand Marnier**).

liqueur coffee **Coffee** served with a **nip** of **spirit** or **liqueur**. (*See* 14.13, 15.24, *and* 15.25.)

liquor [li-cur] Any liquid, but usually an alcoholic drink.

lobster (1) Large salt-water shellfish with big claws, genus *Homarus* (**homard** in French) with flesh and taste like that of **crayfish**. Real lobsters are not found in the waters of the southern hemisphere.

(2) (*Austral.* & *NZ* only) Southern **rock lobster** commonly known as **crayfish** or **cray**. (*See also* **langouste**.)

lobster thermidor *See* **thermidor**.

loin Joint of meat that includes some or all of the ribs. (*See also* **carré**, **rack** *and* **saddle**.)

Lorraine *See* **quiche Lorraine**.

lumpfish roe Eggs of the lumpfish, often referred to as **caviare** (which is actually the much superior sturgeon's roe). Lumpfish roe is dyed red or black in imitation of real caviare.

lyonnaise, à la (*Fr.*) [ah lah lee-on-nayze] In the style of Lyons (large city in SE France); garnished with onions, and often potatoes. (*See also below*.)

lyonnaise, sauce (*Fr.*) [sohs lee-on-nayze] **Reduction** of white wine, **vinegar** and golden onions added to a **demi-glace**. (*See also* **lyonnaise (à la)**, *above*.)

macchiato [makee-ahto] Extra-strong **espresso coffee** served long or short with a dash of cold milk, usually in a glass. (*See* 14.13.)

macadamia (*Austral.*) Nut from rainforest tree of the genus *Macadamia* used in both sweet and savoury dishes and available ready-salted. Also known as bopple nut or Queensland nut. (J. McAdam, *d.* 1865, was secretary of the Philosophical Institute of Victoria.) (*See also* **macadamia oil** *below*.)

macadamia oil Oil of the **macadamia** nut.

macaroon Small almond-flavoured cake or biscuit.

macédoine (*Fr.*) (fem.) [mass-ay-dwaan] **Diced** fruit or vegetables; fruit thus cut and set in jelly; fruit salad. (Macédoine is French for 'Macedonia'.)

macerate [mass-errate] To steep in liquid; to soak food, particularly fruit, in alcohol. (*See also* **marinate**.)

madeira Fortified wine with a distinctive 'burnt' taste (from the Portuguese island of Madeira). (French, **madère**.)

madeleine (*Fr.*) (fem.) [madel-ayn] Small sponge cake shaped like a **scallop** shell.

madère (*Fr.*) (adj.) [mad-air] **Madeira**.

magnum Large bottle of **sparkling wine** (e.g champagne) containing the equivalent of 2 standard (750mL) bottles. (*Magnum* means 'big thing' in Latin.) (*See also* **champagne bottle sizes**.)

maison/à la maison/de maison (*Fr.*) (fem.) [ah lah/ duh may-zo(n)] Home-made; made to the establishment's own special recipe, e.g. **pâté** *maison*. (*Maison* means 'house'.)

maître d'hôtel (*Fr.*) [met-ruh doe-tel] Steward, head-waiter. (*Maître* means 'master'.) (*See also* **beurre maître d'hôtel** *and* **maître d'hôtel (sauce)** *below*.)

maître d'hôtel, sauce (*Fr.*) (fem.) [sohs metruh dohtel] Sauce of melted butter, parsley, and lemon juice. (*See also* **beurre maître d'hôtel** *and* **maître d'hôtel**.)

maize/sweet corn *See* **corn**.

malbec [mahlbek] Black grape variety popular in blends, e.g. **cabernet**-malbec, because it softens the effect of the **tannin**.

malt Grain, esp. barley, steeped in water to germinate and then dried. The process converts starch into maltose. Malt is used for brewing **beer** and to make **malt whisky**. (*See also* **malt vinegar** *below*.)

malt vinegar Strong, dark brown **vinegar** distilled from **malt** and used mostly as a **pickling** agent and traditionally sprinkled over fish and chips. (*See also* **balsamic vinegar, rice vinegar, vinaigrette,** *and* **wine vinegar**.)

malt whisky Traditional kind of **Scotch whisky** made from malted barley only and distilled in a **pot still**.

mange-tout (*Fr.*) (masc.) [monje too] Thin green pea, eaten whole, pod and all. Also called snow pea and sugar pea. (Literally, 'eat everything'.)

maraschino [maras-keenoh] Italian **liqueur** based on distillation of sour (Maraska) cherries.

maraschino cherries Cherries, dyed bright red, preserved in a type of **maraschino** juice.

marbling The streaks of fat contrasting with the lean in meat.

Margarita **Cocktail** made with **tequila, Cointreau,** and lemon juice.

margherita (*Ital.*) Simple style of **pizza** topping containing **tomato**, cheese, and herbs.

marinade (noun) Mixture of liquids (wine, lemon juice, **vinegar**, oil, **soy**) with herbs and seasonings, in which food is **marinated** to enhance its flavour.

marinara (*Ital.*) [marin-ahra] With **seafood**, e.g. spaghetti *marinara*. (*Il mare* means 'the sea'.)

marinate/marinade (verb) To soak food in a **marinade**. (*See also* **macerate**.)

marinière, à la (*Fr.*) [ah lah marin-y-air] Method of preparing shellfish or fish in white wine with onions etc., e.g. **moules** *marinières*.

marjoram Compact shrub with small grey leaves and white flowers both of which are aromatic and are used as a seasoning herb. Similar to, but more subtle than **oregano**, it is one of the ingredients of a traditional **bouquet garni**.

Marmite (*UK*) [mah-mite] **Proprietary** name for a yeast extract similar to Vegemite.

marmite (*Fr.*) (fem.) [mar-meet] Cooking vessel, esp. one with two handles in which soup is cooked.

marmite petite (*Fr.*) [mar-meet pu-teet] (1) **Clear soup** or broth. (*See also* **consommé**.)
(2) Small cooking pot. (*See also* **marmite** *above*.)

marron (1) (*Austral.*) [ma-ron] Type of WA freshwater crayfish larger than a **yabby**.
(2) (*Fr.*) (masc.) [ma-rro(n)] Chestnut (as in *marrons* **glacés**, 'candied chestnuts').

marsala [mar-sah-lah]   Style of fortified red (almost brown) sweet **dessert** wine. Not to be confused with the Indian **masala** (spice).

Martini   (1) Brand of **vermouth**.
(2) **Dry Martini** (cocktail).

maryland (*Austral.*)   Whole thigh and leg joint of chicken. (*See also* **Maryland, chicken** *below.*)

Maryland, chicken (*USA*)   Chicken portions, coated in breadcrumbs, deep-fried. (Maryland is a State in E. USA.) (*See also* **maryland** *above.*)

Maryland cookies   Chocolate-chip biscuits. (Maryland is a State in E. USA.)

marzipan   Thick paste of ground almonds and egg white, used in confectionary, esp. **petits fours**, and to hold decorative icing on fruit cake.

masala (*Ind.*) [ma-sah-lah]   Aromatic spice, e.g. **garam masala** ('hot spice'). Not to be confused with **marsala** (wine).

mascarpone (*Ital.*) [mass-kur-pony]   Fresh, unripened dessert cheese used in place of **cream** in some sweet dishes. (*See also* **crème fraîche** *and* **ricotta**.)

mask   To coat food thoroughly in a sauce before serving. (*See* **nappé**.)

matsutake mushroom   *See* **pine mushroom**.

mayonnaise   Dressing or sauce of egg yolks and oil, flavoured with **vinegar**, salt, **pepper**, and **mustard**.

medallion [med-al-ee-on]   Small round piece of meat shaped like a medallion and usually skinned and boned. (In French, *médaillon* [may-dye-yee-o(n)].)

mélange (*Fr.*) (masc.) [may-lahnzj]   Mixture; medley.

melanzane alla parmigiana (*Ital.*) [melan-zahnay alla parmy-yahna]   Classic baked dish of layered **eggplant**, tomato sauce, **mozzarella**, and **parmigiano**. (*Melanzana* is Italian for 'eggplant'.)

Melba toast   (1) Very thin toast made by splitting toasted bread and grilling the untoasted sides.
(2) Small thick squares of toast available commercially for use in **canapés**.
(Named after Dame Nellie Melba, 1861-1931, the famous Australian opera singer.) (*See also* **peach Melba**.)

menu   (1) The range of food items served in an **establishment**.
(2) The arrangement by which the items are offered (set menu, **à la carte** menu, etc.)
(3) Written list of the food items served (also called the **bill of fare**).
(*See* chapter 2 *and* 6.2-6.4; *see also* **classic menu, menu d'agrément, menu dégustation, prix fixe,** *and* **table d'hôte**.)

menu d'agrément (*Fr.*) (masc.) [menu dag-ray-mo(n)]   Fixed price menu. (*See also* **prix fixe** *and* **table d'hôte**.)

menu dégustation   Small portions of a range of the specialities of the **establishment**.

meringue [me-rang]   Egg white whipped with sugar and baked. (*See also* **pavlova**.)

merlot [mairloh]   Black grape variety noted for its **bouquet** and popular in blends, especially **cabernet**-merlot.

mesclun   Mixed salad greens (especially curly **endive**) of varying colours and flavours, served with a **vinaigrette**.

méthode champenoise [may-toad sham-pen-warz]   Method by which French champagne is made. (*See* 14.6.)

methuselah (meth-ooz-uh-lah)   Large bottle of **champagne** containing the equivalent of 8 standard (750mL) bottles. (Methuselah is the oldest man in the Bible, said to have lived to be 969.) (*See also* **champagne bottle sizes**.)

meunière, à la (*Fr.*) [ah lah mur-nee-air]   Served with a sauce of browned butter, lemon juice, parsley and seasoning. (*Meunière* means 'miller's wife' or 'female miller'.)

mezcal   Mexican spirit distilled from the *mezcal azul* cactus. **Tequila** is a superior type of mezcal.

meze/mezze (*pl.* **mezedes**) (*Grk. & Turk.*) [mez-zay/meze-thes]   Substantial assortment of cold **hors d'oeuvres** including such items as **taramasalata** and **dolmades**, often almost a meal in itself. (Literally, 'half' — a half meal, the **hors d'oeuvre**). (*See also* **antipasto**.)

mignon (*Fr.*) [mee-neeyon]   Small and dainty, as in **filet mignon**.

mignonette (*Fr.*) (fem.) [mee-neeyon-ett]   (1) Coarsely-ground white **pepper**.
(2) Small cuts of meat elaborately prepared (e.g. **mignonnettes d'agneau**).
(3) Potatoes sliced into thin sticks.
(4) Variety of lettuce.

milanese (*Ital.*) [milan-ay-zay]   In the style of Milan (N. Italian city) e.g. **risotto alla milanese**.

mille-feuille (*Fr.*) (fem.) [meel fuh-ee]   Puff-pastry cake layered with whipped **cream** and jam. Some savoury *mille-feuilles* are layered with a meat or fish sauce. (Literally, 'thousand-leaf'.)

minced meat/mince   Any meat ground or minced. Do not confuse with **mincemeat**, *below*.

mincemeat (*UK*)   Fruit mince; sweet spicy mixture of currants, apple, etc. usually with **suet** and **brandy**, used in mince pies at Christmas. Do not confuse with **minced meat**, *above*.

mineral water   Water flavoured with minerals, often thought to be health-promoting. Sparkling mineral water is aerated with carbon dioxide, either 'naturally' (at its source) or by injection. (*See also* **Appolinaris, Evian,** *and* **Perrier**; *see also* 14.18.)

minestra (*Ital.*) [min-ess-tra] **Soup**. (*See also* **brodo**, **minestrone**, *and* **zuppa**.)

minestrone (*Ital.*) [min-ess-troh-nay] Thick vegetable and **pasta** soup. (*See also* **minestra**.)

mint Herb, of which there are many varieties (genus *Mentha*), used as a flavouring or **garnish** in sweet or savoury dishes. (*See* **crème de menthe** *and below*.)

mint sauce Thin sauce, served cold, of finely chopped garden **mint**, **malt vinegar** and sugar, served traditionally as an **accompaniment** to roast lamb.

mint, Vietnamese *Polygonum oloratum*, also known as 'hot **mint**'; used as **garnish** in Vietnamese **cuisine**.

mints, after-dinner Chocolates with **mint**-flavoured centres served with **coffee** after the meal.

minute steak [minit] Tender steak cooked for one minute only. (It is therefore not necessary to ask how the guest prefers the steak cooked.) (*See also* **entrecôte**, **filet mignon**, **porterhouse**, **rump**, **sirloin**, *and* **T-bone**.)

mirepoix (*Fr.*) [meer-pwah] **Diced** carrot, onion, and celery **sautéed** and used to flavour soups and stews. *Mirepoix au gras* is this mixture cooked with ham or bacon. (Created by chef to the Duc de Mirepoix, 1699-1757, French general.)

mirin (*Jap.*) Sweet rice wine, low in alcohol, used only for cooking in Japan. (*See also* **sake**.)

miroir (*Fr.*) (masc.) [meer-wah] Shiny fruit **glaze** completely covering a dessert. (Literally 'mirror'.)

mise-en-place (*Fr.*) (fem.) [meez-on-pluss] The setting out of equipment, garnishes, etc. in preparation for service or cooking. (Literally, 'set in place'.) (*See* 4.8 *and* 13.7.)

miso (*Jap.*) [meessoh] Paste made from fermented **tofu** and used to make **miso shiru**.

miso shiru (*Jap.*) Soup made from **miso** and **stock** often eaten at breakfast time.

misto/mista (*Ital.*) (adj.) Mixed, e.g. **fritto misto**, **insalata mista**.

mL Millilitres.

mocha/mocca [mokkah] (1) Strong variety of **coffee** bean.
(2) A combination of **coffee** and chocolate flavouring (as in mocha **coupe**).
(From Mocha, or Al Mukha, port in Yemen, from which the coffee beans were shipped.)

mocktail Non-alcoholic, or **virgin**, **cocktail**.

môde, à la (*Fr.*) [ah lah mode] In the manner of, e.g. *boeuf à la môde*.

monosodium glutamate *See* **MSG**.

morel [morrell] Variety of mushroom (*Morchella esculenta*) with a crinkled and brownish pointed cap resembling the pitted bark of a tree. (*See also* **cep**, **oyster mushroom**, **pine mushroom**, *and* **truffle**.) (Do not confuse with **morello**.)

morello [mur-elloh] Dark, bitter cherry commonly used in jams and cooked **puddings**. (Not to be confused with **morel**.)

Moreton Bay bug *See* **bug**.

mornay Cheese sauce made with milk or **cream** to which dried **mustard** has been added. (Philippe de Mornay, 1549-1623, colleague of Henri IV of France.) (*See* **gratin**, **gratinée**.)

mortadella (*Ital.*) [mort-a-dell-ah] Lightly **smoked** large Italian sausage, pale in colour with spots of pork fat. It is sometimes flavoured with **parsley**, **pistachios**, **peppercorns**, **coriander** seeds, or green **olives** and served with the **antipasto**. (Mortadella is not a place; the origin of the name is disputed.)

moselle (1) Rather sweet white wine from the Mösel River region of Germany.
(2) **Generic** wine blended to resemble the style of German moselle.

moule (*Fr.*) (fem.) [mool] Mussel, e.g. *moules marinières*.

moussaka (*Grk.*) [moose-ah-kah] Minced meat and eggplant baked with a topping of cheese sauce.

mousse (*Fr.*) (fem.) [moose] (1) Light and frothy dish, usually set with **gelatine**, in which the basic ingredient is folded with whipped **cream**. It can be sweet or savoury (*mousse de saumon* 'salmon mousse'; *mousse au chocolat* 'chocolate mousse').
(2) The bubbles in **sparkling wine**.
(*Mousse* means 'foam', 'lather', or 'effervesence'.)

mousseline (*Fr.*) (fem.) [moose-leen] (1) **Puréed** fish or meat blended with **cream**.
(2) Sauce to which **cream** has been added, e.g. **hollandaise** *mousseline*.

moutarde (*Fr.*) (masc.) [moo-tard] *See* **mustard**.

mozzarella (*Ital.*) [motsa-rella] Italian cheese, waxy in texture which when cooked becomes stringy; the classic topping for pizza. (*See also* **bocconcini**, **cheddar**, **parmesan**, *and* **ricotta**.)

MSG Monosodium glutamate. Salt used to enhance the flavour of meat, much used in Chinese cooking and as an additive in processed foods. Some object to MSG being included in their food since it is thought it may cause an allergic reaction.

muddle **Cocktail**-mixing term. To crush in the bottom of the glass with a special 'muddler' (miniature pestle) or the base of a bar spoon. (*See* **Old Fashioned**.)

muffin (1) (*UK*) Round, flat yeast bun split and toasted and served buttered.
(2) (*USA*) Large cup cake usually containing fruit, e.g. blueberry muffin.

mulled wine Red wine heated gently with sugar, spices, raisins, and **citrus** fruits and served hot. (*See also* **glühwein**.)

mulligatawny (*Anglo-Ind.*) [mully-guh-tawny] Highly seasoned chicken soup with vegetables. (Literally, Tamil for 'pepper water'.)

muscat (1) Australian style of sweet fortified **dessert wine** (e.g. Rutherglen muscat).
(2) One of a number of varieties of grape, also known as **frontignac**.

muscatel/muscadel [muss-kuh-tel] Raisin; dried fruit of **muscat** grape.

muselet (*Fr.*) [moo-sell-ay] Wire muzzle used to hold in the corks of **sparkling wines**. (*See* 15.7.)

mushroom One of various kinds of edible fungus but usually the cultivated mushroom (*Agaricus bisporus*). (French *champignon*.) (*See also* **cep**, **morel**, **oyster mushroom**, **pine mushroom**, *and* **truffle**.)

mustard Yellow or brown **condiment** made from seeds of the mustard plant (genus *Brassica*). There are many different kinds of mustard seeds and mustard styles, including everyday hot English mustard, the milder Australian mustard, sweet American mustard, and various French mustards which are commonly used in cooking. (French *moutarde*.) (*See also* **cress** *and* **Dijon**.)

naan/nan (*Ind.*) [nahn] Flat puffy leavened bread best cooked in a **tandoor**.

nacho (*Mex.*) [nah-choh] **Corn chips** served with spicy sauce of beans, tomatoes, and/or meat topped with grated cheese, soured **cream** or **guacamole**. (*See also* **enchilada**, **taco** *and* **tortilla**.)

nam pla (*Thai.*) [nam plah] Salty, pungent fish sauce used in cooking. (*See also* **nuoc mam**.)

nam prik (*Thai.*) [nam prik] Spicy shrimp sauce served as a **condiment**.

napkin *See* **table-napkin**.

Napoléon (**brandy**) Marketing term without technical or legal meaning used on labels of brandy, particularly **cognac**. (Napoléon Bonaparte, 1769-1821, was Emperor of the French.)

napolitana (*Ital.*) [napol-it-ahna] From Naples, town in N. Italy. **Pizza** *napolitana* contains **tomato**, cheese, herbs, **garlic**, **olives**, and **anchovies**.

nappé(e) (*Fr.*) [nap-pay] Covered evenly with sauce or jelly. (*See* **mask**.)

nashi (*N-E Asia*, esp. *Jap.*) [naashi] Crisp, juicy fruit related to a pear but resembling an apple. There are two varieties, *chojuro* which is a russet colour, and *shinsui* with is smooth and yellowy-green.

nasi (*Malay*) [nahsee] Cooked rice.

nasi goreng (*Malay*) [nahsee gore-eng] Fried rice with chicken meat or prawns, shredded **omelette**, onions and spices. (*Goreng* means 'fried'.)

nasturtium Plant (*Tropaeolum majus*) whose leaves, flowers and seeds are all edible. The leaves have a pungent, peppery taste reminiscent of **watercress**. The flowers are vivid orange and may be torn up in salads. The seeds are **pickled** and used like **capers**.

native peach *See* **quandong**.

natural Uncooked, as in oysters natural. (*See also* **naturel**, *au* .)

nature (*Fr.*) (adj.) [natoor] Plain, unadulterated or without **garnish**; cooked with no sauce. (*See also* **naturel**, *au* .)

naturel, au (*Fr.*) [oh na-toor-el] In a state of nature; food cooked plainly and simply, or not at all, e.g. **huîtres** *au naturel* (oysters **natural**).

navarin (*Fr.*) (masc.) [nav-a-ri(n)] Mutton (lamb) stew with vegetables, originally turnips. (*Navet* means 'turnip'.)

navy bean *See* **haricot**.

neat **Liquor**-mixing term; undiluted (e.g. neat **whisky**).

nebuchadnezzar Largest recognized size of bottle for **sparkling wine**, the equivalent of 20 standard 750mL bottles. (Nebuchadnezzar was the King of Babylon who conquered Judah and carried the Jews off into exile in 586 BC.) (*See also* **champagne bottle sizes**.)

nem nuong (*Viet.*) [nem nung] Grilled minced-pork balls wrapped in **rice paper** with lettuce, cucumber, and **mint**. (*Nem* means 'ham', *nuong* 'grilled'.)

newburg Method of cooking and serving shellfish, esp. **lobster** or **crayfish**, with a sauce of sherry, cream, and egg yolk. (Originally created by a New York chef called Wenburg, the first three letters of his name being transposed in the name of the dish.)

New Zealand spinach Green-leaf vegetable (*Tetragonia tetragonoides*) used in salads or cooked and used as spinach; **warrigal greens**.

niçois(e) (*Fr.*) (fem. adj.) [neece-swaz] Literally from Nice (city in SE France). Typically **provençal** dishes, including **garlic**, **anchovies**, **olives**, green beans and **tomatoes**. The most famous dishes of this type are **salade niçoise** and **poulet sauté** *à la niçoise*.

nip (1) Small measure (of **spirits**); the standard Australian measure or nip is 30mL.
(2) (*UK*) Quarter bottle.

noble rot *See* **botrytis**. (*See also* 14.4.)

noisette (*Fr.*) (fem.) [nwah-zet] (1) Hazel-nut, or coloured or shaped thus. (*See* **beurre noisette** *and* **pommes noisettes**.)
(2) Small round tender piece of meat, usually lamb, cut from the **loin** or rib.

noodle(s) Food paste similar to **pasta** usually cut into thin strands or rolled into thin sheets (used as wrappers in Chinese cooking). Most European noodles are made from wheat flour and eggs though some are made of rice and a few of potatoes. Asian noodles are made from rice or wheat and seldom contain eggs. (From the German *nudel*, meaning 'dumpling'.) (*See also* **udon noodle**.)

nori (*Jap.*) [no-ree] Kind of seaweed, dried and pressed into thin sheets, used as an edible wrapping or casing for **sushi**.

normande, à la (*Fr.*) [ah lah nor-mahnd] In the Normandy (province in N. France) style; with apples and possibly **calvados** as well as **cream**, e.g. **pommes de terre** *à la normande*. (*See also* **normande sauce** *below*.)

normande sauce Rich sauce made with **cream** and fish **stock**. (French, **sauce** *normande*.) (*See also* **normande (à la)**, *above*.)

nose Wine-tasting term; the combination of the **aroma** and **bouquet** of a wine.

nouvelle cuisine (*Fr.*) (fem.) [noo-vell kwiz-een] Style of French cooking introduced in the early 1970s when healthier food was promoted and lighter sauces replaced the old heavy, creamy ones and alcohol was used relatively sparingly. (*See also* **cuisine minceur**.)

nuoc cham (*Viet.*) [nuok chum] **Nuoc mam** with **chilli**, **garlic**, sugar, and lime juice added and used as a dipping sauce. (*Nuoc* means 'water' or 'juice', *cham* 'dip'.)

nuoc mam (*Viet.*) [nuok mum] Salty, pungent fish sauce used in cooking. (*Nuoc* means 'water' or 'juice', *mam* 'sauce'.) (*See also* **nam pla**.)

nutrient Providing nourishment; a nourishing ingredient.

oeuf (*Fr.*) (masc.) [erf] Egg.

oeuf en cocotte [erf ahn ko-kot] Baked egg. (*See* **cocotte**.)

oeuf mollet [erf moll-ay] Soft-boiled egg.

oeufs à la neige (*Fr.*) [erf ah lah nayzj] **Floating islands**. (Literally, 'eggs like snow'.)

off-premises catering Food prepared and brought to a venue ready to serve.

oie (*Fr.*) (fem.) [wah] Goose, e.g. **confit** *d'oie*.

okra Seedpod of *Hibiscus esculentis*, also called **lady's fingers** or **gumbo**. Popular vegetable in Middle Eastern and **creole** cooking.

Old Fashioned Cocktail of **rye whiskey** and soda poured over sugar flavoured with **Angostura Bitters**. The sugar is often **muddled** in the glass, so that an Old Fashioned glass (*see* p. 99) has a specially thick base.

olive (1) Small stoned fruit, often stuffed and served as an **appetizer** or used as a **garnish** in **cocktails**. They may be green (immature) or black (mature). (*See also* **Kalamata**, **Ligurian**, *and* **Spanish** olive.)
(2) **Paupiette** (beef olive).

olive oil Oil extracted from **olives**. 'Pure' olive oil is pressed under heat from the pulp and kernels of lower-grade olives. **Virgin** and extra-virgin oil are finer and simply crushed from the first pressing of the highest grade fruit.

oloroso Golden and sweet style of Spanish **sherry**.

omelette Eggs, beaten with seasonings and fried in hot butter until just set; fillings, e.g. mushrooms or cheese, are sometimes added before the omelette is turned from the pan.

on-the-rocks Cocktail-mixing term: poured over a large quantity of cubed ice (e.g. **Scotch** on-the-rocks).

oregano Leaves of plant similar to **marjoram** used as robust seasoning herb esp. in Mediterranean cooking.

oseille (*Fr.*) (fem.) [oz-ayuh] **Sorrel**.

osso buco (*Ital.*) [oss-oh boo-koh] Rich **casserole** of knuckle of **veal** in a **tomato**, wine, and vegetable sauce, traditionally served with rice garnished with **parsley** and lemon **zest**. (*Osso* is Italian for 'bone' and *buco* means 'hole' — 'bone with a hole' in it.)

ouzo/oyzo (*Grk.*) Aniseed-flavoured **spirit**, similar to **pastis**.

overproof Alcoholic drinks stronger than 57.1% alc/vol, e.g. overproof **rum**.

oyster Bivalve mollusc (shellfish) usually eaten raw. The variety most commonly served in Australia is the Sydney rock oyster (*Saccostrea commercialis*). The New Zealand bluff oyster (*Ostrea luteria*) has a distinctive flavour and is used in soups and seafood casseroles. *See also* **huître**, **Kilpatrick** *and* **natural**.

oyster mushroom Large white mushroom (*Pleurotus ostreatus*) with a slight taste of **oysters**. Also known as abalone mushroom. (*See also* **cep**, **morel**, **pine mushroom**, *and* **truffle**.)

oyzo *See* **ouzo**.

paella (*Span.*) [pie-yella] Rice dish flavoured with **saffron** and containing chicken, **shellfish**, **chorizo**, peas and other vegetables.

paillard (*Ital.* from *Fr.*) [pie-yar] **Escalope** of **veal**. (Paillard was a 19th-century Parisian restaurateur.)

pain (*Fr*) (masc.) [pa(n)] Bread. (*See* **pané**.)

pain au chocolat (*Fr.*) [pa(n) oh shokohlah] **Croissant** containing chocolate. (Literally 'chocolate bread'.)

pakora/pakhora/pakorha (*Ind.*) [pack-or-ah] Savoury **fritter** made of **chick-pea** flour containing spicy **diced** vegetables.

palate Upper part of the mouth; sense of taste.

palm sugar Coarse, dark sugar obtained from the sap of the palmyra palm. It is used in Malaysian and Indonesian cooking. (*See also* **jaggery**.)

pancake Thin flat **batter** cake, usually fried. (*See* **crêpe**.)

pancetta (*Ital.*) [panchetta]   Pork belly rolled and eaten hot or cold; bacon.

pané(e) (*Fr.*) [pan-ay]   Fried in breadcrumbs. (*See also* **pain**.)

panettone (*Ital.*) [panuh-tone-ay]   N. Italian Christmas cake made from yeast and containing dried fruit, spices and nuts.

panforte (*Ital.*) [panfortay]   **Sweetmeat** containing **glacé** fruit and nuts.

papillote (*Fr.*) (fem.) [pap-ee-yot]   (1) Buttered paper; **en papillote**, cooked in buttered paper. (Fish is often served in this way.)
(2) Small frill of paper used to garnish **cutlet** bones.

pappadam/poppadum (*Ind.*) [poppa-dum]   Very light and thin crisp wafer made from **lentil** flour cooked in oil, often served with **curry**.

paprika [pap-reeka]   Red spice (*Capsicum annuum*) bought powdered and used both as a **garnish**, and for its colour and flavour in cooked dishes, esp. Hungarian **goulash**.

parfait (*Fr.*) (masc.) [par-fay]   (1) Creamy iced **pudding**.
(2) Layered fruit and ice-cream dessert served in tall glasses.
(3) Smooth, savoury **pâté**, usually of meat, blended with **cream**.

Parma ham   Fine, raw **smoked** Italian ham (Italian **prosciutto** *di Parma*) from Parma, city in N. Italy.

Parmesan (*Ital.*) [parm-i-zan]   Very hard dry cheese much used in Italian cooking. (Originally from Parma, city in N. Italy.) (*See* **Parmigiano**.)

Parmigiano (**reggiano**) (*Ital.*) [parmi-zjahnoh rezj-ee-ahnoh]   **Parmesan** cheese produced in Parma, N. Italy. (It can only carry this label if produced in the region.)

pasta (*Ital.*)   Staple food of Italy made of durum wheat flour (**semolina**) or potato, mixed with water, and, usually, egg and often sold dried. There are many varieties of pasta. (*See* **cannelloni, fettuccine, gnocchi, lasagne, linguini, penne, ravioli, rigatoni, spaghetti, tagliatelle, tortellini,** *and* **vermicelli;** *see also* **al dente** *and* **noodles**.)

pastis (*Fr.*) (masc.) [pas-teece]   (1) Strong alcoholic drink flavoured with aniseed, similar to **ouzo**, e.g. **Pernod**.
(2) Any of several pastries made in SW France, e.g. *pastis Béarnais*. (Béarn is a province in SW France.)

pasto (*Ital.*)   A meal. (*See also* **antipasto**.)

pastrami (*USA/Yid.*) [pass-trahmee]   **Cured**, spiced roast beef **silverside** rubbed in spices and black **peppercorns**. It is usually sliced and served in **rye** bread sandwiches with **dill pickles**.

pâte (*Fr.*) (fem.) [paht]   Dough, pastry or **batter**. (Not to be confused with **pâté** *below*.)

pâté (*Fr.*) (masc.) [paht-ay]   Paste of **blended** meats or fish, flavoured with seasoning, herbs and, sometimes, alcohol. (Not to be confused with **pâte** *above*.) (*See also* **parfait, rillettes,** *and* **terrine**.)

pâte à choux (*Fr.*) (fem.) [paht ah shoo]   **Choux** pastry.

pâte brisée (*Fr.*) (fem.) [paht breez-ay]   **Short-crust pastry**.

pâté de foie gras (*Fr.*) (masc.) [pat-ay duh fwa gra]   **Pâté** of force-fed goose or duck liver made by **blending** the fattened livers with minced pork and **truffles**. (*Gras* is French for 'fat'.)

pâté en croûte (*Fr.*) (masc.) [pat-ay ahn croot]   **Pâté** baked in a pastry case. (*See* **croûte**.)

pâte feuilletée (*Fr.*) (fem.) [paht fur-yet-ay]   **Puff pastry**.

pâté maison (*Fr.*) (masc.) [pat-ay mayzo(n)]   Homemade **pâté**, made according to the chef's own recipe. (*See* **maison**.)

pâte sablée (*Fr.*) (fem.) [paht sab-lay]   Sweetened **shortcrust pastry**. (*Un sablé* means 'a shortbread'.)

pâte sucrée (*Fr.*) (fem.) [paht soo-cray]   Rich, sweetened **shortcrust pastry**. (*Sucré* means 'sugared'.)

patisserie (*Fr.*) (fem.) [pat-ees-er-ee]   (1) Pastry.
(2) Cake-shop; tea-room.

patty   Small flat cake of meat (like the filling of a hamburger); a little pie.

pauchouse   *See* **pochouse**.

paupiette (*Fr.*) (fem.) [paw-pee-ett]   Thin slice of meat rolled with a stuffing (*paupiettes de* **veau**), sometimes referred to as an **olive** (beef olives).

pavé (*Fr.*) [pavay] (masc.)   (1) Sponge cake or dessert of biscuits sandwiched in layers with creamy filling.
(2) Savoury **mousse** set in **aspic** and garnished with **truffles**.
(*Pavé* means 'paving stone'.)

pavlova (*Austral.* & *N.Z.*)   Soft **meringue** cake filled with **cream** and topped with fruit. (Named for Anna Pavlova, Russian ballerina, 1882-1931.)

paysanne, à la (*Fr.*) (masc.) [ah lah pay-ee-zan]   **Diced** vegetables used as **garnish**, e.g. *potage à la paysanne*; **braised** dishes cooked with vegetables, e.g. **côtes** *de* **veau** *à la paysanne*. (*Paysanne* means 'peasant woman'.)

peach Melba   Poached peach halves enclosing **vanilla** ice-cream coated with raspberry **coulis** (French, *pêches Melba*). The original peach Melba was devised by the famous chef Auguste Escoffier (1846-1935) in honour of the Australian opera-singer Dame Nellie Melba. (*See also* **Melba toast**.)

pecan [pekahn/peecan]   Smooth brown nut from the Mississippi region, USA; hickory nut.

pêche (*Fr.*) (fem.) [paysh]   Peach. (*See also* **peach Melba**.)

Peking   One of the five main styles of Chinese cuisine; Peking cuisine is light and delicate. (Peking, now called Beijing, is a city in N. China.) (*See also* **Cantonese, Fukien, Honan,** *and* **Szechwan.**)

Peking duck (*Chin.*)   The crisp, crackling skin of mandarin duck eaten in a **pancake** with **spring onion**, cucumber, and **hoi sin sauce**. The flesh of the duck is served separately.

penne (*Ital.*) (pl.) [penay]   Short tubes of **pasta** cut at an acute angle. (Literally 'quills'.)

peperoni (*Ital.*) (pl.) [pepper-ohny]   Preserved **sweet peppers**. (*Peperoni* is Italian for 'capsicums'.) (Do not confuse with **pepperoni.**)

pepper   **Condiment** made from the dried berry-like fruit (**peppercorn**) of the pepper plant (*Piper nigrum*). (*See* **peppercorn**; *see also* **capsicum, cayenne,** *and* **sweet pepper.**)

peppercorn   Seed of the **pepper** plant picked and processed at one of three distinct stages:
(1)   *Green* peppercorns picked while the seed is still soft and green; usually bottled in **brine** but occasionally available fresh. (*See* **poivre vert.**)
(2)   *Black* peppercorns picked when the skin has turned yellow and the kernel has hardened. The berry is dried once the skin has been removed.
(3)   Once the berry turns red, the outer coating is washed off and the kernel dried for *white* **pepper**. This has more bite but less **aroma** than the black peppercorn.
Black peppercorns are usually freshly ground from a pepper mill at table. Ground white pepper used to be served in a **cruet** and used at table but freshly-ground black pepper is now preferred by most people. (*See also* **poivre, au.**)

pepperoni (*Ital.*) [pepper-ohny]   Hard, spicy beef-and-pork **salami**. (Do not confuse with **peperoni.**)

peppers   *See* **capsicum, peperoni,** *and* **sweet pepper.**

Pernod [pair-no]   **Proprietary** brand of **pastis**.

Perrier   Brand of French **mineral water**. (*See* 14.18.)

persillade (*Fr.*) (fem.) [pear-sill-ahd]   Mixture of **garlic** and chopped **parsley**.

persillé (*Fr.*) [pear-sill-ay]   Dishes seasoned with a **persillade**, e.g. **boeuf** *persillade*.

pesce (*Fr.*) (masc.) [pesskuh]   Fish.

pesto (*Ital.*) [pest-oh]   Paste made by blending **basil**, **Parmesan** cheese, **pine nuts**, **garlic** and **olive oil**. (*See also* **pistou.**)

petit four (*Fr.*) (masc.) [put-ee foor]   Small fancy cake or biscuit. There are different varieties: plain petits fours are dry and undecorated; fresh petits fours include miniature cakes, iced **marzipan** sweets, and sugar-coated fruits; and savoury petits fours which are served with **apéritifs**. (*Petit* means 'little' and *four* (usually) 'oven', so *petits fours* 'little baked things', 'little cakes'.)

petits pois   *See* **pois.**

pho (*Viet.*) [fo] (short 'o' as in hot)   Soup.

phosphorus [fos-fore-uss]   Non-metallic element found in all foods. Very high intakes can inhibit the absorption of **calcium**.

phyllo   *See* **filo.**

pickle   (1) (noun) **Condiment** of fruit or vegetables preserved in **vinegar** with sugar and spices, e.g. **dill pickle**, Branston pickle.
(2) (verb) To **preserve** vegetables or fruit in a **pickle** solution, e.g. pickled onions. (*See also* **brine, cure,** *and* **smoke.**)

pièce de résistance (*Fr.*) (fem.) [pee-yayss duh ray-zees-tahns]   The main dish of a meal, substantial and usually rather grand. (Literally, 'item of strength'.)

pilaff (*Turk.*) [peelaf]   Middle Eastern dish of spiced rice with meat, chicken, or fish, usually cooked together. (*See also* **pilau.**)

pilau (*Ind.*) [pee-low]   Indian version of **pilaff**, typically including chicken and/or mutton or goat's meat and spiced. (*See also* **biryani.**)

pilsner/pilsener   (1) Pale hop-flavoured **lager** originally made in Pilsen, Bohemia (now Plzen, Czecho-slovakia).
(2) Style of beer glass. (*See* p. 98.)

Pimm's   Properly 'Pimm's No. 1 Cup', an English **proprietary** gin-based flavoured liquor, usually served in summer mixed with lemonade or **ginger ale** and ice, and garnished with cucumber and **mint**.

pine mushroom   Large, golden mushroom (*Armillaria edodes*) which grows under red pine trees. Also known as **matsutake mushroom**. (*See also* **cep, morel, oyster mushroom,** *and* **truffle.**)

pine nut   The seed of the Mediterranean stone pine. Pine nuts are an essential ingredient of **pesto**.

Pink Gin   **Cocktail** of gin served with a dash of **Angostura Bitters**.

pinot noir [pee-no nwaar]   Grape variety used in the famous French red **burgundy** wine. Pinot noir wines are usually soft and light; they are also part of the blend used to make French **champagne**.

pipe   To squeeze **cream**, icing, etc. in decorative patterns on a cake or other food item.

piperade (*Fr.*) (fem.) [peep-ay-rahd]   Stewed **tomato**, **capsicum**, onion, and **garlic** mixed with beaten eggs and cooked slowly over gentle heat.

piquant [pee-kant]   Spicy, appetizing.

piroshki (*Russ.*) [pi-rohsh-kee]   Savoury pasty.

pistachio [piss-tashee-oh]   Fruit of the *Pistacia* tree, native to the Middle East. Pistachio nuts are used in savoury and sweet dishes, esp. cream desserts and sliced meats where their bright green colour enhances their appearance.

pistou (*Fr.*) (masc.) [pees-too] **Provençal** paste **condiment** made of sweet **basil**, and olive oil with **garlic** and **Parmesan** cheese, similar to Italian **pesto**. Pistou soup (**soupe** *au pistou*) is popular.

pita/pitta (*Grk.*) [pitta] Flat round double-layered bread which can be cut open and filled; pocket bread.

pithiviers (*Fr.*) [peeteev-ee-ay] **Puff-pastry** tart traditionally sandwiched with almond cream but often filled with a savoury mixture. The pastry top is usually **scalloped** around the edges and **scored** with curves radiating from the centre. (Pithiviers is near Orléans in Central France.)

pizza (*Ital.*) [peetsa] Plate-like base of dough covered with topping which usually includes cheese, tomato and herbs. (*See* **capricciosa, margherita, marinara,** *and* **napolitana;** *see also* **calzone** *and* **focaccia.**)

platter Large serving dish; a 'sizzling platter' is presented direct from the stove and so is usually made of cast iron. (*See also* **skillet.**)

ploughman's lunch (*UK*) Cheese and **pickle** served with a hunk of bread and **beer,** esp. in local pubs.

plum pudding *See* **Christmas pudding.**

poché(e) (*Fr.*) (adj.) [poshay] Poached.

pochouse/pauchouse (*Fr.*) [poh-shooz] Fish stew from Burgundy cooked with white wine. (Dialect version of *pêcheuse,* 'fisherwoman'.) (*See also* **bouillabaisse.**)

point, à (*Fr.*) [ah pwa(n)] Medium; steak cooked so that it shows a tinge of pink blood. (*See also* **bien cuit, bleu,** *and* **saignant.**)

poire (*Fr.*) (fem.) [pwaar] Pear.

poireau(x) (*Fr.*) (masc.) [pwah-roe] Leek(s).

pois (*Fr.*) (fem.) [pwah] Pea, usually eaten young as *petits pois.* (Literally 'little peas'.)

poisson (*Fr.*) (masc.) [pwah-so(n)] Fish.

poivrade, sauce (*Fr.*) [sohs pwahv-rwahd] Sauce consisting of a **mirepoix** mixed with **vinegar,** wine, and crushed green **peppercorns,** traditionally served with **game.** (*See also* **chevreuil, salmis,** *and* **venaison.**)

poivre (*Fr.*) (masc.) [pwahv-ruh] Pepper.

poivre, au (*Fr.*) [oh pwahv-ruh] With **pepper** or crushed **peppercorns,** e.g. **bifteck** *aux poivres.*

poivre vert (*Fr.*) [pwahv-ruh vair] Green **peppercorn,** e.g. **poulet** *aux poivres verts.*

polenta (*Ital.*) [puh-len-ta] Dough of thick porridge-like consistency made with cornmeal (maize flour). Cooked polenta can be fried or baked and served with meat dishes.

pollo (*Ital.* & *Span.*) Chicken.

pomme (*Fr.*) (fem.) [pom] Apple.

pomme de terre (*Fr.*) (fem.) [pom duh tair] Potato. (*De terre* means 'of the earth'.) Note that in com-

pounds such as those below, the words '*de terre*' are omitted.

pommes Anna (*Fr.*) (fem.) [pom anna] Sliced potatoes cooked with butter in a pan to form a solid cake. It is served in slices. (Dish dedicated to Anna Deslions, socialite in the Second Empire, *c.* 1860.)

pommes duchesse (*Fr.*) (fem.) [pom doo-shess] Potatoes **puréed** with egg yolk and butter, **piped** around the edge of a dish, or into small shapes, and baked in the oven.

pommes frites (*Fr.*) (fem.) [pom freet] Chipped potatoes deep-fried; French fries. (*See* **frite.**)

pommes noisettes (*Fr.*) (fem.) [pom nwa-zet] Small potato balls **sautéed** in butter. (*See* **noisette.**)

pommes sautées (*Fr.*) (fem.) [pom soh-tay] Cooked potatoes fried quickly, often with **shallots** or bacon to flavour. (*See* **sauté.**)

porridge (*Scot.*) [porij] Breakfast dish of oatmeal cooked with milk or water and served hot.

port Kind of **fortified wine,** originally developed in Portugal, often served after dinner. (*See* 14.5.)

porterhouse Large beef steak cut from the **fillet** end of the **sirloin.** (*See also* **entrecôte, filet mignon, minute steak, rump,** *and* **T-bone.**)

portion Amount of food served to guests in any particular menu item.

potage (*Fr.*) (masc.) [pot-ahzj] Soup, particularly thick (cream) soup. (*See* 2.2; *see also* **bisque, garbure, soupe** *and* **vichyssoise.**)

pot-au-feu (*Fr.*) (masc.) [pot oh fur] Classic dish of beef cooked slowly with vegetables in liquid to form a **broth** which is eaten before the meat. (Literally, 'pot for the fire', so 'stewpot' or 'casserole'.)

pot roast Joint of meat baked with vegetables and **stock** in a covered pan.

pot still Traditional **still** used to distil **malt whisky, cognacs** and **armagnacs** whereby the spirit is distilled in batches, unlike the 'continuous still' used to distil most modern **spirits.**

poulet (*Fr.*) (masc.) [poo-lay] Chicken, fowl.

poussin (*Fr.*) (masc.) [poo-sa(n)] Baby chicken.

praline [pray-leen] Confection of **caramelized** almonds or hazelnuts baked hard. It is added to some sweet dishes in the form of a fine, crushed powder. (Devised by Lassagne, chef to Marshal Duplessis-Praslin, *c.* 1630.)

preserve (1) (noun) Preserved fruit; jam, jelly. (2) (verb) To prepare food for storage; to **pickle.**

pretzel Salted stick-like biscuit, shaped into knots and curls, served as an apéritif, especially with beer.

princesse, à la (*Fr.*) [ah lah pra(n)-sess] Garnished with asparagus tips.

Pritikin Style of cooking food named after Nathan Pritikin (1915-85) who maintained that by reducing

cholesterol levels many diseases caused by modern lifestyle could be prevented. The diet is low in fats and animal **protein**, has no added salt or sugar, and is high in fibre. (*See also* **cuisine minceur**.)

prix-fixe (*Fr.*) [pree fiks] Fixed-price meal; **table d'hôte** menu. (*Prix* means 'price'.)

profiterole (*Fr.*) (fem.) [prof-ee-tay-rol] Small **choux-pastry** bun with a sweet creamy filling served in chocolate sauce. Those filled with a cheese mixture or savoury purée are often used to garnish soup.

proof Old measure of alcohol in **liquor** obsolete in Australia, NZ, and UK, but still used in the USA (US 100° proof = 50% alc/vol). (*See also* **overproof**.)

proprietary The property of some person or body. A proprietary **liqueur**, **Grand Marnier** for example, can only be made by the company which owns the right to make it. (*See also* **generic**.)

prosciutto (*Ital.*) [prosh-choot-oh] Raw **smoked** ham sliced very thinly. (*See also* **Parma ham**.)

protein Constituent of food needed for growth and repair, found particularly in meat and dairy products, but also in **soya beans**, **lentils** and peas.

provençale, à la (*Fr.*) [ah lah prov-ah(n)-saal] In the manner of Provence (province in S. France); cooked with tomatoes and **garlic**.

pudding (1) Soft food item of ingredients mixed with or enclosed in flour or suet and usually steamed or baked, e.g. **bread and butter pudding**, **Christmas pudding** and **Yorkshire pudding**. (*See also* **black pudding** *and* **summer pudding**.)
(2) (*UK*) The **sweet** or **dessert** course of a meal. (*See* 2.2.)

puff pastry Delicate airy pastry rolled so that it forms thin layers when cooked. (*See* **pâte feuilletée**.)

pumpernickel (*Ger.*) [poom-purr-nickel] Solid, dark brown or black **rye** bread, often packaged for use as a base for **canapés**, cut into small circles or squares and sliced thinly.

punch Drink of wine or **spirits** with fruit juices or water flavoured with spices and often served hot. (*See also* **glühwein** *and* **mulled wine**.)

pungent With a strong taste or smell.

punt The hollow at the base of some wine bottles. It retains the deposit (if any) thrown by the wine and, especially in the case of **champagne** bottles, may be used to hold the bottle while pouring. (*See* 15.7.)

purée [pew-ray] (1) (*Fr.*) (fem. noun) Any food **blended** to a smooth, thick paste, e.g. *purée de volaille*, 'purée of chicken'.
(2) (*Eng.*) (verb) To **blend** into a purée (e.g. puréed potatoes).

quail Small **game** bird, nowadays farmed, usually served two birds to a guest.

quail egg Egg about one-third the size of standard hen's egg, often served hard-boiled as an **appetizer**. (*See also* **Scotch egg**.)

quandong/quondong (*Austral.*) [kwondong] Small bright-red fruit with a wrinkled stone containing an edible kernel; also known as native peach.

quenelle (*Fr.*) (fem.) [ken-nell] Poached **dumpling** of **puréed** fish, egg white and **cream**. **Veal** or chicken is sometimes used instead of fish.

quiche (*Fr.*) (fem.) [keesh] Open pie or **flan**, filled with savoury custard holding other ingredients.

quiche Lorraine [keesh lor-aine] **Quiche** filled with savoury custard and bacon and topped with cheese. (Lorraine is a province in NE France.)

quince Hard yellow apple-like fruit delicately scented which when cooked turns pink. Often used in pies and **puddings** and makes excellent **preserves**.

quinine Bitter alkaloid obtained from cinchona bark, once the principal treatment for malaria and used as flavouring, e.g. in Indian **tonic**.

race (1) Fenced access in a self-service **establishment** which channels guests in a line past food and beverages towards the till. (Also called 'straight' race.)
(2) (**scrambled**) Self-service system where different types of food or beverage are available at different parts of the counter and are collected separately.

rack (of lamb) Joint of lamb cutlets cut from the rib **loin**. There are usually between four and six chops in the rack. (French **carré** *d*'**agneau**.)

raclette (*Swiss*) (fem.) [rack-let] Cheese **fondue** made by melting a whole Swiss cheese and scraping off pieces as they soften. It is usually eaten with plain potatoes, gherkins, **pickled** onions, and black **pepper**. (*Raclette* is French for a 'scraping'.)

radicchio (*Ital.*) [rad-eek-ee-oh] **Endive** with dark reddish-green leaves and distinctive white veins. Has pungent taste and mixes well with other salad greens.

ragoût (*Fr.*) (masc.) [rag-oo] Stew or **casserole** (e.g. *ragoût d*'**agneau**).

rainbow chard See **silverbeet**.

raita (*Ind.*) [rye-eeta] Yoghurt blended with **garlic** and cucumber and served as a cooling **condiment** with spicy dishes.

ramekin [ram-uh-kin] Small baking dish for one serving; miniature **soufflé** dish. (*See* 3.5.)

rang (*Fr.*) (masc.) [rung] Rank, brigade, team (of waiters). (*See* **chef de rang**.)

rare Meat cooked for only a short time so that the blood runs; underdone. (*See also* **bleu, à point**.)

ratatouille (*Fr.*) (fem.) [rata-too-wee] **Provençal** vegetable stew containing tomatoes, onions, eggplant, **capsicums**, and **zucchini**, flavoured with **garlic** and ground **pepper**.

ravière (*Fr.*) (fem.) [ravee-ayr] Oval or rectangular-shaped serving dish. (*See* 3.5.)

ravioli (*Ital.*) (pl.) [rav-ee-oh-lee] Squares of **pasta** filled with meat, **ricotta** cheese, or a vegetable.

réchaud (*Fr.*) (masc.) [ray-show] Small stove or spirit-lamp used for table-side cooking or to keep food warm. (*Chaud* means 'hot'.) (*See* 3.6 *and* 12.13; *see also* **chafing dish**, **chaud**, *and* **flambé**.)

réchauffé (*Fr.*) [ray-show-fay] (1) (masc. noun) Re-heated dish; a dish made up of left-overs. (*See also* **émincés**.)
(2) **réchauffé(e)** (adj.) Re-heated.
(*Chauffé* means 'heated'.)

red pepper (1) **Cayenne pepper**.
(2) Variety of **sweet pepper** or **capsicum**.

reduce To thicken **stock**, or liquids such as white wine or **vinegar**, by boiling rapidly without a lid thus reducing the quantity through evaporation.

rehoboam [re-huh-boh-um] Large bottle of **sparkling wine** containing the equivalent of 6 standard (750mL) bottles. (Rehoboam was King of Judah 10th century BC.) (*See* **champagne bottle sizes**.)

relevé (*Fr.*) [ruh-lev-ay] (1) (masc. noun) Meat course in the **classic menu** following the **entrée**, usually a dish carved from a joint.
(2) (adj.) Cooking term meaning 'highly seasoned'.

relish Condiment, **sauce**, or **pickle**, usually eaten with plain food. (*See also* **Gentleman's Relish**.)

rémoulade (*Fr.*) (fem.) [ray-moo-laad] **Mayonnaise** sauce seasoned with gherkins, **capers**, **anchovies**, and **herbs**.

rendang daging (*Indon.*) [rendan(g) dahging] Dry-fried beef **curry** cooked in **coconut milk** and spices.

reservation The booking of a table for a meal or bed for the night; the place thus booked.

restaurateur (*Fr.*) (masc.) [res-tara-tur] Manager or owner of a restaurant; the licensee. (Note *not* restaura*n*teur.)

Rhine riesling Popular white wine grape variety, usually known internationally simply as **riesling**. It is used to make **hock**. (*See also* **riesling**.)

rice-paper Edible paper made from the pith of an oriental tree and used in Asian cooking. (*See also* **goi cuon** *and* **nem nuong**.)

rice vinegar Mild **vinegar** used in Asian cooking as a **pickling** agent, or to give an acidic or 'sour' taste to dishes. (*See also* **balsamic vinegar**, **malt vinegar**, **vinaigrette**, *and* **wine vinegar**.)

ricotta (*Ital.*) White, moist, light cheese made mostly from the **whey** of milk. (*See also* **mascarpone**.)

riesling (*Ger.*) [reece-ling] (1) Dry white wine made from the **Rhine riesling** grape, from the Rhine region of Germany. (*See also* **hock**.)
(2) (*Austral.*) **Generic** wine blended to resemble

the style of German riesling. (*See* 14.3.)
(*See also* **auslese** *and* **spätlese**.)

rigatoni (*Ital.*) (pl.) [rigga-toh-nee] **Pasta** made in the shape of short ridged tubes.

rillettes (*Fr.*) (fem. pl.) [ree-yettuh] **Minced meat**, usually pork, cooked in its own fat and made into a **pâté**. Served as cold **hors d'oeuvre**.

risotto (*Ital.*) [riz-ott-oh] Rice, preferably **arborio**, and vegetables (and sometimes meat or fish) cooked in **stock** until the liquid is absorbed by the rice.

risotto alla milanese [riz-ott-oh ala mil-an-ayz-ay] Rice cooked in **stock** with onions, flavoured with **saffron** and **Parmesan** cheese. (*Milanese* means 'in the style of Milan', city in N. Italy.)

rocket Pungent **cress** rather like spinach (*Eruca sativa*) used raw in **mesclun** mix for salad.

rock lobster Salt-water **crayfish** or southern rock **lobster**. (French **langouste**). (*See also* **bug**.)

roe Fish eggs. (*See also* **caviare** *and* **lumpfish roe**.)

roesti/rösti [rur-stee] Swiss potato cake; grated potatoes formed into a cake and fried in butter.

rognon (*Fr.*) (masc.) [roh-nyo(n)] Kidney.

Romanov/Romanoff (*Fr.*) [roam-anoff] (1) **Garnish** of cucumber stuffed with **duxelles**.
(2) Creamed-potato cases filled with mushrooms in a **velouté** sauce, seasoned with **horseradish**.
(3) Strawberries **macerated** in **curaçao** served with **crème chantilly**.
(Romanov was the name of the dynasty which ruled Russia 1613-1917. Many French chefs dedicated dishes to the Imperial family.)

roquefort (*Fr.*) [rok-fore] Smooth and creamy **blue-veined** ewes'-milk cheese. (Roquefort is a district in S. France.) (*See also* **Gippsland blue**, **gorgonzola**, *and* **stilton**.)

rosé (*Fr.*) [rose-ay] Pink wine made by removing the skins of black (red) grapes early in the **fermentation** process resulting in a lighter colour and flavour than in an ordinary red wine.

rosella (*Austral.*) Fleshy red seed pod of *Hibiscus heterophyllus* usually stewed and made into **preserve**.

Rossini *See* **tournedos Rossini**.

rosso Sweet, pink style of **vermouth**.

Rosso Antico **Proprietary** Italian **apéritif** infused with aromatic herbs. (Literally, 'Ancient Red'.)

roti (*Ind.*) [roh-tee] General term for bread, particularly flat unleavened bread like **chapati**; with **dahl** it is the staple food of northern India.

rôti (*Fr.*) (masc.) [roh-tee] Roast meat, e.g. *rôti de* **boeuf**. *Rôtis* (pl.) is a course in the **classic menu**.

rotisserie Device for roasting meat on a rotating spit so that it browns evenly.

rouille (*Fr.*) (fem.) [roo-ee] **Provençal** sauce of **garlic**, oil, and **stock** with red **chillies** and **saffron**

served with fish dishes, esp. **bouillabaisse**. (Literally, 'rust' from its colour.)

roulade (*Fr.*) (fem.) [roo-lahd] Stuffed roll of food. A savoury roulade may be a thin piece of meat stuffed and rolled; a sweet one a chocolate sponge filled with **cream** before rolling.

roux (*Fr.*) (masc.) [roo] Blend of fat and flour which is used to thicken sauces. (*See* **béchamel**.)

rum **Spirit** distilled from sugar-cane or molasses. Rum comes in various styles and colours ranging from colourless (like **Bacardi**) to dark brown Jamaica rum.

rum baba *See* **baba**.

rump steak Tender cut of beef taken from behind the **loin**. (*See also* **entrecôte, filet mignon, porterhouse, sirloin,** *and* **T-bone**.)

russe, à la (*Fr.*) [ah lah rooss] In the Russian style; often shellfish in an **aspic** jelly with **mayonnaise** or a **chaudfroid** sauce served with a **Russian salad**. (*See also* **charlotte russe**.)

Russian salad Salad of **diced** cooked vegetables mixed in **mayonnaise** and flavoured with either caraway or **pickles**.

rye (1) **Cereal** used for making bread; rye bread is rather dark in colour and slightly bitter in taste. (2) Rye **whiskey**; American whiskey distilled (mainly) from fermented rye.

sabayon (*Fr.*) (masc.) [sab-eye-on] Mixture of egg yolks, white wine, and sugar whipped together to form a rich foamy dessert usually served just warm. Similar to Italian **zabaglione**.

sabayon sauce Sauce made from egg yolks blended with alcohol (particularly **champagne**) and usually served with fish.

sablé (*Fr.*) (masc.) [sab-lay] Kind of **shortbread**.

saddle Large cut of meat from the top of the back of the animal. (*See also* **loin**.)

saffron Dried stigma of a kind of crocus flower used as a spice for flavouring. It colours food bright yellow, and is also used as a dye.

saignant(e) (*Fr.*) [say-nyo(n)(tuh)] **Rare** and rather bloody (steak, etc.) but not 'blue'. (*See also* **bien cuit, bleu** *and* **point (à)**.) (Literally, 'bleeding'.)

sake (*Jap.*) [sah-kay] Fermented, colourless rice wine, usually served warm. (*See also* **mirin**.)

salad dressing *See* **French dressing, mayonnaise,** *and* **vinaigrette**.

salade (*Fr.*) (fem.) [sall-ahd] Salad. (*See also* **insalata, niçoise, Caesar, Russian,** *and* **Waldorf**.)

salamander Grill which heats from above, used for browning, etc.

salami (*Ital.*) [salaamee] Highly-seasoned sausage served cold. (*See also* **kabana, King Island, mortadella,** *and* **pepperoni**.)

salmanazar Large bottle size for **sparkling wine**, equivalent of 12 standard (750mL) bottles. (Salmanazar was the Assyrian King who conquered Israel in 721 BC.) (*See also* **champagne bottle sizes**.)

salmis (*Fr.*) (masc.) [salmee] **Râgout** of **game** bird or duck, often finished at table. (*See also* **salmis, sauce**.)

salmis, sauce (*Fr.*) [sohs salmee] Sauce served with a **salmis** made with the cooking juices diluted with wine mixed with an **esapagnole** sauce.

salmonella Group of **bacteria** which can cause food poisoning.

salpicon (*Fr.*) (masc.) [sal-pee-ko(n)] **Diced** pieces of meat, etc. held in a sauce and used to fill **canapés, vols-au-vent**, etc.

salsa (*Ital., Span., & Mex.*) [sals-a] (1) **Sauce**. (*See below*.) (2) Combination of chopped and usually raw vegetables, served as a fresh **chutney**.

salsa di pomodoro (*Ital.*) [sals-a dee pom-uh-dorr-oh] Tomato sauce. (Literally, 'sauce of tomato'.)

salsa verde (*Ital.*) [sals-a vairduh] **Vinaigrette** with **anchovies** and **capers** or finely-chopped parsley added. (Literally 'green sauce'.)

salsa verde cruda (*Mex.*) [salsa vairduh crooda] Uncooked green-tomato sauce served with **tacos, nachos, tortillas,** and **enchiladas**. (Literally 'raw' or 'unripe' 'green sauce'.)

saltimbocca (*Ital.*) [saul-teem-bow-kah] Thin slices of **veal** and **smoked** ham rolled with sage leaves, **sautéed** and simmered in wine. (Literally, 'jump into mouth'.)

sambal/sambol (*Indon.*) [sam-bahl] **Condiment** usually containing **chillies** and onion.

sambal ulek/oelek (*Indon.*) [sam-bahl uluk] Hot **chilli** paste used as a seasoning or **condiment**.

samosa (*Ind.*) [samohsa] Small pastry with spicy filling deep fried and served as a **savoury**.

sashimi (*Jap.*) [sash-eemee] Raw fish arranged in thin bite-sized pieces and served with **daikon radish** and **wasabi**. (Literally, 'pierced flesh'.)

satay (*Malay.*) [sah-tay] Cubes of meat or fish on bamboo skewers, grilled on a charcoal grill, and served with **satay sauce**. (*See* **kebab**.)

satay sauce (*Malay.*) Thick sauce made from crushed peanuts and lemon juice, often served with **satay**.

sauce *See* **béarnaise, béchamel, beurre blanc, beurre noisette, beurre meunière, black bean, bolognaise, bordelaise, capricciosa, carbonara, charcutière, chasseur, chaudfroid, crème anglaise, Cumberland, demi-glace, devilled, diable, espagnole, florentine, French dressing, guacamole, hoi sin, hollandaise, horseradish, ketchup, Kilpatrick, lyonnaise, madère, maître d'hôtel, mayonnaise, meunière, mint, mornay, mousse-**

line, **nam pla**, **nam prik**, **newburg**, **normande**, **nuoc cham**, **nuoc mam**, **poivrade**, **relish**, **rémoulade**, **rouille**, **sabayon**, **salmis**, **satay**, **shoyu**, **soubise**, **soya**, **suprême**, **sweet-and-sour**, **Tabasco**, **tartare**, **teriyaki**, **thermidor**, **Thousand Island**, **velouté**, **venaison**, **vinaigrette**, **Worcestershire**, *and* **zingara**. (*See also below and* **crème** (**à la**), **mask**, **nappé**, **roux**.) (French *sauce* (fem.) [sohs] as in *sauce béarnaise*; Italian and Spanish **salsa** [sals-a].)

saucière (*Fr.*) (fem.) [soh-see-ayr]   Sauce- or gravy-boat. (*See* 3.5 *and* 8.6.)

sauerkraut (*Ger.*) [sour krout]   **Pickled** white cabbage. (Literally, 'sour cabbage').

saumon (*Fr.*) (masc.) [sow-mo(n)]   Salmon.

sauté (*Fr.*) [soh-tay]   (1) (masc. noun) Dish of quickly fried food.
(2) (adj.) (*sauté(e)*) Lightly fried (e.g. **pommes** *sautées*).
(3) (*Eng.*) (verb) Lightly fried — a 'sautéed' mixture, 'sautéed in butter', etc.

sauternes [so-tairn]   (1) Lusciously-rich, sweet white **dessert wine** from Sauternes, district near Bordeaux, SW France. (*See* 14.4.)
(2) (*Austral.*) **Generic** wine in similar style.

sauvignon   *See* **cabernet sauvignon** *and* **sauvignon blanc**.

sauvignon blanc [so-veenee-o(n) blo(n)]   Grape variety used to make dry white wines including **fumé** blanc.

savarin (*Fr.*) (masc.) [sav-a-ra(n)]   Large ring-shaped cake made with yeast dough served soaked in **rum** and filled with **cream** or custard. (Named after Jean-Anthelme Brillat-Savarin, 1755-1826, gastronome and writer.)

savoury   (1) (adj.) Salty, piquant, tasty.
(2) (noun) Small savoury item; **canapé**. (*See also* **classic menu**.)

scald   (1) To dip fruit or vegetables in boiling water to remove impurities or prepare them for skinning or freezing.
(2) To heat (particularly milk) until just at the point of boiling.

scallion   Green (immature) onion; spring onion.

scallop [skol-op]   (1) (noun) Mollusc or shellfish (genus *Pecten*) contained in a big fan-like shell on which it is often served. The 'meat', which is opaque and browny-white when raw, with a 'coral' attached, turns white when cooked. (*French* **coquille**.)
(2) (verb) To decorate with semi-circular shapes; to **score** with such a pattern.

scalloped potatoes (*USA*) [skol-lopt]   Sliced potatoes baked with milk. (*See* **pommes Anna**.)

scallopina (*Ital.*) (*pl.* **scallopini**) [ska-lop-een-ee]   **Escalope** or thin slice of meat lightly crumbed and

sautéed; traditionally a sauce of **marsala**, tomato, and **cream** is served with it.

scampi   Variety of large prawn. (Plural of the Italian *scampo*; in French **langoustine**.)

schnapps (*Ger.*) [shnaps]   N. European flavoured distilled **spirit** made from grain or potatoes, similar to **hollands gin**.

schnitzel (*Ger.*) [shnit-sell]   Thin slice of meat, usually chicken or **veal**. (*See* **Wiener schnitzel**.) (*Schnitzeln* means 'to cut', so schnitzel means 'a slice'.)

scone [skon]   Bread-like cake served in individual portions with jam and butter or thick **cream**. (*See also* **Devonshire tea**.)

score   To cut lines or marks into a surface, esp. in skin or rind.

Scotch   Scotch **whisky**.

Scotch egg (*UK*)   Hard-boiled egg encased in sausage meat, covered with beaten egg and breadcrumbs, deep-fried and served cold.

scrambled race   *See* **race**.

seafood   Collective term for edible fish, shellfish in particular. (*See* **fruits de mer**, **marinara**, **pesce**, *and* **poisson**.)

seal   To sear the surface of meat by intense heat to seal in the juices.

sec (*Fr.*) (fem. **sèche**) [sek/sesh]   Dry (when referred to wine). But note that the word *sec* sometimes is confusingly applied to drinks that are not really dry, e.g. **triple sec** and **champagne**. (*See* 14.6.)

sekt (*Ger.*) [sekt]   German **sparkling wine**.

sémillon [say-me-yo(n)]   Grape variety used to make crisp dry white wines.

semolina (*Ital.*)   Coarsely-ground grains of hard wheat or rice, used to make many **pasta** products, and **couscous**.

service cloth   A (white) cloth or **table-napkin** used by the waiter in foodservice. (*See* 7.4.)

service gear   Utensils used by the waiter in food service, especially **silver service**, usually a tablespoon and fork. (*See* 3.2, 8.2 *and* 8.3.)

service plate   Large plate covered with a **service cloth**, used, for example, to carry cutlery to tables once customers are seated. (*See* 6.11.)

serviette   *See* **table-napkin**.

sesame seed   Small seed from sesame plant, oily and nourishing, widely used in cooking, e.g. to make **halva** or sprinkled on loaves of bread. (*See also* **hummus** *and* **tahini**.)

set menu   Menu allowing no choice to the guests, all items having been pre-selected by the **host**, typically used at **functions**. (*See* 2.12.)

sformato (*Ital.*) [s-form-ahtoe]   Kind of **soufflé**, either sweet or savoury served with accompanying sauce of meat or flavoured **cream**.

shake and strain   Cocktail-mixing term. The ingredients are shaken together with ice in a
cocktail-shaker and strained through a
Hawthorn strainer into the glass. (*See* 14.10.)

shallot   Small brown onion (*Allium ascalonicum*)
much used in French cookery to flavour sauces (e.g.
béarnaise.) and also in E. Asian cuisine. The word is
sometimes incorrectly used as if it meant **spring
onion**. (In French *èschalot*.)

shank   Cut of meat, esp. veal or lamb, from the leg.
(*See also* **carré**.)

sherbet   (1) Sweet flavoured effervescent drink.
(2) (*USA*) Water-ice or **sorbet**.

sherry   Fortified wine made from white grapes,
originally developed in Jerez in Spain. There are
various styles, among them **fino** (dry and pale),
amontillado (medium dry, rather darker), and
oloroso (sweet and golden). Cream sherry is very
sweet and creamy. Australian sherries are usually
simply called 'dry', 'medium', 'sweet', etc. (*See* 14.5.)

shiraz [shi-raaz]   Grape variety, also called hermitage,
suiting warm conditions. It produces robust red
wines which benefit from long maturing.

shirred egg   Baked egg.

shish kebab (*Turk.*) [shish kuh-baab]   Small pieces of
meat, usually lamb, cooked on a skewer. (*See* **kebab**.)

shooter   Layered **cocktail** without ice served in a small
glass or test-tube.

shortbread (*UK*)   Crumbly sweet biscuit of flour
(originally oatmeal) and butter.

shortcake   Dessert of sweet pastry or cake sandwiched
with fruit, esp. strawberries, and **cream**.

shortcrust pastry   Basic pastry mix made by combin-
ing flour, fat, and water. It may be sweetened in
which case sugar is added. Egg or lemon juice may
replace the water. (*See* **pâte brisée**, **pâte sablée**,
and **pâte sucrée**.)

shoyu (*Jap.*) [show-yu]   Popular style of Japanese **soya
sauce**; it is less salty and lighter than the most
common Chinese varieties.

shuck (*USA*)   To remove from shell or cob.

shwarma/chawarma (*Leb.*) [sha-warma]   *See* **döner
kebab**.

sideboard   Table or chest for holding plates and glass,
and from which food is served; a waiter's **station**.
(*See* 1.7 *and* 4.8.)

silverbeet/Swiss chard   Glossy, green-leaf vegetable
with white stalks that look like celery. The stem and
the leaf are edible but are usually prepared separately. The leaves are often used as a substitute for
spinach. Rainbow chard has brightly coloured stems
of red, yellow, and orange. (In French, *blettes*.)

silver service   Formal style of food service whereby
food items are transferred by the waiter to the
guests' plates from service dishes at the table. (*See*
Chapter 8.)

silverside   Boneless hindquarter of beef usually salted
and **pot roast**ed.

sirloin   Choice joint of beef taken from the upper **loin**
which includes the **fillet**. It is often boned and
rolled with the fillet removed. It can be cut into
steaks. (*See also* **entrecôte**, **filet mignon**, **porterhouse**, **rump**, *and* **T-bone**.)

skillet   Frying pan; cast-iron pot.

slivovitz   Plum **brandy** from the Balkans. (*Sljiva*
means 'plum' in Serbo-Croatian.)

sloe gin   Liqueur of sloe berries soaked in **gin**.

smallgoods   Cooked meats and meat products, sausages, salamis, **pâtés**, etc. (*See also* **charcuterie**.)

smoke   To **preserve** or **cure** food, e.g. ham, salmon, or
turkey, by drying it above smoking wood or peat
with mixtures of sugar, spices, and **liquors** added to
impart special flavours.

smoothie   Beverage of blended fruit mixed with milk
and honey.

smorgasbord (*Swed.*)   Self-service buffet. (*See* 10.9).
(Literally, 'lump of butter' (*smörgås*) + 'table'
(*bord*). In Scandinavia a *smörgåsbord* is a very substantial meal of several courses, including especially
dishes of herrings.)

smørrebrød (*Dan.*) [shmuruh-brur(t)]   Open sandwich.

snow pea   *See* **mange-tout**.

snow pea shoots   Small shoots from the **snow pea**
plant, usually served mixed in green salads.

soda-(water)   Water aerated with carbon dioxide.

sodium   Salt.

sommelier (*Fr.*) (masc.) [som-ell-ee-ay]   Expert wine-
waiter.

sorbet (*Fr.*) (masc.) [sor-bay]   Light soft frozen
mixture of **puréed** fruit or fruit juice with some
liquor and **sugar syrup**; **water ice**. Sorbets are
often served between courses to freshen the **palate**.
(*See also* **classic menu**.)

sorrel [sorrul]   Green-leaf vegetable with a slightly
bitter taste. It is used to make soup and, when
young, mixed in green salad. (French *oseille*.)

soubise (*Fr.*) (fem.) [soo-beez]   An onion sauce or
purée of onion and rice.

soufflé (*Fr.*) (masc.) [soo-flay]   Sweet or savoury sauce
mixture to which beaten egg whites have been
added which cause it to rise once baked. It is almost
always served hot, but a cold sweet soufflé is made
from fruit **purée** to which egg white is added, e.g.
soufflé aux fruits (fruit soufflé), *soufflé au fromage*
(cheese soufflé), *soufflé au chocolat* (chocolate
soufflé).

soupe (*Fr.*) (fem) [soop]   Soup, esp. those containing
bread. (*See also* **bisque**, **consommé**, **garbure**,

julienne, marmite petite, pistou, potage, *and* vichyssoise.)

sour cream *See* **cream, soured**.

sourdough Piece of dough left over from a previous batch and used as a 'starter' to leaven a new batch. Sourdough bread has a crisp crust and soft inner crumb, a slightly sour taste, and is usually baked by traditional methods.

sous chef (*Fr.*) [soo shef] Deputy chef. (*Sous* means 'under'.)

Southern Comfort US **proprietary liqueur**, based on **bourbon whiskey** with peach flavourings.

souvlaki (*Grk.*) [soov-lahkee] Grilled or barbecued meat, esp. lamb, wrapped in **pita** bread with **humus** and salad; meat cooked on a skewer. (*See also* **kebab**.)

soya/soy bean Round bean, the same size as a pea, rich in protein, used to make **tofu**, etc.

soya/soy sauce Vital ingredient and popular **condiment** of E. Asian **cuisine**, made from **soya beans** and water with other ingredients such as wheat, **vinegar**, salt, etc. There are many different kinds of soya sauce, including the Japanese **shoyu** and **teriyaki sauce**.

spaetzle/späzle (*Ger.* & *Alsace*) [spaytz-luh] Small poached **dumplings** of flour, eggs, and cream, usually used to **garnish** meat dishes or served as an **entrée**, *au* **gratin**.

spaghetti (*Ital.*) (pl.) [spag-ay-tee] **Pasta** cut into long strings.

spanakopita (*Grk.*) [spana-kohpeeta] Pasty made of **filo pastry** containing spinach and cheese.

Spanish olive Particularly mild-tasting green **olive** suitable for use in **cocktails**.

spare-ribs The rib bones of pork or beef, usually **marinated** and baked.

sparkling wine Wines made effervescent (bubbly) by the natural action of the carbon dioxide gas produced by **fermentation**. **Champagne** is the most famous kind of sparkling wine. (*See* 14.6.) *Compare* **carbonated wine**.

spatchcock Dressed young chicken or **game** bird that is split open and grilled or fried without being allowed to hang and mature.

spätlese (*Ger.*) [shpayt-layz-uh] Sweet dessert wine made from late-picked **riesling** grapes. (*See also* **auslese** *and* **riesling**.) (*Spätlese* means 'late-picked'.)

späzle *See* **spaetzle**.

spice Aromatic or pungent vegetable substance used to flavour food, e.g. **coriander**, **turmeric** or **pepper**.

spirits General term for **distilled** alcoholic liquors, including **brandy**, **gin**, **rum**, **tequila**, **whisky** and **vodka**. (*See* 14.7.)

split Small or half-bottle (285mL) of an effervescent drink like **soda** or **tonic**.

spoom **Sorbet** stirred with **meringue** so that it foams. (In Italian *spuma* [spoo-mah].)

spring roll Deep-fried Chinese-style **pancake** parcel containing minced meat and vegetables. (*See also* **cha gio** *and* **goi cuon**.)

spumante (*Ital.*) [spoo-man-tay] Sparkling; Italian **sparkling wine**.

squab [skwob] Young pigeon.

staphylococcus **Bacterium** causing food poisoning found in human throats and noses, and septic cuts.

starch **Carbohydrate** found in cereals and potatoes.

station (1) Section of the dining-room for which a waiter or team of service staff is responsible. (*See* 1.7.) (2) Table or **sideboard** where a waiter keeps the equipment necessary for service; a waiter's work station. (*See* 4.8.)

steak tartare *See* **tartare** *and* **tartare steak**.

steamboat Style of Chinese cooking where a pan of **broth** is placed on a heat source in the centre of the table into which diners dip raw food until it is cooked. At the end of the meal this **broth**, which has become quite rich, is eaten as soup.

still Apparatus used to distil **spirits**. (*See* **distillation**, **pot still**, *and* 14.7.)

stillroom Store or pantry for small items of food and beverage needed for service but not provided by the kitchen or larder.

stilton (*UK*) Rich, creamy **blue-veined** cheese, now usually served on cheeseboards. Traditionally a whole stilton was presented and scooped out with a spoon, with **port** filling the hollow so created. (Stilton is a village in central England.) (*See also* **Gippsland blue**, **gorgonzola**, *and* **roquefort**.)

stir and strain Cocktail-mixing term. Ice is placed in a mixing glass, the **liquors** are added and stirred until cold, then strained into the serving glass using a **Hawthorn strainer**.

stir fry (1) (verb) E. Asian method of preparing food whereby the ingredients are chopped into small pieces and cooked over a fast heat often in a **wok** while continually being stirred. (2) (noun) A stir-fried dish.

stock **Broth** made by simmering bones and vegetables used as the basis for **sauces**, gravies, soups, and stews.

stout Strong dark **beer** brewed with roasted **malt**.

Stroganov *See* **boeuf Stroganov**.

strudel [stroo-del] Dessert with case of **filo pastry**, e.g. apple strudel (German *Apfel Strüdel*. *Strüdel* means 'whirlpool'.)

sucré(e) (*Fr.*) [sookray] Sugared. (*Sucre* means 'sugar'.)

suet [sooet] Solid fat from around the kidney of beef or mutton, fresh or dried, used in traditional English **Christmas** (plum) **pudding** and in steamed pastry dishes, e.g. steak and kidney **pudding**.

sugarbark (*Austral.*) Garnish of mixed sugars baked until crisp and golden. (Recipe created by Jean-Paul Bruneteau of Rowntrees The Australian Restaurant.)

sugar syrup Sweet **liquor** made of sugar and water, boiled and used when making desserts or poaching fruit and in some **cocktails; gomme syrup**.

sukiyaki (*Jap.*) [sooky-yahkee] Small lumps of meat cooked in oil at table with diners helping themselves from the common pot, **fondue**-style. (*Suki* means 'scoop' and *yaki*, 'grilled'.)

summer pudding (*UK*) Dessert of white bread soaked with fresh red and/or black berries and currants and turned out to serve.

sundae [sunday] Ice cream dessert with topping of fruit, nuts, or syrup.

sun-dried tomato *See* **tomato**.

supper (1) Insubstantial late evening snack or very light meal taken after dinner or tea.
(2) (*UK*) Informal evening meal replacing a more formal dinner.

suprême (*Fr.*) (masc.) [soo-praym] (1) Breast and wing of poultry or **game**, e.g. *suprêmes de volaille* (chicken breasts in sauce).
(2) **Fillet** of large fish. (*See also* **suprême, sauce**.)

suprême, sauce (*Fr.*) [sohs soo-praym] Rich sauce containing **cream** and butter.

sushi (*Jap.*) [soo-shee] Bite-sized rice balls or sandwiches flavoured with **vinegar** and topped with **marinaded** raw fish or some other delicacy, often wrapped in **nori**.

Suzette *See* **crêpes Suzette**.

sweet (1) (adj.) Tasting of sugar; opposite of sour.
(2) (noun) Small item of confectionery usually mainly of sugar or chocolate.
(3) (noun) The sweet or **dessert course** of a meal. (*See* 2.2; *see also* **entremets** *and* **pudding**.)

sweet-and-sour In Chinese cuisine, dishes cooked with a sauce made from sugar, **soy sauce**, and **vinegar** or lemon, usually thickened with cornflour.

sweetbreads Pancreas or thymus of an animal (usually **veal** or lamb) when used in cooking. (*See* **abats**.)

sweet corn/maize *See* **corn**.

sweetmeat Sugar-coated confection; small fancy cake. (*See also* **fondant** *and* **petit four**.)

sweet pepper **Capsicum** or bell pepper; green, red, yellow, or purple pepper. Soft, well-fleshed vegetable (*Capsicum annuum*) related to the hot **chilli**, but not the pepper spice. (*See* **pepper**.)

Swiss chard *See* **silverbeet**.

syllabub (*UK*) [silla-bub] **Dessert** of sweetened **cream** with lemon juice and wine or **brandy**.

Szechwan [sitch-wahn] One of the major styles of Chinese cuisine, and typically hot and spicy. (*See also* **Cantonese, Fukien, Honan,** *and* **Peking**.) (Szech-

wan, now spelt Sichuan, is a province in NW China.)

Tabasco [tab-ass-coh] Spicy **proprietary** sauce made from the pungent tabasco **chilli** pepper. Sold in small bottles, it is used to season meat and egg dishes and **cocktails**. (Tabasco is a state in Mexico.)

tabbouleh/tabouli (*Arab.*) [taboo-lee] Salad of **cracked wheat**, onion, **mint**, tomato, *and* **parsley**.

table d'hôte (*Fr.*) [tahbl doht] Type of menu offering limited choice at a fixed price for the whole meal. (*See* **prix fixe** *and* 2.11.)

table-linen Tablecloth and **napkins**; napery (not necessarily made from linen cloth).

table-napkin Serviette; a cloth placed on diners' laps and used to protect their clothes and to wipe their fingers and mouths.

table wine Wine that is drunk with a meal; unfortified still wine. (*See* **fortified wine, sparkling wine,** *and* **wine**; *see also* 14.3.)

taco (*Mex.*) [tahkoh] Sandwich in a crisp **corn pancake**; small **tortilla** wrapped around a filling usually of meat and/or beans and cheese. Ready-made taco shells are available commercially.

tagliatelle (*Ital.*) (pl.) [tie-ya-telluh] Long ribbons of **pasta** curled around one another.

tahini/tahina (*Arab.*) [tuheen-ee] **Sesame seed** paste, an ingredient of **hummus**. (*Tahina* means 'ground' or 'crushed'.)

tamarind (*Arab.*) Fruit of the tamarind tree (*Tamarindus indica*) the black pulp of which is used in Indian cuisine. It is rarely available fresh in Australia, but is compressed in a block or bottled as a paste.

tandoor (*Ind.*) (noun) [tun-door] Open-topped clay oven.

tandoori (*Ind.*) (adj.) [tun-door-ee] Food that has been cooked in a **tandoor** (e.g. tandoori chicken).

tannin Ingredient of wine, esp. full-bodied red wine, derived from pips and stalks which gives drying, furry sensation to tongue and gums.

tapas (*Span.*) [tap-ass] Substantial cocktail snacks or **appetizers**, often served in bowls from which guests select the food. (*See also* **hors d'oeuvres**.)

tapas bar **Brasserie** or wine-bar at which **tapas** is served.

tapénade (*Fr.*) [tapay-nahd] **Provençal** thick paste of crushed **olives, anchovies, capers, garlic,** and oil.

taramasalata (*Grk.*) [tarra-mah-sall-ah-tah] Soft pink creamy paste of fish **roe** with olive oil and **garlic**, usually served as part of the **hors d'oeuvres** or **meze**.

tarragon Plant with long narrow green leaves used as a flavouring herb. The French variety is much finer, but difficult to grow. Russian tarragon is sturdier, but coarser. Tarragon is one of the ingredients of **fines herbes**.

tartare, à la (*Fr.*) [ah lah tar-tar] Literally, 'in the manner of the Tartars', the once-terrifying nomadic hordes of Central Asia. (*See below.*)

tartare sauce [tar-tahr] **Mayonnaise** sauce made from hard-boiled egg yolks, onion, **chives**, and **capers** served with fish.

tartare steak/steak tartare [tar-tahr] Minced raw beef garnished with **capers**, minced onion, parsley and served with a raw egg-yolk. (In French **bifteck** *à la* **tartare** .)

tarte (*Fr.*) (fem.) [tart] Tart, e.g. **tarte tatin**.

tarte tatin (*Fr.*) [tart tata(n)] Upside-down apple tart. (The Tatin sisters, restaurateurs, popularized the dish in the early 1900s.)

T-bone Beef steak on a T-shaped bone cut from the **fillet** end of the **sirloin**. (*See also* **entrecôte**, **filet mignon**, **porterhouse**, **rump**, *and* **sirloin**.)

tea (1) Mildly stimulating beverage made by infusing the dried leaves of the tea-bush in boiling water. The two main styles are green (or **China**) tea and black (or Indian) tea. There are many varieties, e.g. Assam, **Darjeeling**, **Earl Grey**, **English Breakfast**, **jasmine**, etc. Some drinks are called 'tea' although they are not made with tea-leaves, e.g. **herbal teas**. (*See also* **iced tea** *and* 14.12, 15.19, *and* 15.20.)
(2) Meal at which tea is served, e.g. afternoon tea; the main (informal) evening meal.

tempura (*Jap.*) [tem-poor-ah] Strips of fish, shelled prawns, or vegetables fried in a light **batter** and served very hot, usually with grated **daikon radish**.

teppanyaki (*Jap.*) [tep-an-yak-ee] Meat, fish and vegetables fried at the table. (Literally, 'table-grilled'.)

tequila Mexican **spirit**, of which there are two varieties, white and gold, distilled from the cactus-like **mezcal** azul plant. Tequila is an ingredient of many **cocktails**, e.g. **Margarita**. (*See also* **mezcal**.)

teriyaki (*Jap.*) [terri-yah-kee] Meat or fish **marinated** in **teriyaki sauce** and grilled. (Literally, 'sunshine-grilled' — glazed and grilled.)

teriyaki sauce **Soya sauce** brewed with sweet rice wine, **vinegar**, sugar, and spices.

terrine (*Fr.*) (fem.) [teh-reen] (1) Oblong straight-sided cooking dish with a tight-fitting lid. (Not to be confused with a **tureen**.)
(2) Chopped and minced meat of different varieties (or occasionally fish) mixed with vegetables and seasoning and cooked in a **terrine** until they form a 'loaf' which is sliced and served cold.

thermidor Recipe for **lobster** or **crayfish** served baked in their shells with a creamy sauce and hot **mustard**, often **au gratin**. (Thermidor was the name of the hottest month in the new calendar introduced at the French Revolution.)

Thousand Island dressing (*Canada* & *USA*) Sauce of **mayonnaise** flavoured with **tomato sauce**, onion, and **chilli**. (The Thousand Islands are in the north-east of Lake Ontario.)

thyme [time] Shrub with small powerfully pungent leaves used as seasoning herb, especially in soups and stews, and stuffings. A component of the traditional **bouquet garni**, thyme is also a vital element in **Cajun** cooking.

Tia Maria Rum-based, coffee-flavoured **liqueur** from Jamaica.

timbale (*Fr.*) (fem.) [tam-bahl] (1) Cup-shaped mould.
(2) Food pressed into a timbale, served turned out in the shape of an inverted cup.
(3) Pie-crust baked in a timbale and filled with a creamy savoury mixture (**croûte** *à timbale*).
(4) **Dessert** of fruit or a **cream** presented in a cup-shaped basket made from biscuit or pastry dough.

tira-mi-su (*Ital.*) [teera mee soo] Cake of **macerated** biscuits (**ladyfingers**) sandwiched with a **cream** made of sweetened **mascarpone** and separated eggs. (Literally 'pick-me-up'.)

tisane [tizann] *See* **herbal tea**.

tofu (*Jap.*) [toe-foo] Highly nutritious **curd** made from **soya beans** and which looks like a lump of soft cheese or firm custard. It is a versatile ingredient which tastes of little but absorbs the flavour of accompanying food or sauce.

tokay (1) Classic sweet white unfortified **dessert wine** of Hungary.
(2) Australian **fortified** dessert wine similar to **muscat** made from a variety of grape called tokay in Australia (but muscadelle in Europe).

tomato Versatile vegetable used in many cooked dishes and **chutneys**, and eaten raw in salads. Roma, also known as Italian plum, tomatoes are used fresh and for canning. Other tomato products include tomato **purée** (also known as 'tomato paste') and tomato **ketchup** ('sauce' or 'catsup'). Cherry tomatoes are a miniature variety. Sun-dried tomatoes are preserved in oil. (*See* **salsa di pomodoro**.)

Tom Collins **Cocktail** containing equal measures of **gin** and lemon juice with a dash of **Angostura Bitters**, and **soda**.

tom ka gai (*Thai*) [tum kah gye] Spicy chicken soup with **coconut milk**. (*See also* **tom yam** *below*.)

tom yam (*Thai*) [tum yum] Spicy **clear soup** made with **lemon grass**. (*See also* **tom ka gai** *above*.)

tom yam kung (*Thai*) [tum yum koong] **Tom yam** with prawns added.

tonic Short for '**Indian tonic** water', a non-alcoholic aerated water flavoured with **quinine**, used as a mixer in various **cocktails** and mixed drinks, e.g. **gin**-and-tonic. (It is called 'Indian' because the beverage was developed in India where quinine was used as a protection against malaria.)

torte (*Ger.*) [tor-tuh]   Rich cake made in layers, sandwiched together with **cream** and covered with chocolates, fruit, or nuts. (*Compare* **tourte**.)

tortellini (*Ital.*) (pl.) [tor-tell-een-ee]   **Pasta** filled with meat or cheese, rolled into small packages and served in a sauce.

tortilla (*Mex.*) [tor-tee-ya]   Flat, round **pancake** made of maize (cornmeal) served hot and usually filled with meat or beans and a sauce. (*See also* **enchilada**, **nacho**, *and* **taco**.)

tournedos (*Fr.*) (masc.) [toor-nay-doh]   Small round slice of beef **fillet** from the centre of the 'eye'. (Literally, 'turn (the) back'.) (*See* **bifteck**, **filet mignon**, **médallions**, **mignonnettes**, *and* **noisettes**.)

tournedos Rossini   **Tournedos** served on fried bread, originally garnished with **foie gras** and **truffles**. (Devised by Gioacchino Rossini, 1792-1868, composer of operas and famous gastronome.)

tourné(e) (*Fr.*) [toor-nay]   Turned, shaped.

tourte (*Fr.*) (fem.) [toort]   Round pie or tart. Savoury *tourtes* have a pastry lid, sweet ones usually do not. (Do not confuse with **torte**.)

toxin   Poison.

traminer   One of a group of grape varieties used to make white wine, the most popular of which is **gewürztraminer**.

tranche (*Fr.*) (fem.) [trahnsh]   A slice (of fish, meat, etc.). (*See also* **tronçon** *and* **darne**.)

trattoria (*Ital.*)   Italian restaurant, usually quite small.

trifle   **Dessert** dish of sponge cake (often soaked in sherry) topped with fruit, custard, and cream.

tripe   Lining of cow's stomach. (French *tripe* [treep].)

triple sec   Very sweet white **curaçao**, e.g. **Cointreau**.

tronçon (*Fr.*) (masc.) [tro(n)so(n)]   Slice, usually of large flat fish cut through the bone. (*See also* **darne**.)

trotters   Feet of hoofed animal, esp. pig's feet.

truffle   (1) Edible fungus (**tuber**) found underground, especially near the roots of oak trees, highly prized as a savoury delicacy. (In French *truffe* (fem.) [troof]). (2) Rich, creamy chocolate **sweet**, shaped into a ball; a chocolate truffle. (So called because it resembles the truffle tuber.)

truite (*Fr.*) (fem.) [trweet]   Trout.

truite au bleu (*Fr.*) [trweet oh bluh]   Freshly-caught trout, cleaned and plunged into a **court-bouillon**. (*See also* **bleu**.)

tuber   Vegetable which swells underground, e.g. potato, **Jerusalem artichoke**, or **truffle**.

tuile (*Fr.*) (fem.) [tweel]   Almond wafer curved like a tile and served as a **petit four**. (*Tuile* means 'tile'.)

tumbler   Simple, straight-sided glass for serving water and soft drinks. (*See* p.98.)

tureen [ture-reen]   Deep covered dish from which soup is served at the table. (Do not confuse with **terrine**.) (*See also* 3.5.)

turkey buffet (*Austral.*)   Joint of turkey breast with the legs and wing tips removed; **smoked** turkey breast.

Turkish coffee   Strong, dark, sweet **coffee** served in small cups; **Greek coffee**. (*See* 14.13.)

turmeric   Mildly peppery spice, bright yellow when ground to powder, used in most **curry** mixtures, usually called *haldi* in India.

tutti frutti   Ice-cream mixed with **diced glacé** fruit which has been **macerated** in alcohol. (Literally, 'all the fruits' in Italian.)

tzatziki (*Grk.* & *Turk.*) [tsat-seekee]   Yoghurt mixed with **garlic** and cucumber and served as an **appetizer** or dip with the **meze**.

udon noodle   Thick noodle made of wheat flour, popular in Japan and China. Udon noodles are usually boiled in stock and are often served as a snack.

un/une (*Fr.*) (masc./fem.) [u(n)/oon]   A. (The indefinite pronoun — e.g. *un* **goujon** *de* **poisson**, *une* **quiche**.)

Underberg   **Proprietary** brand of German **bitters**, taken both as a tonic and a **digestif**; it is drunk straight from the bottle in one mouthful.

underliner   Plate, usually with a **doily** on it, placed under another dish, such as a soup bowl; an underplate. (*See* 7.7.)

vacherin (*Fr.*) (masc.) [vasheri(n)]   (1) Round cows'-milk cheese. (*Vache* means 'cow'.) (2) Dessert consisting of layers of crisp **meringue** sandwiched with **cream**, similar to **pavlova**.

vanilla   Sweet and fragrant flavouring obtained from the bean of the vanilla orchid (*Vanilla planifolia*). (*See also below*.)

vanilla bean   Long pod of the **vanilla** containing the seeds producing the distinctive flavour. When the pod is boiled with liquid, dishes so flavoured have a slightly speckled appearance.

vanilla essence   Concentrated extract of the **vanilla bean** used to flavour sweet dishes in place of the bean.

vanilla sugar   Sugar stored in a container with a **vanilla bean** which imparts the vanilla flavour to the sugar.

varietal   Adjective used to describe wine made from a particular variety of grape, e.g. **chardonnay**. (*See also* **generic**.)

veal   Calf's meat. The finest is fed exclusively on milk.

veau (*Fr.*) (masc.) [voh]   **Veal**.

vegan [vee-gan] Strict **vegetarian**; person who eats no animal products at all, not even milk or eggs.

vegetarian Person who does not eat animal (or fish) products, especially the flesh of slaughtered animals. Many vegetarians do eat eggs and consume dairy products (milk, cheese, etc.). *Compare* **vegan**.

velouté (*Fr.*) (masc.) [vuh-loot-ay] Thick velvety sauce made from a light **stock**, rather than milk, and a white **roux** to which **cream** is often added.

venaison (*Fr.*) (fem.) [venay-so(n)] **Venison**; the meat of any large **game** animal. (*See also* **chevreuil, poivrade,** *and* **salmis**.)

venaison, sauce (*Fr.*) [sohs venay-son] **Sauce poivrade** to which fresh cream and red currant jelly have been added, traditionally served with **game** and dishes '*en* **chevreuil**'. (*See also* **venaison**.)

venison [ven-sun] Meat of deer. (*See also* **venaison**.)

verde (*Ital*.) [vairduh] Green.

vermicelli (*Ital.*) (pl.) [vairmi-chelly] Long thin threads of **pasta** sometimes coiled into rings; **noodles**. (Also known as *capellini*.)

vermouth [ver-muth] Flavoured **fortified wine** available in three principal styles: dry (or **French**), sweet (**rosso** or Italian), and **bianco** which is golden and medium sweet. (*Rosso* literally means 'red' and *bianco* 'white'.)

viande (*Fr.*) (fem.) [vee-ond] Meat.

vichyssoise (*Fr.*) (masc.) [vee-shee-swaz] Creamy soup made of **puréed** leeks and potatoes, served chilled and garnished with **chives**. (*See also* **garbure** *and* **potage**.)

Vichy water (*Fr.*) [veeshee] Mineral water from Vichy (spa town in central France). (*See* 14.18.)

Vienna coffee **Coffee** topped with thick, rich **cream**. (Vienna is the capital of Austria.) (*See* 14.13.)

Vietnamese mint *See* **mint, Vietnamese**.

vin (*Fr.*) (masc.) [vi(n)] Wine.

vinaigrette (*Fr.*) (fem.) [vin-uh-gret] Mixture of oil and **vinegar** or lemon juice used to dress salads. Other ingredients, especially **mustard** or herbs, may be added. (*See* **French dressing** *and* **wine vinegar**.)

vindaloo (*Ind.*) [vin-daloo] Very hot S. Indian **curry**, spiced and flavoured with **vinegar**.

vinegar Fermented acidic **liquor** made from wine, cider, **malt**, **spirits**, or rice. (French *vinaigre;* literally, 'sour wine'.) (*See* **balsamic, malt, rice,** *and* **wine vinegar**; *see also* **vinaigrette**.)

vin ordinaire (*Fr.*) [vi(n) or-din-air] Moderately priced everyday wine; **house wine** bought in bulk by an **establishment** and often served from **carafes**.

vintage [vin-tij] (1) (noun) Season when grapes are harvested (as in *the vintage was late this year*).
(2) (noun) Wine made from the season's produce; the year the wine is made (as in *the 1992 vintage*).

(3) (noun) Wine from a single year (as in *1992 was a good vintage*).
(4) (adj.) Wine or **port** of special quality (*vintage wine*); of high quality (as in *a vintage year*).

virgin Without alcohol. (*See* **cocktail** *and* 14.10.)

virgin olive oil Finest olive oil; oil extracted from the first pressing of the olives, and which contains no additives.

vitamin Any of a group of substances found in food which help regulate body processes essential to health and growth. Vitamins are classified by letters and numbers (vitamin A, B_2, C, D_3, E, etc.).

vitello (*Ital.*) **Veal**.

vodka **Spirit** made from grain; in the West usually colourless and flavourless but in Russia and Poland often flavoured. It is most popular as an ingredient in **cocktails**, e.g. a **Bloody Mary**.

volaille (*Fr.*) (fem.) [voll-eye-yuh] Poultry.

vol-au-vent (*Fr.*) (masc.) (*pl.* **vols-au-vent**) [voll oh vahn] Round case of **puff pastry** filled with a savoury mixture held in a creamy sauce and capped with a lid. Tiny ones are served as cocktail **savouries** and larger ones as an **entrée**. (Literally, 'flight in the wind'.) (*See also* **croustade**.)

VSOP Very Superior Old Pale, a technically meaningless term used on labels to market **cognac**.

waffle [wofful] Small crisp cake made of **batter**, baked in a utensil with hinged halves (a waffle-iron). (From Dutch *wafel* meaning 'wafer'.) (*Compare* **jaffle**.)

waiter's friend Tool that is a combination of bottle-opener and corkscrew. (*See* 13.4 *and* 15.16.)

Waldorf salad Salad made with lettuce, **diced** apples, walnuts, celery and **mayonnaise**. (From the Waldorf Hotel, New York, where it was invented.)

warrigal greens Green-leaf vegetable (*Tetragonia tetragonoides*) used in salads or cooked and used as spinach; **New Zealand spinach**.

wasabi (*Jap.*) [woss-ah-bee] Extremely hot Japanese **horseradish**, served in the form of a green paste as a **condiment** to accompany **sashimi** and **sushi**.

water-chestnut The crunchy **tuber** of an Asian sedge (*Eleocharis tuberosa*) commonly used in Chinese cookery. Usually bought canned.

watercress Green leaf vegetable (*Nasturtium officinale*) with small, round leaves and a pungent flavour. (*See also* **cress** *and* **nasturtium**.)

water ice Iced dessert made of **puréed** fruit, **sugar syrup** and egg white. (*See* **sorbet**).

wattle seed (*Austral.*) Milled seed of the wattle (*Acacia*) species. Wattle seed is used to flavour both biscuits and bread, and many sweet dishes, esp. cream desserts.

Wellington *See* **beef Wellington**.

whey Watery unfattening part of milk, separated from the **curd**, used to make some kinds of light cheese, e.g. **ricotta**.

whisky/whiskey **Spirit distilled** from **fermented** corn (barley, rye, wheat or maize). There are many styles. **Scotch** whiskies are by far the most popular. Most Scotch whiskies are blends of **malt whiskies** (made from barley) and grain whiskies (distilled in bulk from fermented wheat and maize). American and Irish whiskey are spelt with an 'e'. Other varieties drop the 'e'. (*See also* **bourbon** *and* **rye**.)

whitebait Sprats; small young fish, usually fried and eaten whole.

white pepper *See* **pepper** *and* **peppercorn**.

Wiener schnitzel [veener shnit-sell] **Veal escalope** coated in breadcrumbs and egg, and **sautéed**. (From Wien — Vienna — capital of Austria.)

wild rice Not a variety of common white rice which the dark brown grains resemble in shape, but *Zizania aquatica*, a grass native to North America. Turns slightly purple when cooked.

wine (1) Alcoholic drink made from fermented grape juice, e.g. **burgundy**, **claret**, **champagne**, etc. (2) Any **fermented** vegetable juice which is **distilled** to make spirits.

wine vinegar **Vinegar** distilled from (grape) **wine** and used in **béarnaise sauce**, **vinaigrette**, etc. Some are infused with herbs, spice, or fruit, e.g. **tarragon**, **chilli**, or **raspberry**. (*See* **balsamic vinegar**, **French dressing**, *and* **malt vinegar**.)

witchetty grub Long fat white grub found on wattle roots. Witchetty grub soup is available canned.

witloof/witlof **Chicory**, white or Belgian **endive** (*Cichorium intybus*). (Flemish for 'white leaf'.)

wok (*Chin.*) Large basin-shaped (hemispherical) frying-pan with a lid and two handles, much used in E. Asian cookery, esp. for **stir-fried** dishes.

won ton (*Chin.*) Small noodle-dough **dumpling**, either boiled in soup or deep fried.

Worcestershire/Worcester sauce [wuster(shuh)] Spicy sauce made of **vinegar**, molasses, sugar, spices, etc. (Worcestershire is a county in W. England.)

wurst (*Ger.*) [voorst] Sausage.

yabby/yabbie (*Austral.*) Small freshwater **crayfish** (*Cherax destructor*) with large pincers so that it looks like a miniature **lobster**.

yam nang mu (*Thai.*) [yum nang moo] Pork skin salad.

Yorkshire pudding (*UK*) Savoury **batter pudding** traditionally served with roast beef.

yum cha (*Chin.*) Banquet usually served mid-morning and lasting over three hours. Many small dishes are served on a central turn-table from which guests help themselves. (*Yum* means 'drink', *cha* 'tea'.)

zabaglione (*Ital.*) [zab-ay-on-nay] Light foamy dessert made by whipping egg yolk, sugar, and alcohol (traditionally **marsala**) over a low heat. Served just warm. (*See* **sabayon**.)

zest (of **citrus** fruit) Outer rind of citrus peel without the pith, and the scented oil it produces. It is used to enhance the citrus flavour.

zingara (*Fr.*) (adj.) [zjan-gahra] Containing **paprika** and tomato. (*Zingaro* means 'gypsy'.)

zucchini Variety of marrow or squash also known as **courgette**. The flowers can be stuffed with a **farce**.

zuppa (*Ital.*) [zuppah] Thick soup. (*See also* **brodo** *and* **minestra**.)

zuppa inglese (*Ital.*) [zuppa inglay-say] **Dessert** or **pudding** made from sponge cake, chocolate and custard; **trifle**. (Literally, 'English soup'.)

INDEX

Items in the Glossary do not appear in the index unless they are also in the main text. Glossary references are only given in the index if the Glossary gives *additional* information to that in the main text.